5 STEPS TO A 5

500

AP U.S. History Questions

to know by test day

Lawrence A.

5 STEPS TO A >5™

500

AP U.S. History Questions
to know by test day

Scott E. Demeter

New York Chicago San Francisco Lisbon London Madrid Mexico City
Milan New Delhi San Juan Seoul Singapore Sydney Toronto

SCOTT E. DEMETER teaches in north Jersey, where he also resides. His major areas of educational focus include honors-level and advanced-placement programs in the areas of American history, world history, and United States government.

ISBN   978-0-07-174207-8
MHID   0-07-174207-7

Library of Congress Control Number 2010935991

Series interior design by Jane Tennenbaum

CONTENTS

INTRODUCTION

Congratulations! You've taken a big step toward AP success by purchasing *5 Steps to a 5: 500 AP U.S. History Questions to Know by Test Day*. We are here to help you take the next step and score high on your AP Exam so you can earn college credits and get into the college or university of your choice.

This book gives you 500 AP-style multiple-choice questions that cover all the most essential course material. Each question has a detailed answer explanation. These questions will give you valuable independent practice to supplement your regular textbook and the groundwork you are already doing in your AP classroom.

This and the other books in this series were written by expert AP teachers who know your exam inside out and can identify the crucial exam information as well as questions that are most likely to appear on the exam.

You might be the kind of student who takes several AP courses and needs to study extra questions a few weeks before the exam for a final review. Or you might be the kind of student who puts off preparing until the last weeks before the exam. No matter what your preparation style is, you will surely benefit from reviewing these 500 questions, which closely parallel the content, format, and degree of difficulty of the questions on the actual AP exam. These questions and their answer explanations are the ideal last-minute study tool for those final few weeks before the test.

Remember the old saying "Practice makes perfect." If you practice with all the questions and answers in this book, we are certain you will build the skills and confidence needed to do great on the exam. Good luck!

—Editors of McGraw-Hill Education

CHAPTER 1

Pre-Columbian/
Native American History

1. What was the main cause of the exposed land bridge connecting Eurasia to North America?

   (A) Extended periods of drought during the last Ice Age lowered ocean levels.

   (B) Plate tectonics temporarily led to a rise in the ocean floor within the Bering Sea.

   (C) Much of the water in the oceans congealed into vast glacial packs.

   (D) Increased snowfall on land during the last Ice Age lowered ocean levels.

   (E) The shift of Eurasian and North American Plates briefly connected the two continents.

2. Which theory best describes the spread of maize as a staple crop through the Native American populations?

   (A) Maize was first developed upon the Siberian Steppes and carried to the Americas via the land bridge.

   (B) Maize was developed in South America and slowly spread throughout the rest of the Americas via pre-Columbian trade routes.

   (C) Maize was developed by the nomadic tribes of North America but was first grown intensively as a staple crop by Native American groups in Central and South America.

   (D) The cultivation of maize occurred separately in isolated pockets throughout the two continents.

   (E) Maize was first developed in the region that is now Mexico and spread through the Americas in a slow and uneven process.

3. With few exceptions, Native American groups of North America would be most accurately described as
   (A) living in dense but isolated pockets throughout the continent
   (B) elaborately developed social groups in centrally organized nation-states
   (C) independent paternal-based social groups living in small semi-nomadic populations
   (D) sporadic with inconsistent development between tribes, lacking a common linguistic base
   (E) lacking dense population concentrations or highly developed social life in the modern sense

4. The Native American Mississippian Valley culture differed from other Native American groups in that it
   (A) illustrated a higher level of hierarchical political organization
   (B) existed in mainly semi-nomadic populations with limited agriculture
   (C) had a developed network of trade with other regional tribes
   (D) based its social structure on maternal lineage
   (E) closely tied its religion to the natural world

5. Which tribe of Native Americans is *not* associated with the Iroquois League?
   (A) Mohawk
   (B) Oneida
   (C) Cayuga
   (D) Seneca
   (E) Powhatan

6. In agricultural terms, how did Native Americans differ from their European counterparts?
   (A) Europeans had a greater diversity in the types of staple crops they used for subsistence.
   (B) Unlike Europeans, Native Americans lacked any efficient means to clear the vast forests to open land for intensive agriculture.
   (C) Europeans achieved greater technologies to alter the landscape in a more aggressive manner.
   (D) Unlike the sedentary European communities, the nomadic lifestyle of the Native Americans limited their ability to develop high-yield strains of vegetation.
   (E) The Native Americans had less agricultural diversity than European farmers.

7. Why is L'Anse aux Meadows significant within North American history?
   (A) It marks the first example of pre-Columbian European contact with Native Americans.
   (B) It marks the first example of the cultivation of maize in North America outside of Mexico.
   (C) It serves as an example of a highly developed Native American nation-state in North America.
   (D) It contains the oldest fossil record of Native American inhabitants on the North American continent.
   (E) It illustrates a rare example of a sedentary Native American community.

8. In what way did pre-Columbian Mesoamerican and Central American civilizations most greatly contrast with European societies?
   (A) The pre-Columbian civilizations in these regions lacked highly developed trade routes, so they developed more independently than European societies.
   (B) Unlike European societies, the pre-Columbian societies in these regions lacked large draft animals to aid in transportation or agriculture.
   (C) Unlike European societies, the pre-Columbian societies in these regions failed to develop sophisticated systems within the sciences such as mathematics or astronomy.
   (D) Unlike European societies, the pre-Columbian societies in these regions never established a developed system of class or labor division.
   (E) Unlike European societies, pre-Columbian societies in these regions failed to develop an understanding of metalworking.

9. In Native North American culture along the Eastern Seaboard, the Three Sisters would most accurately refer to
   (A) the sustainable agricultural technique of growing maize, beans, and squash
   (B) the matrilineal lines upon which most clans were based in this region
   (C) the trade and cultural network established between Native Americans living in North America and those in Central and South America
   (D) the spiritual belief in three major forces that defined the natural world
   (E) a creationist myth common among eastern tribes

10. Which of the following statements best describes the view of Native Americans in North America concerning property?
    (A) A portion of lands should remain untouched for the use of future generations.
    (B) Land should be transferred through paternal lines.
    (C) The right of an individual to use the land was temporary.
    (D) The crops grown by the individual became the property of the clan.
    (E) The transfer of land was allowed only within one's own clan.

11. The large cliff dwelling structures of the North American Southwest are associated with which one of the following tribes?
    (A) Anasazi
    (B) Navaho
    (C) Hopi
    (D) Zuni
    (E) Apache

12. The Native American clan in North America was primarily based on
    (A) a kinship network
    (B) multiple nuclear families based on paternal lines
    (C) a single religious leader and his followers
    (D) a single chieftain and his warriors with their spouses and children
    (E) a defined tribal council of elders, the sons, and spouses

13. The early American Indian civilizations of Mexico and Peru were based on which agricultural product?
    (A) Wheat
    (B) Maize
    (C) Cattle
    (D) Horses
    (E) Coffee

14. Which tribe is most associated with the American Southwest?
    (A) Navajo
    (B) Ojibwa
    (C) Powhatan
    (D) Pequot
    (E) Wampanoag

15. Wampum is mostly associated with the
   (A) Eastern Woodland tribes
   (B) Southwestern tribes
   (C) Central Plains tribes
   (D) Northern Pacific tribes
   (E) Central American tribes

CHAPTER 2

Early Exploration and Spanish and French in the Colonies of the New World

16. Why did the European Crusades directly lead to the Age of Exploration?

(A) European nations needed to develop more efficient means to travel to newly acquired lands in the Middle East.

(B) Islamic control of the Middle East and North Africa cut off Europe from the Mediterranean Sea during the 11th century.

(C) Lost navigational technologies of the Greeks and Romans were discovered during the Crusades in newly conquered lands.

(D) Returning crusaders brought exotic spices, perfumes, and fabrics, creating a new European demand for these commodities.

(E) Maps defining safe passages to eastern lands were discovered by Europeans during the Crusades.

17. The end of the feudal systems that defined the European Middle Ages was primarily caused by

(A) the arrival of the Black Death in 1300

(B) the demands of serfs for wages in coinage

(C) the emergence of trade and a middle class of merchants

(D) disruption of traditional trade routes such as the Silk Road

(E) the end of absolute rule by the monarchies in European nations

18. The 1215 signing of the Magna Carta directly affected the future American government by

(A) allowing for the emergence of joint stock companies and other entrepreneurial commerce

(B) guaranteeing basic liberties to all citizens regardless of social class

(C) providing a clear system of checks and balances within the national government

(D) legitimizing citizen revolts against aristocratic or authoritarian rule

(E) providing for a defined separation between the church and state

19. The Columbian Exchange would best be described as
    - (A) the trade network established between Europe and the Americas
    - (B) the new agricultural goods brought to Europe from the Americas
    - (C) the exchange of biological, ecological, and other commodities brought to Europe and the Americas
    - (D) the introduction of European diseases that decimated indigenous populations in the Americas
    - (E) the arrival of European agricultural goods and livestock in the Americas

20. The Spanish colonial system of forcing Native Americans to work for individual Spaniards in the Americas was known as
    - (A) peonage
    - (B) indentured servitude
    - (C) *encomienda*
    - (D) *ejido*
    - (E) indigenous diaspora

21. The Spanish conqueror most associated with the destruction of the Incan Empire was
    - (A) Francisco Pizarro
    - (B) Hernán Cortés
    - (C) Francisco Vásquez de Coronado
    - (D) Vasco Núñez de Balboa
    - (E) Amerigo Vespucci

22. In 1494, Pope Alexander's Treaty of Tordesillas established the line of demarcation granting
    - (A) all of the land north of the meridian not already claimed by Christian nations to the Spanish
    - (B) all of the land east of the meridian not already claimed by Christian nations to the Spanish
    - (C) Portugal the right to establish a colonial empire in South America
    - (D) all of the land west of the meridian not already claimed by Christian nations to the Spanish
    - (E) a partition between Spanish, Portuguese, and French lands in the Americas

23. Which explorer is credited with being the first to reach the Pacific Ocean in the Americas?

    (A) Vasco Nuñez de Balboa
    (B) Francisco Vásquez de Coronado
    (C) Amerigo Vespucci
    (D) Vasco da Gama
    (E) Bartholomeu Dias

24. Which of the following explorers claimed Louisiana Territory for France?

    (A) Jacques Cartier
    (B) Louis Joliet
    (C) Jacques Marquette
    (D) Sieur Robert Cavelier de La Salle
    (E) Samuel de Champlain

25. In what way did early Spanish colonization differ from that of the early French efforts during the 1600s?

    (A) Unlike the French, the Spanish made religious conversion a major focus of settlement.
    (B) Unlike the Spanish, the French focused on establishing larger permanent communities in their colonies.
    (C) The French focused less on the accumulation of wealth and more on territorial expansion than did the Spanish.
    (D) Unlike the Spanish, the French based much of their colonial economy on the fur trade.
    (E) Unlike the Spanish, French colonization was in part motivated by French Protestants escaping religious persecution.

26. The system of trails that linked the Spanish settlements in and along the Pacific coast of what is today Mexico and the United States was called

    (A) El Carretera Norteña
    (B) El Rastro Terrestre
    (C) El Camino Real
    (D) El Camino de Cruces
    (E) The Old Spanish Trail

27. The primary function of the Spanish pueblo during Spanish colonial control of Mexico was to

    (A) serve as military posts to protect villages and missions
    (B) serve the Catholic Church in converting indigenous populations
    (C) serve as mainly outposts for traders
    (D) serve as centers of cultural education
    (E) serve as protected lands for Native Americans

28. What role did the Catholic Church play in Spain's rule of its colonial possessions in North America?
    (A) The pope indirectly ruled the colonies through the Spanish monarchy, requiring papal approval for all policies in the colonies.
    (B) Responsibilities to the Catholic Church dominated expansion policies into the northern territories.
    (C) The papacy provided the majority of funding for Spanish exploration.
    (D) The Spanish monarchy ordered priests to convert the indigenous population to Catholicism.
    (E) The Spanish missions reported to the pope rather than the Spanish monarchy.

29. Which of the following statements best describes the reason the Dutch settlers in North America practiced religious tolerance?
    (A) They were following the policy of tolerance practiced by the French and British in their New World possessions.
    (B) Religious tolerance was a method to entice more settlers to their North American colonies.
    (C) The Dutch believed religious tolerance would maintain order within their New World possessions.
    (D) Religious tolerance allowed for investment in colonization from joint stock companies.
    (E) The major religion of the Dutch called for religious tolerance.

30. Which explorer's expedition is most associated with first circumnavigating the globe?
    (A) Vasco da Gama
    (B) Amerigo Vespucci
    (C) Francis Drake
    (D) Ferdinand Magellan
    (E) Bartholomeu Dias

CHAPTER 3

Early English Colonies

31. Which statement is the most accurate concerning the North American colonies?

   (A) Most of the colonies were able to become profitable within the first years of their creation.
   (B) Most of the colonies started as proprietary but became royal colonies by the mid-18th century.
   (C) Most of the original colonies began as royal colonies.
   (D) Most of the colonies started as independent colonies but later received charters.
   (E) Most of the colonies started as proprietary colonies but became independent by purchasing their charters.

32. The Middle Passage refers to which of the following?

   (A) The passage of African people across the Atlantic to the Americas
   (B) The passage of Irish Catholics to the United States
   (C) The movement of African-Americans out of the southern United States to northern cities
   (D) The forced passage of Cherokee Indians west
   (E) The sought waterway connecting the Atlantic and Pacific Oceans

33. Which of the following statements does *not* describe slavery in the North American colonies?

   (A) Slaves in Georgia and South Carolina's coastal region primarily worked on large plantations in dangerous and brutal conditions.
   (B) In Virginia, slaves made up a minority of the population and had varied jobs.
   (C) In New England, slaves worked mainly in urban areas and ports.
   (D) The slaves contributed to the growth of the Atlantic economy as shipbuilders and dock workers in the middle colonies.
   (E) Strict slave laws prevented slave revolts through the 1700s.

34. The land explored by Sir Walter Raleigh was named Virginia in honor of

(A) Queen Elizabeth
(B) the Virgin Mary in Christian tradition
(C) the first female born by English settlers in North America
(D) Queen Mary
(E) the untouched appearance of the land upon Raleigh's arrival

35. The purpose of the headright system was to

(A) open up more land for tobacco cultivation
(B) ensure the separation between slaves and indentured servants
(C) establish a basic system of laws within the Piedmont region of Virginia
(D) keep non-Protestants from taking part in colonial government
(E) encourage increased migration to the Virginia Colony

36. Which of the following is true concerning the First Great Awakening?

(A) The First Great Awakening brought separatism and secession from established churches.
(B) The First Great Awakening brought the renewed persecution of witches.
(C) The First Great Awakening led to the strong reemergence of Catholicism.
(D) The Church of Jesus Christ of Latter Day Saints was created in direct response to the First Great Awakening.
(E) The First Great Awakening created a greater appreciation for the emotional experiences of faith.

37. Which of the following changes was a direct result of Bacon's Rebellion?

(A) Southern colonies began to farm tobacco as a staple export.
(B) A balance of power no longer existed between Native Americans and colonists in New England.
(C) Southern labor shifted from African slaves and began to rely more on indentured servants.
(D) Southern labor moved away from indentured servants and began to rely more on African slaves.
(E) Virginia transformed from a proprietary colony into a royal colony.

38. John Rolfe's main contribution to the Jamestown settlement was

(A) guiding the first settlers through the Starving Time
(B) devising the headright system to increase the population
(C) serving as Virginia's first colonial governor
(D) founding the first legislative body within the colonies
(E) introducing tobacco as the colony's first staple crop

39. "When London Merchants Urge Repeal" (January 17, 1766) referred to "this Trade, consisting of British Manufactures exported, and of the Import of raw Materials from America, many of them used in our Manufactures, and all of them tending to lessen our Dependence on neighboring States," what economic system was specifically being described?

(A) Stochastic
(B) Mercantilism
(C) Qualitative
(D) Keynesian
(E) Laissez-faire

40. In what way did the Jamestown Colony and the Massachusetts Bay Colony differ greatly?

(A) Unlike Jamestown, Massachusetts Bay was established as a joint stock company.
(B) Jamestown became a royal colony, while Massachusetts remained a proprietary colony.
(C) Unlike Jamestown, Massachusetts Bay maintained peaceful relations with the Native Americans within the region.
(D) Massachusetts Bay did not suffer from the same hardships as Jamestown during its first years.
(E) The practice of slavery was legal in Jamestown but not in Massachusetts Bay.

41. Which of the following individuals was *not* involved in the religious revivals in the colonies?

(A) John Peter Zenger
(B) John Woolman
(C) Jonathan Edwards
(D) George Whitefield
(E) Gilbert Tennent

42. All of the following innovations and discoveries are associated with Benjamin Franklin *except*

(A) bifocal glasses
(B) the flexible catheter
(C) North Atlantic Ocean current patterns
(D) the principle of conservation of charge
(E) interchangeable parts

43. Which of the following statements is *not* true about the colony of Pennsylvania?

(A) It increased its population through heavy advertising by paid agents.

(B) Because of Quaker beliefs, it strongly supported upholding land treaties with the Native Americans.

(C) It allowed Catholics and Jews to vote and hold public office.

(D) It did not require taxes to fund a state-held church.

(E) It imposed the death penalty on those who committed murder or treason.

44. Which of the following terms best describes colonies such as Pennsylvania and Maryland that were granted to a group by the English monarchy and given the right of self-government?

(A) Royal colonies

(B) Proprietary colonies

(C) Corporate colonies

(D) Chartered colonies

(E) Joint stock colonies

45. Which North American colony was intended to serve as a penal colony for debtors?

(A) Connecticut

(B) South Carolina

(C) Georgia

(D) Rhode Island

(E) Florida

46. Which of the following statements was *not* true of education in the New England colonies prior to the American Revolution?

(A) Towns of over 50 families were required to support an elementary school.

(B) Towns of over 100 families were required to support a grammar school.

(C) Elementary education was offered to both male and female children.

(D) New England schools served as an early example of a true secular education.

(E) New England had a higher literacy rate than the southern colonies.

47. American colonists began to use African slaves primarily because

(A) the papacy created an edict calling for the use of African slaves in Catholic-controlled lands

(B) the African slaves were more accustomed to agriculture than the Native Americans

(C) the Native Americans were decimated by European disease, while the Africans developed immunity

(D) the practice of indentured servitude was outlawed by the pope

(E) the European population was too limited to provide the needed labor

48. What is the African diaspora?

(A) The strict slave codes put into place to maintain order on plantations

(B) The passage of slaves from West Africa to the Americas

(C) The use of Africans in mines and on plantations as forced labor

(D) The dispersal of Africans throughout the Americas under the system of slavery

(E) The papal order to force Africans into the system of slavery

49. What was the major reason for Catholics migrating to the Americas from England during the 1600s?

(A) The return of a Catholic sovereign to the English monarchy granted them greater rights to establish colonies.

(B) The papacy called upon English Catholics to migrate as a protest to Anglican rule.

(C) The Catholic migrants would provide Catholic nations such as France and Spain with military support within their colonial possessions.

(D) Catholic nations in Europe granted them lands within the southern region of the New World.

(E) English Catholics wanted to escape the persecution they faced under Anglican rule.

50. The Puritans of New England felt the freedom to practice religion should be extended to

(A) only Puritans

(B) only Protestants

(C) only Christians

(D) only Christians and Jews

(E) all people

51. John Winthrop referred to Massachusetts Colony as "a city on the hill" because

    (A) Boston's elevation made it clearly visible from the Atlantic Ocean

    (B) its views of religious freedom made it a safe haven for the oppressed

    (C) the colony's fair treatment of Native Americans was to be an example for others

    (D) the colony was to serve as an example of Christian virtue and charity

    (E) the term distinguished Massachusetts from the lower-elevation Tidewater settlements in Virginia

52. Which of the following statements best describes women in colonial New England?

    (A) They were less likely to attend church than men.

    (B) They did not participate in outdoor farmwork.

    (C) They could own property and form contracts if they were widowed.

    (D) They were discouraged from learning to read.

    (E) They were allowed to vote in town hall assemblies.

53. What was the major purpose of the Toleration Act of 1649?

    (A) It was a way to suppress rebellions such as the one led by Nathaniel Bacon.

    (B) It was an attempt to maintain order in Boston after the passage of the Coercive Acts.

    (C) It protected Catholic rights in Maryland from the influx of Protestant colonists.

    (D) It extended voting rights to non-Protestants in New England.

    (E) It improved the conditions of indentured servants in the middle colonies.

54. Which of the following is the most accurate statement about the southern colonies during the late 17th century?

    (A) The economy was equally mixed between farming, trade, and small manufacturing.

    (B) African slaves were strictly segregated from white indentured servants.

    (C) The economy was dominated by skilled labor in port towns.

    (D) Tobacco, rice, and indigo served as the major staple crops.

    (E) The growth of upland cotton dominated the economy.

55. Which of the following statements best describes Roger Williams's view of "liberty of conscience"?

    (A) All people have freedom of speech.
    (B) People must be protected from unreasonable search and seizure.
    (C) Religious freedom requires a separation of church and state.
    (D) The press should be free to report honestly about political figures.
    (E) Men could avoid military service on religious grounds.

56. Which of the following statements best describes the ideas that caused the division between Anne Hutchinson and the Puritan church?

    (A) Hutchinson wanted to grant citizens of all faiths the right to vote.
    (B) Hutchinson openly promoted the idea of an individual personal relationship with God without the guidance of church leaders.
    (C) Hutchinson openly protested the witch trials taking place in New England.
    (D) Hutchinson rejected treaties with the Native Americans as being unfair.
    (E) Hutchinson promoted the return of Catholic traditions within the Puritan church.

57. The primary staple crops produced in the middle colonies included which of the following?

    (A) Wheat, oats, and barley
    (B) Cotton, tobacco, and tomatoes
    (C) Rice, tobacco, and indigo
    (D) Wheat, flax, and barley
    (E) Tomatoes, soy, and rye

58. The majority of colonists who migrated to Maryland and Virginia during the 17th century would be best described as

    (A) wealthy planters
    (B) indentured servants
    (C) women
    (D) African slaves
    (E) bankers and financiers

59. What advantage of colonies in the South was *not* shared by New England farmers?
    (A) Unlike the South, New England lacked ability to use slave labor.
    (B) Unlike the South, there was a lack of labor available to work in agriculture in New England.
    (C) Unlike the South, strict Puritan laws limited the type of agriculture allowed in New England.
    (D) Unlike the South, New England soil did not permit the growth of large quantities of cash crops.
    (E) Unlike the south, New England colonial charters did not allow for high-volume agriculture.

60. Bacon's Rebellion is most associated with which early colony?
    (A) Virginia
    (B) Maryland
    (C) North Carolina
    (D) Massachusetts
    (E) Pennsylvania

61. In colonial Virginia, the Piedmont referred to
    (A) foothills of the Appalachian Mountains in western Virginia
    (B) the area in eastern Virginia along the major rivers
    (C) coastal highlands in the southern part of Virginia
    (D) wide-open plains in western Virginia
    (E) a trade route between Virginia and Maryland

62. Which of the following statements was *not* true of the Tidewater in colonial Virginia?
    (A) It was located on the James and Rappahannock Rivers.
    (B) It was adjacent to the Chesapeake Bay.
    (C) Many of the wealthiest Virginian plantations were located in this region.
    (D) Many poorer farmers and former indentured servants were forced to locate in the Tidewater.
    (E) It was east of the Piedmont region and the Appalachians.

63. Which of the following statements is *not* true of the House of Burgesses in colonial Virginia?
    (A) It consisted initially of 22 representatives.
    (B) All laws passed by the body could be vetoed by the governor.
    (C) It was responsible for electing the governor.
    (D) Only landowning males could vote for representatives.
    (E) The powers of the House of Burgesses were limited when Virginia became a royal colony.

64. King Philip's War could be best described as
    (A) an uprising of poor famers against wealthy plantation owners
    (B) the colonial conflict resulting from the European War of Spanish Succession
    (C) the first of a series of wars between the English and French colonies in North America
    (D) an early revolt by enslaved Africans in the southern colonies
    (E) a conflict between Native Americans and New England settlers

65. Which early colonial trial is most associated with the First Amendment's idea of freedom of the press?
    (A) The trial of John Peter Zenger
    (B) The trial of Anne Hutchinson
    (C) The Salem Witch Trials
    (D) The Boston Massacre trial
    (E) James Otis's challenge of writs of assistance

CHAPTER 4

The Era of Discontent

66. Which of the following actions best illustrates the policy of salutary neglect?

    (A) Lack of enforcement of the Navigation Acts prior to 1763
    (B) Creation of royal colonies such as the Carolinas
    (C) The practice of non-importation within the colonies after 1765
    (D) The use of vice admiralty courts to prosecute smugglers
    (E) Lack of interference with indigenous populations west of the Appalachians prior to 1763

67. Which of the following actions does *not* illustrate the strategy employed by Lord William Pitt during the French and Indian War (1756–1763)?

    (A) Taking over the French forts located along both sides of the Mississippi River
    (B) Making peace with important Native American allies
    (C) Changing the British fighting style to better match the frontier
    (D) Fighting in North America rather than on the European mainland
    (E) Establishing control of the Saint Lawrence Seaway

68. Which of the following was *not* a provision of the Coercive Acts?

    (A) The closing of Boston Harbor
    (B) The establishment of martial law in the colonies
    (C) The creation of colonial-controlled legislatures
    (D) The quartering of British troops by colonists
    (E) The allowance of trials to be held in jurisdictions other than where a crime was committed

69. The main purpose of the Albany Congress of 1754 was to
    (A) draw up a treaty with the Native Americans
    (B) protest restrictions on western settlements put in place by the British Parliament
    (C) develop common defensive measures against the Spanish after they acquired lands west of the Appalachian Mountains from France
    (D) create a confederation that could militarily challenge British control in the North American colonies
    (E) establish a strong governing body that would replace parliamentary control of the colonies

70. Non-importation is best illustrated by
    (A) American colonists refusing to purchase goods from Britain after the Stamp Act
    (B) the British Parliament limiting the sale of gunpowder to colonists under the Coercive Acts
    (C) the 1807 law banning the importation of slaves from Africa
    (D) the strict limits placed on the number of Catholics allowed into the Massachusetts Bay Colony
    (E) the strict immigration restrictions on Japanese citizens established under the Gentlemen's Agreement

71. Which of the following was *not* an intention of the Proclamation of 1763?
    (A) Reducing conflicts between British colonists and Native Americans
    (B) Keeping British colonists loyal to the British government
    (C) Limiting the growth of manufacturing within the North American colonies
    (D) Enforcing the authority of the Church of England within the colonies
    (E) Ensuring British control over colonial trade

72. Which of the following British laws illustrates an attempt to keep the colonists from purchasing goods from other colonial powers?
    (A) The Sugar Act
    (B) The Quartering Act
    (C) The Quebec Act
    (D) The Coercive Acts
    (E) The Currency Act

73. The main purpose of the _____ was to create a united treaty with the Iroquois and serve for the common defense against the French.
    (A) Albany Congress
    (B) First Continental Congress
    (C) Second Continental Congress
    (D) Committees of Correspondence
    (E) Articles of Confederation

74. Which of the following powers was vested within the Articles of Confederation?
    (A) The power to tax
    (B) The power to regulate interstate trade
    (C) The power to regulate foreign trade
    (D) The power to raise a standing army
    (E) The power to declare war

75. What was the 18th-century principle of virtual representation?
    (A) The British government represents all citizens regardless of their actual representation in Parliament.
    (B) Although slaves lack the right to vote, they need to be considered when conducting an official government census.
    (C) Paper currency has value as long as it is backed by precious metal.
    (D) Only those males who own land can rightly participate in government and vote.
    (E) All British subjects have the right to a jury trial.

76. The purpose of the Declaratory Act was to
    (A) require that colonists provide housing and board to British troops
    (B) create a new tax on sugar and molasses from the French West Indies
    (C) establish a tax on household goods such as lead, paint, tea, and glass
    (D) state that the British government had the authority to create laws without colonial representation
    (E) make it illegal for colonies to issue their own paper currency

77. Which of the following actions was a result of the Boston Tea Party?
    (A) All of the other colonies rejected the Bostonians' actions.
    (B) The tea tax was repealed.
    (C) The British government reopened Boston Harbor for trade.
    (D) The Coercive Acts were issued.
    (E) Britain opened negotiations with Boston concerning taxation.

78. The death of Crispus Attucks is associated with which of the following events?
    (A) Lexington and Concord
    (B) The Boston Massacre
    (C) Shays' Rebellion
    (D) Gabriel Prosser's Rebellion
    (E) The Whiskey Rebellion

79. Which of the following colonists defended the British soldiers involved in the Boston Massacre?
    (A) James Otis
    (B) John Dickenson
    (C) John Adams
    (D) Samuel Adams
    (E) Andrew Hamilton

80. The main purpose of the Olive Branch Petition was to
    (A) create peace between western settlers and Native American tribes
    (B) end the war between the British and French in the Ohio River Valley
    (C) avoid the escalation of violence between Britain and the colonies
    (D) reconcile Britain and the colonies after the Boston Massacre
    (E) reconcile northern and southern states prior to the Civil War

81. The reason British troops were ordered to Concord in 1775 was to
    (A) impose marshal law on the town
    (B) defeat the Continental army in one decisive attack
    (C) capture a store of militia weapons
    (D) disrupt colonial intelligence
    (E) capture the Second Continental Congress

82. Writs of assistance refer to
    (A) general search warrants
    (B) requirements to house and feed soldiers
    (C) stamps that proved taxes were paid on goods
    (D) agreements to serve for the common defense of the colonies
    (E) agreements to establish colonies overseas

83. The Third Amendment to the U.S. Constitution relates most directly to

   (A) the Quartering Act
   (B) the Navigation Act
   (C) the Stamp Act
   (D) the Quebec Act
   (E) the Tea Act

84. Which was *not* an advantage of the British during the American Revolution?

   (A) They had a superior navy.
   (B) They had more Native American allies.
   (C) They successfully utilized loyalist support.
   (D) They had a greater treasury.
   (E) They had greater manufacturing capabilities.

85. Which of the following battles did *not* include the presence of George Washington?

   (A) Trenton
   (B) Brandywine
   (C) Monmouth
   (D) Saratoga
   (E) Yorktown

86. Which of the following advantages did the colonists have during the American Revolution?

   (A) More accurate rifles
   (B) Developed manufacturing
   (C) An experienced military
   (D) More Native American alliances
   (E) A large treasury

87. Which of the following statements best describes the role African-Americans played in the American Revolution?

   (A) The colonists actively enlisted black slaves to build up the Continental army's strength.
   (B) The British army adopted a policy of enlisting runaway slaves and offered emancipation to gain support.
   (C) African-Americans uniformly supported the patriot cause of freedom from Britain.
   (D) After the war, Britain returned most of the slaves who attempted to seek refuge in Canada.
   (E) African-Americans did not play a significant role during the American Revolution.

88. After 1778, the British military adopted a strategy of

(A) using Native American allies to regain control of the West and then march east to the Atlantic
(B) ending the revolution by cutting off New England from the rest of the colonies
(C) adopting a defensive strategy and winning through attrition
(D) capturing key southern ports with the aid of loyalist militias, and then advancing northward
(E) convincing Benedict Arnold to turn West Point over to the British

89. General Charles Cornwallis was forced to surrender at Yorktown mainly because

(A) the British failed to capture key southern ports such as Charleston and Savannah
(B) the Hessians no longer offered their support after Saratoga
(C) the French navy won control of the Chesapeake Bay
(D) the Spanish agreed to reinforce Washington's army
(E) the Americans successfully recaptured New York City

90. Which of the following groups would most likely support the Articles of Confederation?

(A) Those who held strong anti-monarchical views
(B) Men who served as officers during the revolution
(C) Citizens who held government-issued securities
(D) New England merchants and bankers
(E) Politicians who feared rule by the masses

91. What movement most directly influenced the writing of the Declaration of Independence?

(A) Scholasticism
(B) Humanism
(C) The Enlightenment
(D) Transcendentalism
(E) Romanticism

92. Which of the following issues was *not* addressed in the Declaration of Independence?

(A) The disbanding of colonial governments
(B) The principle that all men deserve access to equal wealth
(C) The quartering of troops by colonists
(D) The idea of taxation without representation
(E) The trade restrictions being placed on the colonies

93. Which of the following battles was a decisive win for the Americans?
    (A) Brandywine
    (B) Monmouth
    (C) Bunker Hill
    (D) Trenton
    (E) Long Island

94. The role of General Friedrich Von Steuben during the American Revolution would be best described as
    (A) leading the Hessian troops at the Battle of Trenton
    (B) leading the colonial militias at Saratoga
    (C) training the Continental army at Valley Forge
    (D) leading French forces at Yorktown
    (E) defeating the British navy in the Chesapeake Bay

95. Which Revolutionary War battle is considered the turning point in favor of the American colonists?
    (A) Brandywine
    (B) Monmouth
    (C) Saratoga
    (D) Bunker Hill
    (E) Long Island

96. Molly Pitcher is most associated with which American Revolutionary battle?
    (A) Monmouth
    (B) Trenton
    (C) Springfield
    (D) Saratoga
    (E) Bunker Hill

97. Which of the following terms was *not* part of the 1783 Treaty of Paris?
    (A) Britain agreed to remove troops from U.S. territory.
    (B) The importation of slaves was banned.
    (C) The borders of the United States were established.
    (D) The United States agreed to pay existing debts owed to England.
    (E) The United States agreed not to persecute loyalists remaining in the country.

98. Which of the following events serves as an example of a citizen revolt following the American Revolution before the signing of the Constitution?
    (A) Shays' Rebellion
    (B) Gabriel Prosser's Rebellion
    (C) Bacon's Rebellion
    (D) The Whiskey Rebellion
    (E) The Boston Massacre

99. The Northwest Ordinance of 1787 was responsible for
    (A) removing Native Americans from the Ohio River Valley
    (B) allowing for slavery in the Ohio River Valley
    (C) removing British troops remaining on American territory
    (D) establishing the procedure for creating new states
    (E) closing the land west of the Appalachian Mountains from settlement

100. Which power was *not* vested within the Articles of Confederation?
    (A) Declaring war
    (B) Regulating trade
    (C) Making foreign treaties and alliances
    (D) Establishing a post office
    (E) Regulating Native American affairs

CHAPTER 5

The Constitution and Early U.S. Government

101. The United States officially gained its independence with the
- (A) Treaty of Westphalia
- (B) Treaty of Versailles
- (C) Treaty of Ghent
- (D) Treaty of Paris
- (E) Treaty of Tordesillas

102. Which of the following is *not* a legacy of the Articles of Confederation?
- (A) Creation of the Great Seal
- (B) Establishment of the reservation system for Native Americans
- (C) Creation of the U.S. Treasury
- (D) Allowing the statehood of western territories
- (E) Establishment of a post office

103. Which state did *not* attend the 1787 Philadelphia convention?
- (A) New York
- (B) South Carolina
- (C) Georgia
- (D) Rhode Island
- (E) New Hampshire

104. The New Jersey Plan would most likely be supported by
- (A) states with large populations
- (B) states with small populations
- (C) states that were mostly agricultural
- (D) states in the South
- (E) states in the North

105. Which statement concerning the Virginia Plan is *not* correct?

(A) It was drafted by James Madison.
(B) It was a bicameral body.
(C) Representatives were based on population.
(D) It was a unicameral body.
(E) It gave the legislative branch the power to tax.

106. At the Constitutional Convention, the Great Compromise referred to

(A) the counting of slave populations in censuses for representation
(B) the ratification of the U.S. Constitution
(C) the agreement of northern and southern states to allow the expansion of slavery in the South
(D) the creation of the Senate and the House of Representatives
(E) the creation of checks and balances

107. Which of the following people is referred to as the Father of the Constitution?

(A) James Madison
(B) Benjamin Franklin
(C) Thomas Jefferson
(D) George Washington
(E) John Adams

108. What is judicial review?

(A) The Supreme Court's power to strike down laws that are unconstitutional
(B) The requirement that the Senate approve all Supreme Court nominations
(C) The president's right to appoint judges to the Supreme Court
(D) The establishment of lower federal circuit courts
(E) The process of removing justices from the Supreme Court

109. The main purpose of the Three-Fifths Compromise was to

(A) establish the number of votes needed to approve legislation
(B) appropriate congressional seats
(C) formalize a number of state votes needed to ratify the Constitution
(D) develop a method to amend the Constitution
(E) create a system to override a presidential veto

110. Which of the following statements best describes the overall impact of the Three-Fifths Compromise?
    (A) The institution of slavery became officially recognized under the Constitution.
    (B) The compromise provided a clear method for amending the Constitution.
    (C) The compromise provided a clear method for overriding a presidential veto.
    (D) The compromise gave the southern states a clear majority in the House of Representatives.
    (E) The compromise secured the northern states' support for the Constitution.

111. Which of the following beliefs would *not* be held by the Antifederalists?
    (A) The Necessary and Proper Clause gave the central government too much power.
    (B) The government should be able to hold a standing army in times of peace.
    (C) A Bill of Rights was necessary.
    (D) The executive branch threatened states' rights.
    (E) Power was best vested in the hands of state governments.

112. Which of the following framers of the Constitution would most likely view a Bill of Rights as a threat to individual liberties?
    (A) Patrick Henry
    (B) George Mason
    (C) Samuel Adams
    (D) James Monroe
    (E) Alexander Hamilton

113. The powers of the president are outlined in which article of the Constitution?
    (A) Article I
    (B) Article II
    (C) Article III
    (D) Article IV
    (E) Article V

114. Which of the following individuals was *not* a member of the first presidential cabinet under the Constitution?

   (A) Edmund Randolph
   (B) Alexander Hamilton
   (C) John Marshall
   (D) Thomas Jefferson
   (E) Henry Knox

115. The Judiciary Act of 1789 established

   (A) judicial review
   (B) a federal court system
   (C) the Supreme Court
   (D) the chief justice
   (E) writs of assistance

116. Alexander Hamilton's debt plan consolidated the nation's Revolutionary War debts into one debt to be paid off by

   (A) American merchants
   (B) the individual states
   (C) the national government
   (D) newly discovered gold deposits in the West
   (E) foreign investors

117. Which of the following led directly to an undeclared naval war between the United States and France?

   (A) Jay's Treaty
   (B) Pinckney's Treaty
   (C) The XYZ Affair
   (D) The Whiskey Rebellion
   (E) The Treaty of Alliance

118. Which of the following statements is most accurate concerning the Alien and Sedition Acts?

   (A) The acts were passed by a Republican Congress.
   (B) The acts loosened the requirements for U.S. citizenship.
   (C) The acts were passed to protect John Adams from his critics.
   (D) The acts furthered U.S. citizens' First Amendment rights.
   (E) All of the acts expired in 1800.

119. Who was the French foreign minister who interfered with the United States' neutrality in the war between Britain and France during the French Revolution?

   (A) Edmond-Charles Genêt
   (B) Charles Talleyrand
   (C) Georges Clemenceau
   (D) Ferdinand Maximilian
   (E) Maximilian Robespierre

120. Which of the following policies or actions would have been the most popular among people living in the western United States prior to 1812?

   (A) The Force Bill
   (B) Hamilton's economic program
   (C) Pinckney's Treaty
   (D) The Missouri Compromise
   (E) The Alien and Sedition Acts

121. Which group directly profited from the creation of the first national bank?

   (A) Poor farmers
   (B) Jeffersonian Republicans
   (C) People of the northern United States
   (D) People of the southern United States
   (E) People of the western United States

122. Which of the following actions did not directly address a territorial concern?

   (A) Jay's Treaty
   (B) The Whiskey Rebellion
   (C) The Louisiana Purchase
   (D) Pinckney's Treaty
   (E) The Adams-Onís Treaty

123. Which of the following policies was supported by James Madison?

   (A) Creation of a national bank
   (B) Jay's Treaty
   (C) Passing of the Alien and Sedition Acts
   (D) Creation of the Kentucky and Virginia Resolutions
   (E) Issuance of government bonds to help pay the domestic debt

124. The Virginia and Kentucky Resolutions were passed in order to
  (A) promote an excise tax on whiskey
  (B) nullify the power of the federal government
  (C) support the Alien and Sedition Acts
  (D) call for the absorption of the state debts by the federal government
  (E) affirm the power of the federal government

125. Which of the following groups would most likely support the policies of Alexander Hamilton?
  (A) States that independently paid off their debt from the Revolution
  (B) Western farmers
  (C) Entrepreneurs in manufacturing
  (D) People who harbored strong anti-monarchical sentiments after the revolution
  (E) Strict constitutionalists

126. The *Marbury v. Madison* decision strengthened the power of the
  (A) executive branch
  (B) judicial branch
  (C) legislative branch
  (D) legislative and judicial branches
  (E) judicial and executive branches

127. The appointment of John Marshall enabled the Federalists to retain power in which area of government?
  (A) House of Representatives
  (B) Senate
  (C) electoral college
  (D) judicial branch
  (E) executive branch

128. Which of the following policies is most associated with the Native American chief Handsome Lake?
  (A) Full assimilation into American society
  (B) Abstention from alcohol
  (C) Ending land treaties with the U.S. government
  (D) Total rejection of white society
  (E) Voluntary relocation west of the Mississippi River

129. Which of the following statements describes a result of the Embargo of 1807?

   (A) The embargo stopped the smuggling of goods into the United States.
   (B) The embargo was only against the British.
   (C) The embargo led to an increase of trade in the southern states.
   (D) The embargo was strongly supported by New England.
   (E) The embargo benefited northern manufacturing.

130. Of the following people, who is most associated with the War Hawks prior to the War of 1812?

   (A) Charles Sumner
   (B) Elbridge Gerry
   (C) Henry Clay
   (D) Daniel Webster
   (E) Thomas Jefferson

131. Which of the following was *not* a direct reason for the United States to declare war on Britain in 1812?

   (A) Britain's support of Native American uprisings
   (B) A desire to take Spanish-held lands in North America
   (C) British impressments of American sailors
   (D) British actions during the XYZ Affair
   (E) Election of the War Hawks in 1810

132. Which group of people would most support the Hartford Convention?

   (A) New England merchants
   (B) Southern plantation owners
   (C) Western frontiersmen
   (D) Native Americans in the Northwest
   (E) Democratic Republicans

133. "The Star-Spangled Banner" is most associated with which battle location?

   (A) New Orleans
   (B) Fort McHenry
   (C) Thames
   (D) Bladensburg
   (E) Lake Erie

134. Which treaty ended the War of 1812?

    (A) The Treaty of Paris
    (B) The Treaty of Greenville
    (C) The Treaty of Ghent
    (D) Jay's Treaty
    (E) Pinckney's Treaty

135. Which of the following statements does *not* describe a direct result of the War of 1812?

    (A) The United States gained further fishing rights along the eastern Canadian coast.
    (B) American domestic manufacturing increased.
    (C) The border between Canada and the United States was restored to the prewar locations.
    (D) British impressments of American ships increased.
    (E) The United States gained parts of western Florida.

136. What was the name of the ship overtaken by slaves during the early 19th century in the Americas?

    (A) *Leopold*
    (B) *Amistad*
    (C) *Merrimac*
    (D) *Chesapeake*
    (E) *Constitution*

137. Which of the following projects was not part of the transportation revolution prior to the Civil War?

    (A) Erie Canal
    (B) Cumberland Road
    (C) Baltimore & Ohio Railroad
    (D) Clermont
    (E) Transcontinental Railroad

138. Which construction project connected New York City to the Great Lakes?

    (A) Erie Canal
    (B) Baltimore & Ohio Railroad
    (C) Cumberland Road
    (D) National Highway
    (E) Transcontinental Railroad

139. Which of the following statements does *not* describe a result of the cotton gin?

(A) Cotton became a staple export crop.
(B) The demand for western lands increased.
(C) Eli Whitney made huge profits.
(D) The demand for slave labor increased.
(E) Greater pressure was exerted on removing Native Americans from the South.

140. Which of the following best describes the practice of slavery from the end of the American Revolution to 1793?

(A) The number of slaves was gradually decreasing in the South.
(B) All northern states abolished the practice of slavery.
(C) Most slaves worked on cotton plantations.
(D) The federal government did not formally acknowledge the practice of slavery.
(E) The importation of slaves was formally banned.

141. Which religious group is most associated with the Second Great Awakening?

(A) Seventh-Day Adventists
(B) Quakers
(C) Amish
(D) Lutherans
(E) Pentecostals

142. Which of the following was a goal of Gabriel Prosser's Rebellion?

(A) Protesting excise taxes placed on whiskey
(B) Voicing disapproval of high tariffs
(C) Opposing government actions deemed unconstitutional
(D) Creating a massive slave uprising in Virginia
(E) Protesting direct taxes imposed by state governments

143. The main purpose of passing the Twelfth Amendment to the Constitution was to

(A) correct irregularities in presidential elections
(B) prevent individuals in one state from suing another state in federal courts
(C) allow the federal government to purchase new lands from foreign powers
(D) end the importation of slaves from outside of the nation
(E) outlaw forced labor and involuntary servitude

CHAPTER 6

The Era of Good Feelings to the Age of Jackson

144. Which of the following statements about the Treaty of Ghent is *not* true?

(A) It ended the War of 1812.

(B) It settled the border disputes involving the Louisiana Territory.

(C) It failed to address British impressments.

(D) It did not address the idea of freedom of the seas.

(E) It was signed by Britain and the United States.

145. Which of the following was a major result of the *McCulloch v. Maryland* decision?

(A) It addressed Native American territorial rights.

(B) It stated that the national bank was illegal.

(C) It prevented states from interfering with business contracts.

(D) It enforced the principle that the federal government has authority over state governments.

(E) It established the federal government's right to regulate interstate commerce.

146. Which of the following Supreme Court decisions directly dealt with Native American territorial rights?

(A) *McCulloch v. Maryland*

(B) *Worcester v. Georgia*

(C) *Dartmouth College v. Woodward*

(D) *Marbury v. Madison*

(E) *Gibbons v. Ogden*

147. Which of the following Supreme Court decisions directly established the federal government's right to regulate interstate commerce?

(A) *McCulloch v. Maryland*
(B) *Plessy v. Ferguson*
(C) *Dartmouth College v. Woodward*
(D) *Gibbons v. Ogden*
(E) *Schenck v. United States*

148. Which of the following was *not* a provision of the initial Monroe Doctrine?

(A) The Western Hemisphere was closed to colonization.
(B) The Americas were politically different from the nations of Europe.
(C) European intervention in the Western Hemisphere would be regarded as a threat to U.S. security.
(D) The United States would not intervene in European wars and conflicts.
(E) The United States would use military intervention in the Western Hemisphere if needed.

149. Which of the following statements about the Missouri Compromise is *not* true?

(A) Maine was admitted into the Union as a free state.
(B) Missouri joined the Union as a slave state.
(C) Slavery was allowed in the old Northwest Territory.
(D) Slavery was outlawed north of latitude 36°30' north.
(E) The Missouri Compromise was deemed unconstitutional after the *Dred Scott* decision

150. Which of the following was a direct result of the Missouri Compromise?

(A) The state of Maine was created.
(B) Slavery was allowed only in states south of Missouri's northern border.
(C) Kentucky outlawed slavery.
(D) The balance of free and slave states ended.
(E) California was admitted into the Union as a free state.

151. Which president was responsible for signing the Missouri Compromise?

(A) John Quincy Adams
(B) James Madison
(C) James Monroe
(D) Andrew Jackson
(E) James K. Polk

152. The first national labor union in the United States was the
    (A) International Workers Union
    (B) National Trades Union
    (C) National Workers Union
    (D) Knights of Labor
    (E) National Labor Union

153. Which of the following people was most directly responsible for bringing industrialism to the United States?
    (A) Benjamin Franklin
    (B) Samuel Slater
    (C) Eli Whitney
    (D) Thomas Edison
    (E) Henry Ford

154. Industrialism emerged in the northern states prior to the Civil War as a result of the following conditions *except*
    (A) availability of water power from streams and rivers
    (B) availability of capital
    (C) a shortage of labor
    (D) poor agricultural conditions
    (E) access to developed ports and railroads

155. Oliver Evans is most associated with which invention?
    (A) The mechanized flour mill
    (B) The cotton gin
    (C) Interchangeable parts
    (D) The first commercial steamboat
    (E) The first textile mill in the United States

156. The first federally funded telegraph connected which two cities?
    (A) Washington, D.C., and Richmond, Virginia
    (B) New York City and Philadelphia
    (C) Philadelphia and Baltimore
    (D) Philadelphia and Washington, D.C.
    (E) Washington, D.C., and Baltimore

157. Which of the following is *not* part of the economic theory referred to as the American System?

(A) High tariffs

(B) Road building

(C) Encouragement of new enterprises

(D) The national bank

(E) Cheap sale of public lands

158. Which president is most associated with the Era of Good Feeling?

(A) John Adams

(B) Thomas Jefferson

(C) Andrew Jackson

(D) James K. Polk

(E) James Monroe

159. What territorial gain was made with the Adams-Onís Treaty?

(A) Florida

(B) The Philippines

(C) California

(D) Port of New Orleans

(E) Puerto Rico

160. The Cumberland Road connected the Eastern Seaboard to what western river?

(A) Mississippi River

(B) Missouri River

(C) Ohio River

(D) Delaware River

(E) Platte River

161. What was a common theme in the nullification theories held by Thomas Jefferson and John C. Calhoun?

(A) The right of the individual to speak against the government

(B) The right of judicial review within the Supreme Court

(C) The right of states to strike down federal laws they see as unconstitutional

(D) The authority of the federal government over the states

(E) The right of the Congress to pass all laws necessary and proper

162. The Preemption Act most directly dealt with

(A) the sale of government land
(B) the right of the United States to attack nations perceived as a threat
(C) the passage of strict slave laws to suppress future slave uprisings
(D) the federal government's right to remove Native Americans from lands planned for future expansion
(E) the states' right to nullify federal mandates

163. Which of the following inventions did *not* help fuel the agricultural boom in the first half of the 19th century?

(A) The cotton gin
(B) The steel plow
(C) The mechanical reaper
(D) The steamboat
(E) The cigarette-rolling machine

164. Which of the following was an observation of Alexis de Tocqueville concerning American society?

(A) The ability of newcomers to own land
(B) The lack of religious influence in society
(C) The perpetual gap between the rich and poor
(D) The fair treatment of Native Americans
(E) The continued notion of European aristocracy

165. Which of the following statements best defines the Cult of Domesticity?

(A) Women should exemplify the notions of virtue in fulfilling their duties to the family.
(B) The United States should assume an isolationist policy in foreign affairs.
(C) Agriculture and manufacturing should primarily benefit local economies.
(D) High protective tariffs were needed to protect American manufacturing.
(E) Slave women needed to be taught how to fulfill their duties as mothers.

166. Mary Lyon is most associated with establishing which of the following advancements for women?

(A) Access to suffrage
(B) Property ownership
(C) Access to higher education
(D) Access to practicing medicine
(E) Ability to sit on juries

167. Which of the following best describes the goals of the American Colonization Society during the early part of the 19th century?

(A) Expanding the United States' influence in the Pacific
(B) Returning free blacks to Africa
(C) Expanding American intervention in Latin America
(D) Promoting the practices of Manifest Destiny
(E) Expanding American missionaries in Asia

168. Which of the following people was *not* a candidate in the 1824 presidential election?

(A) John Quincy Adams
(B) John C. Calhoun
(C) Henry Clay
(D) William Crawford
(E) Andrew Jackson

169. Which of the following statements best describes the result of the 1824 presidential election?

(A) John Quincy Adams won the popular vote.
(B) No candidate won the majority of electoral votes.
(C) The election was decided by the Senate.
(D) Andrew Jackson won the majority of electoral votes.
(E) John Quincy Adams had his strongest support in the South.

170. Which president is associated with the creation of a Kitchen Cabinet?

(A) John Quincy Adams
(B) Franklin D. Roosevelt
(C) Ulysses S. Grant
(D) Andrew Jackson
(E) Franklin Pierce

171. What new style of campaigning came about in the 1828 presidential election?

(A) Massive infighting among candidates within the same party
(B) Greater focus on candidates' debates and speeches
(C) Greater focus on specific current issues
(D) Stronger emphasis on rallies, slogans, and parades
(E) Movement away from malicious attacks between candidates

172. Which of the following objectives best describes Andrew Jackson's policy toward Native Americans?
    (A) Complete destruction
    (B) Removal to reservations in the West
    (C) Assimilation into American society
    (D) Protection of traditional land claims
    (E) Return of lost lands from unfair treaties

173. Which of the following is *not* considered part of Andrew Jackson's legacy?
    (A) Creation of a two-party political system
    (B) The modern media-driven election campaign
    (C) Reduction of influence in the executive branch over the branches of the federal government
    (D) Increase in the average person's access to political power
    (E) Establishment of the second national bank

174. The Tariff of Abominations of 1828 was opposed mainly because
    (A) it mainly benefited western states
    (B) it hurt northern manufacturers' long-term growth
    (C) it hurt the sale of southern cotton
    (D) it restricted the sale of slaves
    (E) it benefited British imports

175. Andrew Jackson differed from previous presidents in that he
    (A) was a slave owner
    (B) was a wealthy landowner
    (C) came from a family of poor immigrants
    (D) built a successful career in law and politics
    (E) was a college graduate

176. Who did Andrew Jackson choose to be his successor after his second term?
    (A) William Henry Harrison
    (B) Martin Van Buren
    (C) John Tyler
    (D) John C. Calhoun
    (E) Henry Clay

177. Which of the following statements best describes Andrew Jackson's views of the national bank?

(A) It mainly benefited northern bankers.
(B) It served common man.
(C) It symbolized southern power and strength.
(D) It protected the nation's democratic government.
(E) It was needed to protect U.S. currency.

178. Which of the following played a role in the creation of the Whig Party?

(A) The renewal of the national bank
(B) The increased authority of the House and Senate under President Andrew Jackson
(C) Supporters of the executive branch
(D) Concerns over the Force Bill and states' rights
(E) Sharp economic growth during the years 1833–1834

179. Which of the following was *not* a result of the end of the Second Bank of the United States?

(A) Creation of state "pet" banks
(B) A bank panic
(C) Creation of the Whig Party
(D) The Specie Circular
(E) Philadelphia becoming the center of American banking

180. What was the Specie Circular?

(A) A state institution chosen to hold funds from the national bank
(B) An executive order requiring that government land be paid for in gold or silver
(C) A railroad scandal that used stocks to bribe elected officials
(D) A bill that authorized the use of military force to uphold federal law
(E) The basing of currency on both a gold and a silver standard

181. Which of the following groups would *not* be a supporter of the Whig Party?

(A) Northern industrialists
(B) Supporters of the national bank
(C) States' rights activists
(D) Supporters of a powerful executive branch
(E) Supporters of term limits

CHAPTER 7

Antebellum Reform Movements

182. Which of the following objectives was *not* a goal of Tecumseh's confederacy?

(A) Creating a broad alliance to stop settlers
(B) Stopping future treaties that ceded land
(C) Working for the common defense of the confederacy
(D) Returning to traditional cultural practices
(E) Establishing a new settlement west of the Mississippi River

183. Which belief would most be associated with William Lloyd Garrison?

(A) Federal regulation of slavery
(B) Strict constitutional interpretation
(C) Secession of the South
(D) Ending federal tariffs
(E) Abolition of slavery

184. The term *domestic feminism* during the first half of the 19th century could best be defined as

(A) women adopting a more assertive role in the home
(B) women gaining greater access to local politics and regional elections
(C) women gaining broader rights in the area of property ownership
(D) women being awarded primary custody of their children
(E) the advancements of the suffrage movement within the nation

185. Which of the following statements best illustrates the average size of white families during the first part of the 19th century?

(A) Families generally grew larger.
(B) Urban families generally grew smaller, while rural families grew larger.
(C) Urban families increased in size, while rural families grew smaller.
(D) Both urban and rural families became smaller.
(E) Trends in family size remained consistent with those of the colonial period.

186. Lucretia Mott and Elizabeth Cady Stanton held the first U.S. convention on the rights of women at which location?

(A) Seneca Falls, New York
(B) New York City
(C) Washington, D.C.
(D) Niagara Falls, New York
(E) Boston, Massachusetts

187. The main focus of the temperance movement was to

(A) promote equality between races
(B) promote equality between genders
(C) pacify sectionalism within the United States
(D) limit the influx of immigrants
(E) prohibit the consumption of alcohol

188. Which of the following people is most associated with providing treatment for the mentally ill?

(A) Horace Mann
(B) Dorothea Dix
(C) Lucretia Mott
(D) Elizabeth Blackwell
(E) Jane Addams

189. Which of the following people is considered a leader in education reform in the early 19th century?

(A) Henry David Thoreau
(B) Horace Mann
(C) John Dewey
(D) Dorothea Dix
(E) Jane Addams

190. Which of the following was a main goal of the educational reform movement of the early 1800s?

(A) Providing vocational training
(B) Creating responsible new citizens
(C) Teaching young people to read the Bible
(D) Creating coeducational schools
(E) Ending public funding of schools

191. Which field was *not* traditionally open to women for employment during the early 19th century?

    (A) Nursing
    (B) Textile work
    (C) Teaching
    (D) Secretarial work
    (E) Domestic service

192. Which of the following views of public education was *not* supported by Horace Mann?

    (A) Schools should be publicly funded.
    (B) Elementary education should be offered to affluent males only.
    (C) Education should be nonsectarian.
    (D) Students should be taught citizenship and self-discipline.
    (E) Teachers should be well trained.

193. What was the main goal of early-19th-century utopian communities?

    (A) Rehabilitating nonviolent criminals
    (B) Providing better services for low-income families
    (C) Serving as sociological studies
    (D) Achieving religious, social, economic, and/or political perfection
    (E) Furthering American-style democracy in the non-Western world

194. Which of the following people would be most associated with the utopian communities of the early 1800s?

    (A) Robert Owen
    (B) Horace Mann
    (C) Frederick Douglass
    (D) Elijah P. Lovejoy
    (E) David Walker

195. John Humphrey Noyes is most associated with which of the following utopian societies?

    (A) New Harmony
    (B) The Oneida Community
    (C) The Icarian Community
    (D) The Spring Farm Colony
    (E) The Brook Farm Community

196. _____ has been referred to as the Black Moses for helping lead over 300 African slaves to freedom.

(A) Harriet Tubman
(B) Dorothea Dix
(C) Frederick Douglass
(D) Stephen Douglas
(E) John Brown

197. Which of the following issues caused major divisions in the early abolitionist movement?

(A) Debate over ending the slave trade
(B) The role of Native Americans
(C) Providing job training for former slaves
(D) The role of women within the movement
(E) The economic benefits of slavery

198. Many Northern workers rejected the goals of the abolitionist movement because

(A) Congress imposed a gag rule
(B) African-Americans lacked education
(C) they feared competition for jobs
(D) the Constitution clearly supported slavery
(E) southern cotton production was needed to keep the factories running

199. Which of the following characteristics is associated with the 19th-century transcendentalist movement?

(A) The importance of empirical understanding over emotion
(B) The focus on established principles for greater understanding
(C) The emphasis on emotion and instinct
(D) The embrace of American culture and society
(E) The embrace of the doctrines of northern religious institutions

200. Which of the following people would *not* be considered a part of the 19th-century transcendentalist movement?

(A) Ralph Waldo Emerson
(B) Nathaniel Hawthorne
(C) Henry David Thoreau
(D) Margaret Fuller
(E) Frederick Henry Hedge

201. Which of the following is *not* considered part of Ralph Waldo Emerson's transcendentalist views?

(A) Rejection of divinity
(B) Independence of spirit
(C) Importance of self-reliance
(D) Focus on individualism
(E) A close connection with nature

CHAPTER 8

Antebellum Cultural Movements and Manifest Destiny

202. During the early 19th century, laws created in the Southern states concerning free blacks were primarily intended to

(A) guarantee legal status to free blacks
(B) establish guidelines for abolition within the state
(C) establish clear rules and regulations for the treatment of slaves
(D) persuade free blacks to relocate to Northern states
(E) aid the reclaiming of runaway slaves

203. What was the notion of popular sovereignty during the 19th century?

(A) Slavery would be decided by the Missouri Compromise.
(B) Inhabitants of territories becoming states would decide on the issue of slavery.
(C) The practice of slavery was to be outlawed in all U.S. states.
(D) Congress decided whether slavery would be legal in all new states.
(E) The issue of slavery would be decided through a national ballot.

204. Which of the following was *not* a focus of the reform movements of the early 1800s?

(A) Abolitionism
(B) Temperance
(C) Furthering the Establishment Clause
(D) Improving treatment of the mentally ill
(E) Prison reform

205. During the 19th century, settlement patterns of new immigrants were mostly based on

(A) areas where populations of their native communities had already been established

(B) regions where employment was most readily available

(C) the U.S. port they migrated to first

(D) areas where the climate was most similar to that of their native country

(E) regions where the government offered the best land grants

206. Between the 1820s and 1850s, the largest population of immigrants to the United States originated from what country?

(A) Russia

(B) France

(C) Poland

(D) Italy

(E) Ireland

207. Which of the following political parties based its entire platform on the issue of immigration?

(A) Whigs

(B) Democrats

(C) Free-Soilers

(D) Know-Nothings

(E) Republicans

208. The Hudson River School art movement of the mid-19th century addressed all of the following themes *except*

(A) the depiction of pastoral settings

(B) notions of realism and the common man

(C) the peaceful coexistence of humans and nature

(D) the ideas of American exploration and settlement

(E) notions of the transcendentalist authors

209. The influential collection of poems *Leaves of Grass*, considered a revolutionary work, was written by

(A) Samuel Clemens

(B) Henry David Thoreau

(C) Herman Melville

(D) Walt Whitman

(E) Emily Dickinson

210. The themes found in James Fennimore Cooper's literary works can be described as

    (A) being based heavily on European influence

    (B) being focused mainly on industrialization and urbanization

    (C) viewing nature as something to be conquered through expansion

    (D) describing the conflict between nature and progress

    (E) rejecting the notion of the pioneer spirit

211. Which 19th-century author is generally credited with creating the genre of the detective novel?

    (A) Edgar Allan Poe

    (B) Herman Melville

    (C) Nathaniel Hawthorne

    (D) James Fennimore Cooper

    (E) Ralph Waldo Emerson

212. The administration of which president is credited with opening Japan to trade with the United States?

    (A) James Polk

    (B) Millard Fillmore

    (C) Franklin Pierce

    (D) James Buchanan

    (E) Zachary Taylor

213. Who is generally credited with being one of the first people to popularize the phrase *Manifest Destiny*?

    (A) James Monroe

    (B) John Quincy Adams

    (C) Andrew Jackson

    (D) John L. O'Sullivan

    (E) Henry Clay

214. James K. Polk cited which U.S. policy to justify Manifest Destiny?

    (A) The Monroe Doctrine

    (B) Washington's pledge of neutrality

    (C) The Missouri Compromise

    (D) The American System

    (E) The Preemption Act

215. Which group would most likely support Manifest Destiny?

(A) Whigs
(B) Abolitionists
(C) Northern manufacturers
(D) Democrats
(E) Native Americans

216. Which of the following ideas would *not* be considered a justification for Manifest Destiny?

(A) The merit of American democratic institutions
(B) The notion that the United States was to be a "city upon a hill"
(C) The need to develop America's infrastructure
(D) Belief in a divine mandate to expand
(E) The goal of furthering the Monroe Doctrine

217. The founder of the Church of Jesus Christ of Latter Day Saints was

(A) Brigham Young
(B) Wilford Woodruff
(C) Joseph Smith
(D) John Smyth
(E) John Wesley

218. Which overland trail brought settlers to the Willamette Valley?

(A) Oregon Trail
(B) Mormon Trail
(C) Santa Fe Trail
(D) California Trail
(E) Chilkoot Trail

219. The slogan "Fifty-Four Forty or Fight!" dealt with which disputed U.S. border with another nation?

(A) Maine and Canada
(B) Oregon and Canada
(C) Alaska and Canada
(D) Texas and Mexico
(E) California and Mexico

220. Which of the following statements best describes the main reason Southerners supported the annexation of Texas?

(A) They wanted a safer route across the country.

(B) They wanted new seaports to help trade with Asia.

(C) They wanted better access to trade with Mexico.

(D) They wanted more territory and land where slavery had been established.

(E) They felt annexation would aid in Native American relocation.

221. Which of the following actions did *not* inspire the War for Texas Independence?

(A) Mexico outlawed the practice of slavery.

(B) Mexico passed excessive taxes on American goods.

(C) Pancho Villa led raids on American settlements, forcing the U.S. military to intervene.

(D) Mexico stopped allowing Americans to migrate into Texas.

(E) The Mexican government dissolved all state government.

222. The Battle of the Alamo was significant because

(A) it was an overwhelming victory by Americans seeking independence

(B) Americans obtained much-needed supplies in their fight for independence

(C) it launched James Bowie to national prominence, later allowing him to win a Senate seat

(D) it convinced the U.S. government to support the Texas independence movement

(E) it served as a rallying cry to recruit more support for the Texas independence movement

223. Which battle resulted in Texas's gaining independence from Mexico?

(A) the Alamo

(B) San Jacinto

(C) San Antonio de Béxar

(D) Goliad

(E) Guadalupe Hidalgo

224. Which of the following treaties ended the fighting during the Texan independence movement?

(A) Treaties of Velasco

(B) Treaty of San Juan

(C) Treaty of the Wilmot

(D) Treaty of San Jacinto

(E) Treaty of Ghent

225. Which of the following was *not* a reason that Britain considered annexing Texas?

(A) It would curb U.S. westward expansion.
(B) It would allow Britain to gain a new slave state.
(C) It would discredit the Monroe Doctrine.
(D) Britain would gain new territories in North America.
(E) Annexation would lessen Britain's dependence on American cotton.

226. Which of the following was *not* a cause of delaying the annexation of Texas?

(A) Resistance to the creation of another Southern state
(B) A U.S. neutrality pledge with Mexico
(C) Lack of support from the Whig Party in the Senate
(D) British trade and defensive treaties with Texas
(E) Abolitionists' opposition to creating another slave state

227. Which of the following people actively opposed the Mexican-American War?

(A) John Calhoun
(B) Daniel Webster
(C) Zachary Taylor
(D) Stephen Kearny
(E) James K. Polk

228. Which of the following events occurred first?

(A) Brigham Young led the Mormons to Utah.
(B) Joseph Smith was lynched.
(C) The Mormon church caused resentment through the practice of polygamy.
(D) James Buchanan ordered the U.S. military into Utah to suppress the Mormons.
(E) The Mormon church rejected the practice of polygamy.

229. Which of the following was the central issue of the presidential election of 1844?

(A) Slavery
(B) Temperance
(C) Women's suffrage
(D) Westward expansion
(E) Anti-Masons movement

230. The Mexican-American War ended with the signing of what treaty?
    (A) Treaty of Guadalupe Hidalgo
    (B) Treaty of San Juan
    (C) Treaty of the Wilmot
    (D) Treaty of San Jacinto
    (E) Treaty of Ghent

231. The Wilmot Proviso stated that
    (A) slavery would be allowed in the land taken from Mexico
    (B) slavery would be allowed in New Mexico Territory and Texas, but not California
    (C) the line between slave states and free states would be drawn at 36°30′ north
    (D) plantation owners in Texas could retain their current slaves, but no new slaves could be imported
    (E) slavery would not be allowed in the land taken from Mexico

232. Which Mexican-American War general was given the nickname Old Rough and Ready?
    (A) Winfield Scott
    (B) Robert E. Lee
    (C) Zachary Taylor
    (D) Stephen Kearny
    (E) Antonio Santa Anna

233. Which land actions gave the United States possession of the southern part of Arizona and New Mexico, west of the Rio Grande and south of the Gila River?
    (A) Gadsden Purchase
    (B) Treaty of Guadalupe Hidalgo
    (C) Platte Purchase
    (D) Hay-Herrán Treaty
    (E) Webster-Ashburton Treaty

234. Frederick Jackson Turner's Frontier Thesis focused on
    (A) European ideals in North America
    (B) the frontier and American democracy
    (C) the issue of slavery and westward expansion
    (D) the expansion of industrialism and the worker
    (E) cultural diversity among western settlers

235. Which military leader is credited with leading the army into California during the Mexican-American War?

(A) Stephen Kearny
(B) Winfield Scott
(C) Zachary Taylor
(D) James Polk
(E) Robert E. Lee

CHAPTER 9

The Mid-19th Century and Causes of the Civil War

236. Which of the following did *not* lead to the creation of the Monroe Doctrine?

(A) France's desire to reassert itself in the Western Hemisphere
(B) Russia's ambitions in the Pacific Northwest
(C) England's interest in annexing Texas
(D) Emergence of independent Latin American states
(E) Formation of the Holy Alliance in Europe

237. During the early 1800s, immigration in the United States was unrestricted primarily because

(A) such restrictions were deemed unconstitutional
(B) labor unions called for new immigrant labor
(C) southern plantations needed additional workers
(D) the industrial economy was creating new jobs
(E) the view that the United States was a melting pot became prominent

238. The British activity of rounders evolved into which American leisure activity during the first part of the 19th century?

(A) Horse racing
(B) Boxing
(C) Baseball
(D) Lacrosse
(E) Wrestling

239. Improvements in transportation and communication during the first part of the 19th century affected economic relations between regions of the United States by

(A) making the regions more interdependent

(B) making the regions more self-sufficient and independent

(C) making industrial regions economically dominant over agricultural regions

(D) making agricultural regions economically dominant over industrial regions

(E) furthering individual states' ability to regulate interstate commerce

240. The quote "I know of no more encouraging fact than the unquestioned ability of a man to elevate his life by conscious endeavor" best illustrates which 19th-century movement?

(A) Transcendentalism

(B) Pragmatism

(C) The social gospel

(D) The Gospel of Wealth

(E) Social Darwinism

241. Why did the Mormons choose Utah as the place to establish their communities?

(A) Utah's high mountains offered protection from the severe western weather.

(B) Utah contained large, expansive quantities of land for agriculture.

(C) Utah had many river systems for transportation.

(D) Utah's remote location made it less likely to be settled by other groups.

(E) The church's founder was given the land as a charter by the federal government.

242. Which of the following provisions was *not* considered part of personal-liberty laws during the mid-19th century?

(A) Forbidding the use of state jails to imprison alleged fugitives

(B) Citing the state's right of nullification

(C) Interfering with state officials to stop them from enforcing the strict law against fugitives

(D) Forcing bounty hunters to provide proof that captives were fugitives

(E) Ensuring that the accused was given the right to trial by jury

243. Which of the following actions was *not* considered part of the Compromise of 1850?

(A) Citizens of New Mexico and Utah were granted popular sovereignty.
(B) Slave trade was abolished in Washington, D.C.
(C) Texas's borders were extended to Santa Fe.
(D) California was admitted into the Union as a free state.
(E) The Fugitive Slave Act was created.

244. Dred Scott sued for his freedom, arguing that

(A) the institution of slavery was immoral and unjust
(B) he had been forced into slavery through illegal means
(C) he had been a resident of a state where slavery was illegal
(D) slavery was a violation of constitutional rights
(E) his owner had abused and tortured him

245. The *Dred Scott* decision ruled that

(A) accused fugitive slaves had a right to trial by jury
(B) only Congress had the right to prohibit slavery
(C) the federal ban on the importation of slaves was unconstitutional
(D) African-Americans were not citizens and did not have legal protection
(E) state laws banning slavery were illegal

246. Which of the following was *not* a cause of the financial crash of 1857?

(A) Influx of gold from the California Gold Rush
(B) Overproduction of grain
(C) Land and railroad speculation
(D) Decline in the price of cotton overseas
(E) Inflation of currency

247. *Uncle Tom's Cabin* was authored by

(A) Henry David Thoreau
(B) Henry Ward Beecher
(C) Harriet Beecher Stowe
(D) Emily Dickinson
(E) Elijah Lovejoy

248. Which of the following was *not* a theme found in *Uncle Tom's Cabin*?

(A) The notions of Christian values within the abolitionist movement
(B) Feminist beliefs that females were equal in intellect and bravery
(C) The evils of the Fugitive Slave Act
(D) The role of the North and South working together to end slavery
(E) Representation of slavery as a dehumanizing institution

249. Which of the following statements about *Uncle Tom's Cabin* is the most accurate?

(A) It was written in response to John Brown's raid at Harpers Ferry.
(B) It illustrated the political beliefs of the Know-Nothing Party.
(C) It motivated others to write novels refuting the book's assertions.
(D) The author was forced to publish the work under a pseudonym.
(E) It was ill received in both the North and South.

250. Which of the following statements was *not* an argument against the Fugitive Slave Act?

(A) The law made it easy for freedmen to be kidnapped.
(B) The law violated the *Dred Scott* decision.
(C) Accused fugitive slaves lacked the rights of due process.
(D) Methods of returning fugitive slaves were cruel and dehumanizing.
(E) The practice further institutionalized the practice of slavery.

251. Which of the following would *not* be considered an event illustrating the tensions that directly led to the Civil War?

(A) Bleeding Kansas
(B) Bleeding Sumner
(C) John Brown's raid on Harpers Ferry
(D) Publication of *Uncle Tom's Cabin*
(E) Nat Turner's rebellion

252. The Kansas-Nebraska Act was unpopular in northern states because

(A) it furthered the Missouri Compromise
(B) it could increase the number of slave states
(C) it created a transcontinental railroad in the south
(D) the northern states disapproved of Stephen Douglas seeking southern support
(E) it weakened the influence of northern business interests

253. Which of the following most directly led to the creation of the American Party?

(A) The increased number of Irish immigrants in the United States
(B) Publication of *Uncle Tom's Cabin*
(C) Enactment of the Compromise of 1850
(D) John Brown's raid at Harpers Ferry
(E) Passage of the Fugitive Slave Act

254. The Freeport Doctrine stipulated that
    (A) popular sovereignty superseded the Kansas-Nebraska Act
    (B) the *Dred Scott* decision voided the notion of popular sovereignty
    (C) slavery could be prevented by states passing laws unfriendly toward the practice
    (D) the Kansas-Nebraska Act was unconstitutional under the *Dred Scott* decision
    (E) the Fugitive Slave Act was unconstitutional in territories gained from Mexico

255. Which of the following was *not* true of the Kansas-Nebraska Act?
    (A) It was overturned by the *Dred Scott* decision.
    (B) It repealed the Missouri Compromise of 1820.
    (C) It allowed for popular sovereignty within the region.
    (D) It allowed for the creation of a transcontinental railroad.
    (E) It was an attempt to gain southern support for Stephen Douglas.

256. Which of the following statements best explains Abraham Lincoln's opposition to the Crittenden Compromise?
    (A) It was deemed a violation of states' rights.
    (B) It allowed for popular sovereignty to be overturned after a territory gained statehood.
    (C) It would cause Kentucky to secede from the Union.
    (D) It would reinstate the Missouri Compromise.
    (E) It allowed for the institution of slavery to expand.

257. Which of the following best describes the goal of John Brown's raid of Harpers Ferry?
    (A) Raiding the military arsenal to supply later slave uprisings
    (B) Liberating the slaves being held there
    (C) Defeating the southern militias stationed in the region
    (D) Taking the pro-slavery governor hostage to bargain for the release of slaves within the state
    (E) Preventing pro-slavery groups from influencing popular sovereignty in western territories

258. The Free-Soil Party's platform could best be described as

(A) opposing the expansion of slavery into western territories

(B) calling for the expansion of the Homestead Act, providing cheaper land sales in the West

(C) calling for the restriction of immigrants coming into the United States

(D) advocating the notion of popular sovereignty in western territories

(E) opposing protective tariffs and high domestic excise taxes

259. Which of the following was *not* a position supported by the Republican Party prior to the Civil War?

(A) Higher wages for labor

(B) Protective tariffs

(C) Construction of a transcontinental railroad

(D) Stemming the influx of immigrants

(E) Halting the expansion of slavery

260. Which of the following most accurately summarizes James Buchanan's legacy as president?

(A) A sympathizer of abolitionism who pandered needlessly to the pro-slavery South

(B) A strict constitutionalist, which may have limited his ability to preserve the Union

(C) An accomplished leader in fiscal matters, but weak in diplomacy between the states

(D) A strong proponent of education and the expansion of colleges

(E) A great unifier of the Democratic Party, though faced with insurmountable challenges

CHAPTER 10

The Civil War

261. Which of the following statements best describes the presidential administration of Franklin Pierce?

(A) It supported both the abolitionist movement and expansion.

(B) It supported slavery but was conciliatory toward abolitionism.

(C) It supported the abolitionist movement but was conciliatory toward slavery.

(D) It supported slavery but did not support expansion.

(E) It supported both slavery and expansion.

262. The government established by the Confederacy during the Civil War was most similar to

(A) the Articles of Confederation

(B) the Second Continental Congress

(C) the U.S. government under the Constitution

(D) the British parliamentary government

(E) a military dictatorship

263. The first shots fired during the Civil War are associated with which location?

(A) Gettysburg

(B) Fort McHenry

(C) Appomattox Court House

(D) Fort Sumter

(E) Fort Lee

264. Which of the following Civil War battles occurred first?

(A) Battle of Shiloh

(B) Battle of Fredericksburg

(C) Battle of Chancellorsville

(D) First Battle of Bull Run

(E) Battle of Antietam

265. Why did the North need to maintain control of the border states during the Civil War?

(A) Control of the border states would have given the South access to much-needed centers of industry.

(B) President Lincoln needed the region's political support to maintain the presidency.

(C) The North relied on the slave labor in the region for production.

(D) The border states created an impenetrable buffer zone between the North and South.

(E) The land of the border states was vital for the completion of a transcontinental railroad.

266. Which of the following was a Union advantage over the Confederacy during the Civil War?

(A) The Union could fight mainly a defensive war.

(B) The Union had more experienced generals.

(C) The Union had a better-funded treasury.

(D) Britain offered the Union its military support.

(E) The Union had greater support from its citizens.

267. Which of the following statements best describes the impact of the Emancipation Proclamation?

(A) All slaves were freed in both the North and the South.

(B) The practice of slavery was ended in the border states only.

(C) The slaves of the Confederacy were freed.

(D) All slaves who joined the Union army would be freed.

(E) Slaves were freed in the North but not in the border states.

268. Lincoln's primary objective for suspending the writ of habeas corpus was to

(A) suppress Southern sympathizers in border states

(B) better control the newspapers in the North

(C) bolster the size of the army with a draft

(D) be allowed to end slavery officially in the capital

(E) increase taxes to better fund the war effort

269. During the Civil War, "Copperheads" referred to

(A) supporters of the Anaconda Plan

(B) Northern supporters of the Confederacy

(C) Radical Republicans who supported the Union

(D) police officers who broke up the draft riots

(E) coinage minted with engravings of the presidents

270. In George McClellan's race for the presidency, he stated he would
     (A) call for a total Union victory
     (B) suspend habeas corpus in rebellious regions
     (C) reinstitute slavery in the border states
     (D) call for negotiations ending the war
     (E) employ a naval blockade around the Confederacy

271. The use of total warfare during the Civil War was best illustrated by
     (A) Pickett's Charge under Lee
     (B) the naval blockade under Scott
     (C) the March to the Sea under Sherman
     (D) the Peninsula Campaign under McClellan
     (E) Burnside's Charge at Fredericksburg

272. Which of the following battles was a clear Union victory?
     (A) First Battle of Bull Run
     (B) Battle of Fredericksburg
     (C) Battle of Chancellorsville
     (D) Battle of Shiloh
     (E) Battle of Cold Harbor

273. Which of the following was an advantage the South had in the Civil War?
     (A) The size of the Southern population
     (B) Development of the Southern infrastructure
     (C) A unified and strong central government
     (D) The support of Britain and France
     (E) Experienced military leadership

274. What was the primary strategy of the Confederacy during the early part of the Civil War?
     (A) Drafting large numbers of Southerners to match the size of the Union army
     (B) Waging a war of attrition against the Union
     (C) Attacking the North through the Mississippi River
     (D) Creating a naval blockade along the northern Atlantic coast
     (E) Capturing key shipping ports in New England

275. General McClellan was ultimately removed from his command by President Lincoln because

    (A) Lincoln believed McClellan was overly cautious and too slow to engage

    (B) McClellan's loss at the First Battle of Bull Run was seen as a military embarrassment

    (C) McClellan was caught selling military secrets to Confederate spies

    (D) Lincoln thought McClellan's strategies were too risky

    (E) McClellan's political views were unpopular in the North

276. Of the following battles, which two were considered a major turning point in the Civil War?

    (A) Battles of Cold Harbor and Antietam

    (B) First and Second Battles of Bull Run

    (C) Battles of Gettysburg and Vicksburg

    (D) Battles of Shiloh and Hampton Roads

    (E) Battles of Fort Sumter and Fredericksburg

277. The Gettysburg Address most notably

    (A) declared the end of slavery in the South

    (B) reaffirmed the notions of freedom and equality

    (C) demanded that the British and French side with the Union

    (D) called for the South to surrender immediately

    (E) announced a plan for reconciliation with the South

278. The focus of the Union's Anaconda Plan was to

    (A) divide the Confederacy along the Mississippi River

    (B) lead an overland campaign taking the Confederate capital

    (C) take a defensive approach and win through attrition

    (D) incite slave riots in the South

    (E) bring Mexico into the war, opening a second front

279. The *Merrimac* and *Monitor* are most associated which battle?

    (A) Memphis

    (B) Port Hudson

    (C) Hampton Roads

    (D) Fort Donelson

    (E) New Orleans

280. Dorothea Dix is remembered most in the Civil War for

(A) her role as a Confederate spy
(B) her contributions as a nurse
(C) helping to invent smokeless cartridges
(D) her leadership in eastern battles
(E) promoting abolitionist literature

281. Abraham Lincoln differed from Jefferson Davis in that Davis

(A) supported negotiating a peaceful end to the war by 1863
(B) had great experience in government and leadership
(C) was better at gaining and directing popular support to his advantage
(D) was a strict constitutionalist
(E) was unable to work with government and the public

282. Which of the following did *not* aid the economy of the North during the Civil War?

(A) The Morrill Tariff
(B) The Legal Tender Act
(C) The Force Bill
(D) The National Bank Act
(E) The issuing of greenbacks

283. Which of the following statements was *not* true of the Confederacy during the Civil War?

(A) It lacked sufficient textile factories for troop uniforms.
(B) It had few rifle factories.
(C) It suffered from food shortages.
(D) It was plagued by large slave uprisings.
(E) Its currency lacked value.

284. Which of the following statements best describes the role of African-Americans during the Civil War?

(A) African-Americans were readily conscripted into combat duty early on both sides.
(B) At the war's start, the North quickly created numerous African-American combat units.
(C) While the Union desegregated its military, the Confederacy refused.
(D) African-Americans were not allowed to serve in either side's navy.
(E) The Emancipation Proclamation increased African-American enlistments in the North.

285. Which of the following was *not* an innovation used during the Civil War?

(A) Canned foods
(B) The Gatling gun
(C) The zeppelin
(D) The torpedo
(E) The submarine

286. Which event marked the end of the Civil War?

(A) General Lee's men were surrounded at Appomattox.
(B) The Army of Northern Virginia was defeated at Gettysburg.
(C) General Grant's army won a victory at Vicksburg.
(D) The Union army completed General Sherman's March to the Sea.
(E) President Lincoln delivered the Gettysburg Address.

CHAPTER 11

Post Civil War and Reconstruction

287. President Lincoln's plan for Reconstruction was opposed by some Radical Republicans because they

   (A) felt it was too harsh on Southerners
   (B) felt it was too lenient on the South
   (C) believed it was too generous to the freedmen
   (D) believed it would be impractical to carry out
   (E) worried it would raise taxes too high

288. What post–Civil War event is most associated with Ford's Theatre?

   (A) Andrew Johnson's impeachment
   (B) Lee's official surrender to Grant
   (C) Abraham Lincoln's assassination
   (D) Finalization of the Compromise of 1877
   (E) The first Ku Klux Klan meeting

289. The Reconstruction plans of both Lincoln and Johnson included

   (A) a requirement that a majority of citizens sign sworn statements of allegiance
   (B) a call for immediate elections in former Confederate states
   (C) the passage of the Civil Rights Act
   (D) The requirement that Southern states ratify the Thirteenth Amendment
   (E) the redistribution of land

290. Which of the following actions was taken by state governments in the South to improve economic conditions?

   (A) Reinstituting slavery
   (B) Lowering cotton prices
   (C) Redistributing land
   (D) Constructing railroads and businesses
   (E) Lowering taxes

291. Which of the following would be considered an achieved success of Reconstruction in the South?

(A) Racist policies were ended.
(B) Industrialization was successfully implemented.
(C) African-Americans were given redistributed land.
(D) A public school system was successfully created.
(E) Tensions with the North were ended.

292. The Ku Klux Klan formed during Reconstruction with the purpose of

(A) fighting Union armies stationed in the South
(B) keeping African-Americans from exercising rights
(C) taking control of Southern state governments
(D) restarting the Confederacy
(E) helping poor whites improve their economic status

293. Which of the following statements describes a provision of the 1867 Reconstruction Act?

(A) The law divided the South into districts run by the Union military.
(B) The law established a system to end Reconstruction.
(C) The law allowed for the legalization of Black Codes.
(D) The law created a system for Southern generals to receive pardons.
(E) The law created a system of sharecropping to boost the Southern economy.

294. The purpose of the Force Acts was primarily to

(A) limit the actions of the Ku Klux Klan
(B) impose segregated accommodations in the South
(C) limit the president's ability to fire cabinet members
(D) divide the South into military districts
(E) force Southerners to take loyalty oaths

295. The practice of slavery was officially ended in the United States with

(A) the Emancipation Proclamation
(B) passage of the Twelfth Amendment
(C) passage of the Thirteenth Amendment
(D) passage of the Fourteenth Amendment
(E) passage of the Fifteenth Amendment

296. Following the Civil War, the rights of freedmen were restricted by Southern governments through

    (A) refusal to ratify the Thirteenth Amendment
    (B) the holding of constitutional conventions
    (C) creation of Black Codes
    (D) refusal to pay debts remaining from the war
    (E) division of the South into military districts

297. Which action under Reconstruction officially overturned the *Dred Scott* decision?

    (A) Lincoln's Reconstruction plan
    (B) Johnson's Reconstruction plan
    (C) The Thirteenth Amendment
    (D) The Fourteenth Amendment
    (E) The Fifteenth Amendment

298. During the period of Reconstruction, the term *scalawags* referred to

    (A) Southern whites who supported Radical Republicans
    (B) opportunistic Northerners who moved to the South after the Civil War
    (C) former slaves who were elected into local offices in the South
    (D) former Confederate officials who took loyalty oaths and received pardons
    (E) former slaves who moved to find work in Northern cities

299. Which government action extended suffrage to African-American males during Reconstruction?

    (A) The creation of the Freedman's Bureau
    (B) The passage of the Thirteenth Amendment
    (C) The passage of the Fourteenth Amendment
    (D) The passage of the Fifteenth Amendment
    (E) The passage of the Sixteenth Amendment

300. President Johnson was impeached officially because he

    (A) refused to send the military to the South, as required by the 1867 Reconstruction Act
    (B) illegally removed a cabinet member from office
    (C) illegally used Reconstruction funds for personal gain
    (D) vetoed the Radical Republican plans for Reconstruction
    (E) illegally assumed power upon President Lincoln's death

301. The 1869 Supreme Court decision in *Texas v. White* stated that

    (A) Texas, based on its annexation into the Union, still had the right to secede

    (B) the notion of "separate but equal" was legal

    (C) the Ku Klux Klan was protected under the First Amendment

    (D) citizens could not be denied rights based on race or color

    (E) it was illegal for states to secede from the Union

302. Which of the following actions was *not* taken by Ulysses S. Grant as president during Reconstruction?

    (A) Passing legislation to protect the rights of African-Americans to vote

    (B) Passing legislation to suppress the influence of the Ku Klux Klan

    (C) Extending pardons to a broader number of Confederates

    (D) Increasing the size of the Northern military in the South

    (E) Overseeing the ratification of the Fifteenth Amendment

303. During Reconstruction, the Wade-Davis Bill stated that Southern states could reenter the Union after

    (A) they ratified the Fourteenth Amendment

    (B) they ratified the Fifteenth Amendment

    (C) a third of the voters took loyalty pledges

    (D) half of the voters took loyalty pledges

    (E) two-thirds of the voters took loyalty pledges

304. During Reconstruction, most former slaves found employment mainly as

    (A) factory workers

    (B) sharecroppers

    (C) skilled craftsmen

    (D) members of the military

    (E) wage laborers

305. The Depression of 1873 most directly resulted in

    (A) Ulysses S. Grant failing to be renominated for president

    (B) Republicans losing control of the Senate in the following election

    (C) Republicans losing control of the presidency in the following election

    (D) Republicans losing control of the House of Representatives in the following election

    (E) Republicans breaking up into divided factions

306. Which corruption scandal is most associated with the administration of Ulysses S. Grant?

(A) Whiskey Ring Scandal
(B) Teapot Dome Scandal
(C) Star Route Scandal
(D) Whitewater Scandal
(E) XYZ Affair

307. During the Reconstruction Era, the fastest-growing sector of the economy was

(A) cotton production
(B) tobacco production
(C) the shipping industry
(D) the railroad industry
(E) the cattle industry

308. In return for helping Rutherford B. Hayes win the presidency, the Republicans promised the Democrats that

(A) they would stop enforcing laws that suppressed activities of the Ku Klux Klan
(B) they would repeal the 1875 Civil Rights Act
(C) the occupation of the South by federal troops would be ended
(D) the U.S. Treasury would adopt a policy of bimetallism to help Southern farmers
(E) the practice of separate but equal would be upheld

309. Which of the following was *not* a result of the Compromise of 1877?

(A) Military occupation of the South ended.
(B) The Republicans maintained control of the White House.
(C) The Force Acts were overturned.
(D) Another transcontinental railroad was authorized to be constructed in the South.
(E) Reconstruction was ended.

310. In the case *United States v. Cruikshank*, the Supreme Court found that

(A) the 1875 Civil Rights Act was unconstitutional
(B) the federal government could not discriminate based on race
(C) "separate but equal" was legal
(D) only states could enforce the Ku Klux Klan Act of 1871
(E) voter qualification requirements were illegal

311. What are Jim Crow laws?

    (A) Actions created by the federal government but not enforced by the states

    (B) Laws creating segregated accommodations

    (C) Laws created to further ensure equal rights

    (D) Laws limiting actions of groups such as the Ku Klux Klan

    (E) Actions or laws enforced only through social conventions

CHAPTER 12

The Gilded Age and the American West

312. The Pendleton Act was created in response to the

(A) Whiskey Ring Scandal
(B) Colfax Massacre
(C) Battle of Wounded Knee
(D) Battle of Little Big Horn
(E) assassination of President Garfield

313. The Civil Service Commission ended the spoils system by

(A) allowing the president to offer supporters government jobs
(B) requiring anyone applying for a government job to take a competitive exam
(C) forbidding the government from hiring employees who belonged to the same party as the president
(D) cutting the number of jobs within the federal government
(E) not hiring people who were acquainted personally with the president

314. Which of the following was *not* part of the Populist Party's platform?

(A) Institution of a secret ballot
(B) Adherence to a gold standard
(C) Government ownership of the railroads
(D) Banking reform
(E) A graduated income tax

315. Which of the following transformed the practice of post–Civil War agriculture?

(A) The government ended all homestead acts.
(B) The U.S. Treasury moved off the gold standard.
(C) The size of the average farm decreased.
(D) The use of machinery on farms increased.
(E) There was a lack of open land in the Great Plains.

316. During the late 19th century, the reduction in price of American agricultural products led to
- (A) farmers facing less of a debt burden
- (B) more workers shifting to agricultural work
- (C) farmers being compelled to increase production
- (D) less land being cultivated
- (E) farmers experiencing greater profit

317. Which of the following factors played the largest role in increasing the settlement of the Great Plains?
- (A) Construction of railroads
- (B) Removal of the Great Plains Indians
- (C) Increase in foreign demand for agricultural goods
- (D) Increase in price of agricultural goods
- (E) Extended period of economic inflation

318. Which of the following statements best describes the condition of western cattle ranching during the 1880s?
- (A) Open-range grazing became standard practice.
- (B) Cattle ranching was plagued with natural and man-made obstacles.
- (C) Cattle ranching continued to be highly lucrative for small farmers.
- (D) Cattle ranching limited the land available for farmers to settle.
- (E) Cattle ranching was extremely lucrative for cowboys.

319. During the late 19th century, a "robber baron" would be best defined as
- (A) a powerful industrialist
- (B) the leader of a large criminal organization
- (C) a large agricultural landowner
- (D) the head of a large political machine
- (E) a leader of a large labor union

320. The goal of the Sherman Antitrust Act was to
- (A) encourage the creation of labor unions
- (B) encourage the growth of trusts
- (C) create greater fairness in industry
- (D) increase tax review on large businesses
- (E) allow for the creation of vertical monopolies

321. In response to the 1894 Pullman strike, the U.S. government

(A) nationalized the company

(B) tried the company owners under antitrust laws

(C) used federal troops to operate the trains until the strike ended

(D) used federal troops to subdue the workers

(E) forced the striking workers to collectively bargain

322. The Transcontinental Railroad was completed in 1869 when the Central Pacific Railroad and the Union Pacific Railroad met at

(A) Promontory Point, Utah

(B) Independence, Missouri

(C) Santa Fe, New Mexico

(D) Indianapolis, Indiana

(E) Topeka, Kansas

323. Which author is credited with coining the term *Gilded Age*?

(A) Upton Sinclair

(B) Ida Tarbell

(C) Samuel Clemens

(D) Lincoln Steffens

(E) Edward Bellamy

324. A monopoly is best defined as

(A) a market situation where there is only a single provider of a good or service

(B) an arrangement of similar businesses created to regulate production and control pricing

(C) negotiation by workers as a group with business owners over compensation

(D) a group of investors who own shares of a business and receive a percentage of its profit

(E) a business that provides a necessity to the general public

325. Andrew Carnegie engaged in the practice of vertical integration by

(A) monopolizing a single product by eliminating all competition

(B) controlling all aspects of the production process from beginning to end

(C) artificially inflating the value of his companies' stock to attract investors

(D) fixing railroad rates and rebates to decrease costs

(E) using private detective agencies to break strikes

326. Horizontal integration is best illustrated by
   (A) Andrew Carnegie controlling all aspects of the production process
   (B) John D. Rockefeller eliminating all competing firms that produced the same products
   (C) Cornelius Vanderbilt issuing noncompetitive railroad rebates
   (D) John P. Morgan artificially inflating the price of his own stocks
   (E) Henry Frick using private detective agencies to break strikes

327. Which of the following people is *not* correctly matched to the industry or business he is historically associated with?
   (A) John D. Rockefeller—oil
   (B) John P. Morgan—investment
   (C) Gustavus Swift—tobacco
   (D) Andrew Carnegie—steel
   (E) Cornelius Vanderbilt—railroads

328. In what way did the Knights of Labor differ from the American Federation of Labor (AFL)?
   (A) Unlike the AFL, the Knights of Labor limited membership to skilled labor only.
   (B) Unlike the Knights of Labor, the AFL limited membership to skilled labor only.
   (C) Unlike the Knights of Labor, the AFL allowed women to be members.
   (D) Unlike the Knights of Labor, the AFL allowed African-Americans to be members.
   (E) Unlike the Knights of Labor, the AFL allowed farmers to be members.

329. Which of the following was *not* a result of the Haymarket Square riot of 1886?
   (A) Passage of an eight-hour workday for workers
   (B) Increase in membership of the Knights of Labor
   (C) Greater association of labor unions with anarchists
   (D) Passage of antitrust legislation
   (E) Enactment of child labor laws

330. Which of the following inventions is *not* associated with Thomas Edison?
   (A) Phonograph
   (B) Incandescent lightbulb
   (C) AC electric power
   (D) Motion picture camera
   (E) Universal stock ticker

331. The primary function of the Grange movement was to

(A) allow western state governments to sell land quickly

(B) purchase large areas of land in the West to sell later for a profit

(C) herd cattle from the South to railroad centers

(D) help farmers create cooperatives

(E) allow Americans and immigrants to buy land directly from the federal government

332. The function of the Morrill Land-Grant Act of 1862 was to

(A) assist states with establishing colleges

(B) promote the construction of a transcontinental railroad

(C) help farmers establish cooperatives

(D) provide direct land sales from the federal government

(E) provide land for landless former slaves

333. Which of the following statements was *not* true of the 1862 Homestead Act?

(A) It provided a system for the federal government to provide land directly to settlers.

(B) It made land available to citizens and to immigrants who planned to become citizens.

(C) Farmers were given ownership of land after living on it for five years.

(D) To claim land, farmers had to build a dwelling and cultivate the land.

(E) Land speculators were effectively kept from abusing the act.

334. The main purpose of the Interstate Commerce Act was to

(A) better regulate free-range cattle grazing

(B) move western Native American groups to reservations

(C) control unfair railroad rate and rebate practices

(D) increase taxes on businesses that profited from interstate commerce

(E) limit union actions that could negatively affect interstate commerce

335. Farmers of the late 19th century did *not* benefit from the

(A) Farmers' Alliances

(B) Grange

(C) Homestead Act

(D) McKinley Tariff

(E) Populist Party

336. The *Wabash* case, decided by the Supreme Court in 1886, led to the passage of which law?
- (A) Hepburn Act
- (B) Elkins Act
- (C) Comstock Law
- (D) Interstate Commerce Act
- (E) Homestead Act

337. Which Native American nation is most associated with Wounded Knee?
- (A) Sioux
- (B) Crow
- (C) Nez Percé
- (D) Apache
- (E) Shoshoni

338. The 1887 Dawes Severalty Act was passed to
- (A) help Native Americans retain their cultures
- (B) compensate Native Americans for prior illegal land contracts
- (C) move Native Americans onto western reservations
- (D) force Native Americans to adopt Western culture and farming practices
- (E) extend constitutional protections to Native American males

339. What was a bonanza farm?
- (A) A farm established by squatters under the Homestead Act
- (B) A large, professionally managed farm owned by investors
- (C) A series of independent farms operated as a cooperative
- (D) A small, independent farm that practiced sustenance agriculture
- (E) A government-run farm used to teach agriculture

340. What was a primary motivation for the Kansas Exodus of many African-Americans to the West following the Civil War?
- (A) Finding employment as sharecroppers
- (B) Establishing bonanza farms
- (C) Escaping the racial tensions of the South
- (D) Finding employment in railroad construction
- (E) Creating an independent state for African-Americans

341. What did the events that took place between Chief Joseph of the Nez Percé and the federal government illustrate about U.S.–Native American relations in the late 19th century?

(A) The government became more active in protecting traditional Native American lands.

(B) Native Americans became more willing to accept the reservation system.

(C) Native Americans were willing to abandon traditional practices for sedentary agriculture.

(D) Violent conflicts continued to be waged between the Native Americans and the government.

(E) New farming innovations decreased the need for encroachment onto Native American lands.

342. What was the main focus of the Ghost Dance movement?

(A) Restoring the traditional way of life to Native Americans and repelling white settlement

(B) Educating white Americans on the cultural practices of Native Americans in hopes of preserving those practices

(C) Negotiating a peaceful end to disputes over land between settlers and Native Americans

(D) Ending the famines that plagued Native American reservations

(E) Illustrating the new alliance between Native Americans and the Department of Indian Affairs

343. Frederick Jackson Turner's thesis argued that America's frontier

(A) was a major obstacle that stood in the way of progress

(B) was a fundamental factor in American government and individualism

(C) would continue despite the closing of the West

(D) allowed immigrants to retain their culture

(E) was the driving force behind the American Civil War

344. William Jennings Bryan lost his 1896 campaign for the presidency because he

(A) lacked ability as a persuasive speaker

(B) supported the silver standard

(C) was unable to win the support of western farmers

(D) could not win the support of eastern urban centers

(E) was seen as a pawn of the railroad industry

345. "We shall answer their demands for a gold standard by saying to them, you shall not press down upon the brow of labor this crown of thorns. You shall not crucify mankind upon a cross of gold." This quotation is associated with which late-19th-century leader?

(A) Eugene V. Debs
(B) William Jennings Bryan
(C) William McKinley
(D) Booker T. Washington
(E) W. E. B. DuBois

346. Tammany Hall of the late 19th century was

(A) the base of organization for the Populist Party joining with the Grange movement
(B) the location where President Garfield was assassinated, causing the end of the spoils system
(C) the headquarters for the newly formed NAACP
(D) the location that became the basis of the *Plessy v. Ferguson* decision
(E) a Democratic political machine that controlled New York City politics

CHAPTER 13

U.S. Imperialism and the Progressive Movement

347. Which of following policies would *not* have been supported by Alfred T. Mahan?

    (A) Creation of a modern navy
    (B) Creation of a large modern land army
    (C) Construction of a canal through Central America
    (D) Establishment of coaling stations throughout the Pacific
    (E) Establishment of trade with Asian nations

348. Seward's Folly refers to the

    (A) United States' annexation of Hawaii
    (B) Whiskey Ring Scandal
    (C) United States' purchase of Alaska
    (D) events that led to the Spanish-American War
    (E) Gadsden Purchase

349. Which of the following ideas would *not* be part of the Roosevelt Corollary?

    (A) The United States would continue limiting European influence in the Western Hemisphere.
    (B) The Monroe Doctrine would be expanded to include Asia as well as the Americas.
    (C) Latin America would be seen as an agent for U.S. commercial interests.
    (D) The United States had the right to intervene in Latin American conflicts.
    (E) The United States could act as an international police force.

350. The expression "Speak softly and carry a big stick, and you will go far" implied that

(A) protests and strikes were inefficient methods of bringing about reform
(B) the United States should adopt a policy of isolationism as well as militarism
(C) force should be the primary tool of American diplomacy
(D) military power should be available for retaliation if necessary
(E) rhetoric was no match for the power of political machines

351. To build the Panama Canal, the United States backed a revolution in

(A) Colombia
(B) Guatemala
(C) Nicaragua
(D) Costa Rica
(E) Honduras

352. The Hay-Bunau Treaty allowed for the

(A) U.S. military base in Guantanamo Bay
(B) opening of trade in Japan
(C) construction of the Panama Canal
(D) Open Door Policy in China
(E) Cuban nation to remain independent

353. Dollar Diplomacy is most associated with the presidency of

(A) Theodore Roosevelt
(B) William McKinley
(C) William Taft
(D) Woodrow Wilson
(E) Herbert Hoover

354. Moral Diplomacy was best illustrated by

(A) Woodrow Wilson's use of the military in Nicaragua and Haiti
(B) William Taft's urging of U.S. banks to refinance Haiti's national debt
(C) Woodrow Wilson's response to the Tampico Incident
(D) the United States' refusal to recognize the government of Victoriano Huerta
(E) Herbert Hoover's removal of troops from Nicaragua

355. The focus of the 1907 Gentlemen's Agreement was to

(A) make it easier for Chinese immigrants to find work in western cities

(B) ban Japanese immigrants from entering the United States

(C) limit Asian immigrants' right to own property

(D) create an Open Door Policy of trade in China

(E) reduce the number of immigrants coming from Japan

356. The Supreme Court's decision in the "insular cases" stated that

(A) all people living under U.S. control are granted equal rights and protections

(B) all people living under U.S. control have a right to full citizenship

(C) Cuba could join the United States as a protectorate if it chose to by popular vote

(D) some people living under U.S. control would not receive equal rights and protections

(E) while Puerto Ricans would be given full rights as citizens, Filipinos would not

357. Which of the following factors provided economic justification for U.S. expansion in the second part of the 19th century?

(A) Increased production led to the need for new markets abroad.

(B) U.S. industry was suffering from a severe shortage of labor.

(C) The U.S. domestic markets were flooded with less expensive imports.

(D) The United States would be considered an industrial power only if it had colonies.

(E) Failures of western farms caused food shortages within the United States.

358. Which of the following actions illustrated the usage of the Monroe Doctrine in the second half of the 19th century?

(A) Matthew Perry opening up trade relations with Japan

(B) The United States dominating sugar production in Hawaii

(C) Polk citing the doctrine as justification for Manifest Destiny

(D) John Hay's insistence on the Open Door Policy

(E) The United States' arbitration in the Venezuelan boundary dispute with Britain

359. Why was the Open Door Policy important to the United States?

(A) It gave the United States colonial territory in Asia.

(B) It ensured the United States would have access to Chinese markets.

(C) It locked European nations out of Chinese markets.

(D) It allowed China to invest in the United States.

(E) It further secured the legitimacy of the Monroe Doctrine.

360. Which leader's atrocities helped lead the United States to war with Spain during the end of the 19th century?

(A) Porfirio Diaz
(B) José Martí
(C) Emilio Aguinaldo
(D) Valeriano Weyler
(E) Victoriano Huerta

361. The destruction of which of the following American ships directly resulted in the Spanish-American War?

(A) The USS *Constitution*
(B) The USS *Maine*
(C) The USS *Maddox*
(D) The USS *Chesapeake*
(E) The USS *Olympia*

362. The quote "You furnish the pictures, and I'll furnish the war" illustrates what type of late-19th-century journalism?

(A) Muckraking journalism
(B) Yellow journalism
(C) Movie news reels
(D) Citizen journalism
(E) Red journalism

363. Following the Spanish-American War, Cuban independence was protected with the

(A) decision in the "insular cases"
(B) signing of the 1898 Treaty of Paris
(C) passage of the Platt Amendment
(D) signing of the Hay-Bunau Treaty
(E) passage of the Teller Amendment

364. Which of the following territories were acquired by the United States as a result of the Spanish-American War?

(A) Guam, the Philippines, and Cuba
(B) Hawaii, Guam, and the Philippines
(C) Cuba, Puerto Rico, and the Philippines
(D) The Philippines, Guam, and Puerto Rico
(E) Cuba, Hawaii, and Guam

365. Which of the following would *not* be an argument of the Anti-Imperialist League?

   (A) Imperialism caused the need for an expanded military.
   (B) Imperialism hurt manufacturers' ability to obtain raw materials.
   (C) Imperialism would encourage people from different races to enter the United States.
   (D) Imperialism violates America's belief of self-determination.
   (E) Imperial empires are too costly to maintain.

366. Which of the following statements best defines Andrew Carnegie's ideas in his essay "The Gospel of Wealth"?

   (A) Frivolity is the right of those who have accumulated wealth.
   (B) The rich should use their wealth in a way they see best fit to better society.
   (C) Charity is primarily the domain of religious organizations.
   (D) Charitable giving to the poor should address only their basic needs.
   (E) The "rags to riches" success story, with its promise of wealth through hard work, is possible for everyone.

367. Though Booker T. Washington and W. E. B. DuBois both believed in improving conditions for African-Americans, in what way did their views differ?

   (A) They both fought for social equality, but only DuBois fought for economic equality as well.
   (B) They both fought for social equality, but only Washington fought for economic equality as well.
   (C) DuBois fought only for social equality, while Washington fought only for economic equality.
   (D) DuBois focused on achieving political equality in the South, while Washington focused on political equality in the North.
   (E) DuBois felt African-Americans should focus only on vocational training, while Washington called for liberal arts education.

368. The major focus of the Niagara Movement was to

   (A) further the views of the Anti-Imperialist League
   (B) promote nativism and stem immigration
   (C) achieve civil liberties for all African-Americans
   (D) grant suffrage to women
   (E) promote conservation of American natural resources

369. The National Association for the Advancement of Colored People (NAACP) was created primarily to

(A) fight discrimination in American legal courts
(B) create a political party to represent African-Americans
(C) promote the "Back to Africa" movement
(D) establish African-American universities
(E) further the cultural advancements of the Harlem Renaissance

370. The Supreme Court's decision in *Plessy v. Ferguson*

(A) ended segregation in the United States
(B) upheld the doctrine of "separate but equal"
(C) allowed African-Americans to serve in the armed forces
(D) stated that "separate but equal" applied only to private businesses
(E) overturned the earlier *Dred Scott* decision

371. Which of the following is *not* an example of a political reform made during the Progressive Era?

(A) The initiative
(B) The referendum
(C) The recall
(D) Party nominating conventions
(E) The direct election of senators

372. Florence Kelley's efforts helped lead many states to end the practice of

(A) yellow-dog contracts
(B) the Australian ballot
(C) child labor
(D) segregation of public facilities
(E) machine politics

373. Which of the following muckraker journalists is *not* correctly matched with the focus of his or her reporting?

(A) Ida Tarbell—the unscrupulous practices of the road industry
(B) Lincoln Steffens—political corruption
(C) Upton Sinclair—abuses in the meatpacking industry
(D) Samuel Hopkins Adams—fraudulent and dangerous medicines
(E) Jacob Riis—the harsh conditions of New York's slums

374. The Supreme Court's decisions in *Muller v. Oregon* and *Bunting v. Oregon* stated that

(A) child labor is illegal

(B) employers need to provide pensions to employees

(C) law enforcement officers can be used as strike breakers

(D) only the federal government can regulate interstate commerce

(E) states can limit working hours

375. Which of the following was a *not* a provision of the Clayton Antitrust Act?

(A) Labor unions are subject to antitrust laws.

(B) People may not sit on multiple boards of companies within the same business.

(C) Price discrimination was declared illegal.

(D) Companies must notify federal regulators prior to merging.

(E) Holding companies were clearly defined.

376. Of the following individuals, who would be considered a Progressive Era governor?

(A) Samuel Jones

(B) Eugene V. Debs

(C) Robert La Follette

(D) Gifford Pinchot

(E) Louis Brandeis

377. Which of the following objectives was *not* considered part of Theodore Roosevelt's Square Deal?

(A) Controlling the corporations

(B) Providing consumer protection

(C) Protecting business from extreme union demands

(D) Expanding America's international influence

(E) Conserving America's natural resources

378. Both the Elkins Act and the Hepburn Act increased the government's ability to

(A) use federal troops to break strikes

(B) limit the power of corrupt political machines

(C) regulate unfair business practices by railroads

(D) limit child labor in mines and factories

(E) control the flow of immigrants into the United States

379. Which of the following policies of Theodore Roosevelt was continued by William Taft?

(A) Roosevelt's strong advocacy for women's suffrage
(B) The continued attempts to break up monopolies and trusts
(C) Support for Gifford Pinchot in his conservation efforts
(D) Continuation of Big Stick Diplomacy
(E) Furthering the policy of New Nationalism

380. Woodrow Wilson's main objective in calling for the establishment of the Federal Reserve was to

(A) better enforce the Federal Trade Act
(B) better organize the federal banking system
(C) rescue farmers suffering from the recession
(D) nationalize the American banking system
(E) recover the losses from the Underwood Tariff

381. How did Woodrow Wilson's reform platform during the 1912 campaign differ from that of Theodore Roosevelt?

(A) Unlike Wilson, Roosevelt supported strong executive leadership.
(B) Unlike Roosevelt, Wilson supported the federal government's regulation of business.
(C) Unlike Roosevelt, Wilson thought trusts should not be regulated.
(D) Unlike Roosevelt, Wilson called for an increased tariff.
(E) Wilson rejected Roosevelt's platform of New Nationalism.

382. Jane Addams's Hull House was established primarily to

(A) create educational programs to aid poor immigrants
(B) fight the overconsumption of alcohol in the nation's slums
(C) promote women's suffrage
(D) provide a halfway home for recently released criminals
(E) offer a basic education to African-Americans

383. The 1911 fire in the Triangle Shirtwaist factory directly resulted in the

(A) outlawing of sweatshops in New York
(B) decline of the International Ladies' Garment Workers' Union
(C) push for comprehensive safety laws
(D) deaths of only female employees in the fire
(E) decline in political machines in New York

384. Susan B. Anthony was arrested in 1872 for

(A) helping to organize a strike against railroad wage cuts

(B) violating southern segregation laws

(C) allowing African-American children to attend white schools

(D) illegally voting in a presidential election

(E) distributing birth control to unmarried women

385. William Howard Taft lost his support of the progressive Republicans because of his

(A) action in the 1902 coal strike

(B) support of the Payne-Aldrich Tariff

(C) response to the Triangle Shirtwaist factory fire

(D) signing of the McKinley Tariff

(E) support of women's suffrage

386. Which of the following was *not* an accomplishment of George Washington Carver?

(A) Several hundred industrial uses for the peanut

(B) An improved method of crop rotation

(C) Establishment of the Tuskegee Institute

(D) Creation of industrial plant-based dyes

(E) Affordable high-protein diets for poor farmers

CHAPTER 14

The First World War and the Roaring Twenties

387. Which of the following was *not* a direct factor leading to World War I?

(A) The rise of militarism
(B) The creation of secret alliances
(C) Increased jingoism within states
(D) The rise of fascism within European states
(E) The race for colonial possessions

388. Which of the following was *not* a reason for the initial American neutrality during the First World War?

(A) Wilson hoped neutrality would allow him to lead the peace at the end of the war.
(B) American military treaties prevented direct involvement.
(C) Neutrality allowed American businesses to trade with both sides of the conflict.
(D) Support by the U.S. population was divided between the two sides.
(E) Americans generally supported a policy of isolation.

389. The United States responded to the sinking of the *Lusitania* and other passenger ships by

(A) immediately declaring war on Germany
(B) forcing the creation of the Sussex Pledge
(C) entering a formal alliance with the Allied powers
(D) issuing the Zimmerman Telegram
(E) declaring war on Mexico

390. Which of the following events most directly brought the United States into the First World War?

(A) Britain's use of a naval blockade
(B) Germany's resumption of unrestricted submarine warfare
(C) The success of the communist revolution in Russia
(D) The collapse of the French army
(E) Italy's decision to join the Allied powers

391. Who led the American Expeditionary Force during World War I?

(A) Eisenhower
(B) Foch
(C) Pershing
(D) Haig
(E) Butler

392. What was the Great Migration during the First World War?

(A) The increased number of European migrants coming to America, hoping to escape the war
(B) The mass exodus of midwestern farmers looking for factory jobs in war industries
(C) The increased numbers of African-Americans moving into northern cities
(D) The massive transition of women to do work once solely carried out by men
(E) The movement of ethnic Germans out of the United States during the war

393. Which of the following statements best illustrates a challenge faced by the United States following the First World War?

(A) The United States found itself the world's largest debtor nation.
(B) The United States found itself with a severe labor shortage.
(C) The United States lacked a plan to reintegrate soldiers into society.
(D) The U.S. government continued to tightly control the economy.
(E) The infrastructure of the United States was shattered by the war.

394. The purpose of Selective Service during the First World War was to

(A) raise money for the war effort through the sales of war bonds
(B) create more selective requirements for young men wishing to serve in the military
(C) call on females to work in industries that were once open only to males
(D) institute a draft to bolster the number of men in the military
(E) create job opportunities for soldiers returning from war

395. A main reason many Republican senators objected to the plan for the League of Nations was that

(A) Article X would be too expensive for the United States to uphold
(B) it could pull the United States into future conflicts
(C) Russia would be allowed to play a leadership role in the league
(D) Germany would be allowed to retain its military
(E) the United States would have to reduce its military

396. Why was the Battle of Château-Thierry significant for the American military?

(A) It stopped the German advance that nearly captured Paris.
(B) It was the first time African-Americans could serve in integrated combat units.
(C) The conclusion of the battle forced Germany to surrender.
(D) It was the first time the U.S. Air Force used aerial bombardment.
(E) It convinced Italy to join the fighting on the side of the Allies.

397. Which of the following was a major power of the War Industry Board during World War I?

(A) Hosting massive rallies to sell war bonds
(B) Censoring seditious materials
(C) Setting government prices on agricultural goods
(D) Eliminating the practice of daylight savings time
(E) Setting production quotas and allocating raw materials

398. Eugene V. Debs was arrested during World War I for

(A) selling fraudulent war bonds
(B) violating the Espionage and Sedition Acts
(C) organizing a strike during the war
(D) selling American secrets to the Germans
(E) declaring his candidacy against Woodrow Wilson

399. A major goal of Woodrow Wilson's League of Nations was to

(A) provide agricultural aid internationally to countries in need
(B) provide all nations with open access to trade
(C) create military equality among the world's major powers
(D) promote international security and peace among nations
(E) root out communism and socialism globally

400. The Republican administrations of the 1920s would best be described as

(A) possessing a foreign policy based on expansion and heavy domestic business regulation
(B) supporting isolationism and laissez-faire business policies domestically
(C) strongly focused on building up the armed forces
(D) open to increased immigration and less stringent quotas
(E) strongly against high tariffs and pro labor

401. The Palmer Raids of the 1920s were a response to

(A) organized crime developing after Prohibition
(B) government corruption as illustrated in the Teapot Dome Scandal
(C) fears of communism following the Russian Revolution
(D) the reemergence of the Ku Klux Klan during the 1920s
(E) the reemergence of trusts following the First World War

402. The use of installment plans during the 1920s was significant to the economy because it

(A) caused the average wage of workers to decline
(B) illustrated a rejection of materialism and luxury for pragmatism
(C) greatly limited the number of people who had access to credit
(D) served as a catalyst for a new consumer-based economy
(E) illustrated the need for lower tariffs to promote trade

403. The Supreme Court decision of *Schenck v. United States* established the precedent for the idea that

(A) "separate but equal" is constitutional
(B) speech that presents a "clear and present danger" is not protected
(C) labor unions are exempt from antitrust laws
(D) "separate but equal" is by nature discriminatory
(E) groups such as the Ku Klux Klan are protected under the First Amendment

404. Which of the following events illustrates the nativist sentiments of the 1920s?

(A) The feats of Charles Lindbergh and Amelia Earhart
(B) The reemergence of the Ku Klux Klan and the passage of the National Origins Act
(C) The passage of the Volstead Act and the Eighteenth Amendment
(D) The Washington Naval Conference and the Kellogg-Briand Pact
(E) The works produced by the Lost Generation and the Harlem Renaissance

405. What was the 1920s Harlem Renaissance?

(A) The refusal of African-Americans to submit quietly to the practices of Jim Crow laws

(B) The emergence of civic-minded African-American business leaders

(C) A group of civil rights leaders determined to use the courts to end discrimination

(D) The migration of African-Americans from the South to northern cities

(E) A period of artistic achievement in multiple fields by African-Americans

406. The trial of Sacco and Vanzetti illustrated America's fear of

(A) African-Americans' migration to northern cities

(B) the reemergence of hate groups such as the Ku Klux Klan

(C) the growing support for women's suffrage

(D) immigrants who possessed radical or leftist beliefs

(E) treaties that might bring the United States into more European conflicts

407. The impact of the Fordney-McCumber and Hawley-Smoot Tariffs could be best described as

(A) upsetting the balance of trade among European nations

(B) crippling Europe's ability to pay off its war debts and damaging American industry

(C) illustrating America's willingness to disarm following the First World War

(D) illustrating America's fear of leftist immigrants following the Red Scare

(E) greatly benefiting midwestern farmers during the 1920s

408. Why was the Kellogg-Briand Pact significant?

(A) The nations involved agreed not to use the threat of war against each other.

(B) It limited the sizes of the participating nations' navies.

(C) Because of it, the United States abandoned military intervention in Latin America.

(D) It called for the voluntary disarmament of nations.

(E) It led to the passage of the Nineteenth Amendment.

409. A primary reason for Henry Ford's success in the automobile industry was that he

(A) offered consumers a wide variety of models and colors
(B) strongly supported the unionization of his workers
(C) adopted a strategy of horizontal integration
(D) adopted a strategy of vertical integration
(E) would not hire African-American or female employees

410. The purpose of the Nineteenth Amendment was to

(A) create a federal income tax
(B) outlaw the consumption of alcohol
(C) end Prohibition
(D) grant suffrage to women
(E) provide for the direct election of senators

411. The Scopes Trial illustrated the nation's debate over

(A) religious conservatism versus modern scientific theories
(B) immigration and fears of leftist radicals
(C) the rural verses urban split within the nation
(D) the proper role of government and the New Deal
(E) women's suffrage versus the Cult of Domesticity

412. Warren G. Harding's administration is most associated with which scandal?

(A) Crédit Mobilier Scandal
(B) Whiskey Ring Scandal
(C) Star Route Scandal
(D) Teapot Dome Scandal
(E) Execution of Sacco and Vanzetti

413. The groups of American authors disillusioned by society following the First World War are referred to as

(A) the Harlem Renaissance
(B) the Beat Generation
(C) the Lost Generation
(D) Romanticists
(E) transcendentalists

414. The election of Herbert Hoover over Al Smith illustrated

    (A) America's general rejection of Prohibition

    (B) discontentment with Republican policies

    (C) nativist opinions concerning religion

    (D) fears of impending economic uncertainty

    (E) rejection of isolationist policies

CHAPTER 15

The Great Depression and the Second World War

415. At the start of the Great Depression, Black Tuesday occurred when

(A) investors began to buy large numbers of stocks on margin

(B) bankers responded to Black Thursday by offering loan and mortgage forgiveness

(C) President Hoover declared a national bank holiday to stabilize the market

(D) investors raced to sell their stock holdings

(E) the Federal Reserve moved off the gold standard

416. The Dust Bowl of the Great Depression occurred because

(A) the region was hit with heavy rains and tornadoes

(B) farmers could no longer afford to plant their fields

(C) intense agriculture had depleted the topsoil

(D) farmers lacked modern irrigation capabilities

(E) increased crop prices led to severe overproduction

417. African-Americans during the Depression often experienced

(A) access to low-paying industrial jobs once available only to whites

(B) increased discrimination in employment and in relief programs

(C) a migration from the North back to southern farms

(D) greatly improved civil rights and opportunities

(E) the end of many of the Jim Crow laws in the South

418. When faced with the stock market crash and the start of the Depression, Hoover supported

(A) government deficit spending to help bring relief

(B) lowering tariffs to revive international trade

(C) creating federal relief programs for the average worker

(D) encouraging voluntary reforms within private businesses

(E) declaring a bank holiday to stabilize the market

419. The main goal of the Bonus Army at the start of the Depression was to

    (A) allow veterans to receive their promised army pensions early

    (B) distribute food aid to the multitude of people suffering from malnutrition

    (C) protest the socialist undertones of the New Deal

    (D) provide federal aid to farmers who had lost their farms

    (E) support the Norris–La Guardia Anti-Injunction Act to protect unions

420. The main purpose of the Reconstruction Finance Corporation was to

    (A) provide low-cost mortgages to homeowners facing foreclosure

    (B) provide government credit to secure failing banks

    (C) raise farm prices by encouraging farmers to reduce output

    (D) provide work relief for the unemployed through public projects

    (E) provide old-age pensions and unemployment benefits

421. How did Presidents Hoover and Roosevelt differ in their attempts to respond to the Great Depression?

    (A) While Hoover felt that aid should be supplied directly to the people, Roosevelt felt that government should only try to stabilize the corporations and banks.

    (B) While Roosevelt felt that aid should be supplied directly to the people, Hoover felt that government should only try to stabilize the corporations and banks.

    (C) Hoover's reforms focused on providing aid to farmers, while Roosevelt focused on industrial workers.

    (D) Hoover supported the nationalization of banks, while Roosevelt called for the redistribution of wealth through taxation.

    (E) Roosevelt believed that the Depression should be corrected by voluntary self-regulation in business, while Hoover advocated heavy government regulation.

422. What is the practice of buying on margin?

    (A) Purchasing stocks without any prior knowledge of the company

    (B) Using bank loans to purchase stocks

    (C) Pooling money with a group of investors to buy stock

    (D) Buying stocks when they are low and selling them when they are high

    (E) Purchasing consumer goods using an installment plan

423. Which of the following New Deal agencies was created to assist businesses most directly?

(A) Civilian Conservation Corps
(B) Home Owners' Loan Corporation
(C) National Recovery Administration
(D) Tennessee Valley Authority
(E) Works Progress Administration

424. What was Franklin Roosevelt's "Brain Trust"?

(A) The heads of Roosevelt's executive agencies
(B) A collection of intellectuals who served as unofficial advisers
(C) The appointed heads of the agencies created under the New Deal
(D) Those who opposed Roosevelt's New Deal policies
(E) Students who attended colleges with New Deal grants

425. How did the Second New Deal differ from the First New Deal during the Depression?

(A) It contained a greater number of social welfare benefits.
(B) Unlike the First New Deal, it focused primarily on tax laws that benefited the rich.
(C) It offered stricter controls over labor unions and less regulation of businesses.
(D) It repealed most of the acts passed under the First New Deal.
(E) Unlike the First New Deal, its primary focus was on balancing the budget.

426. Huey Long and Upton Sinclair criticized the New Deal on the grounds that

(A) it was moving the country too far in the direction of socialism
(B) shifting the tax burden onto the wealthy was unfair
(C) they disagreed with tighter government regulations on private banks
(D) they disagreed with the notion of social security
(E) they believed the reforms did not go far enough to redistribute wealth

427. What did economist John Maynard Keynes say was necessary to restart the economy during the Depression?

(A) Using government spending to increase consumer demand for goods
(B) Cutting taxes on businesses and investors so they could grow
(C) Adopting bimetallism to provide relief to farmers
(D) Establishing greater protection for organized labor
(E) Maintaining a strict policy of laissez-faire and letting the economy recover naturally

428. During the Great Depression, the "Black Cabinet" referred to

 (A) African-Americans in high-level government positions
 (B) African-Americans who served in Roosevelt's executive cabinet
 (C) African-Americans who openly opposed the New Deal
 (D) supporters of the civil rights leader A. Philip Randolph
 (E) Democrats who were highly critical of the New Deal

429. Frances Perkins gained prominence during the Great Depression by

 (A) photographing the plight of the urban and rural poor in the midst of the Depression
 (B) criticizing New Deal policies as a member of the American Liberty League
 (C) becoming the first African-American to hold a cabinet position
 (D) becoming the first woman to hold a cabinet position
 (E) performing in front of the Lincoln Memorial after being refused at Constitution Hall

430. The main purpose of the Lend-Lease Program was to

 (A) isolate the Soviet Union militarily
 (B) attempt to convince Italy to maintain neutrality
 (C) aid nations deemed vital to American security
 (D) provide aid against communist insurgencies in Spain
 (E) end the Depression through wartime production

431. The Atlantic Charter was an agreement between

 (A) the United States and France
 (B) the United States and Britain
 (C) Britain and France
 (D) the United States and Greenland
 (E) Greenland, Britain, and France

432. In response to the Japanese invasion of Manchuria in 1931, the United States

 (A) declared war on Japan
 (B) adopted its Good Neighbor Policy
 (C) adopted the first Neutrality Act
 (D) froze all Japanese assets and ceased trade
 (E) adopted the Stimson Doctrine

433. Due to the forceful advancement of the Japanese military, General Douglas MacArthur was forced to withdraw from

(A) the Philippines

(B) Korea

(C) French-held Indochina

(D) Pearl Harbor

(E) Manchuria

434. The main goal of the America First Committee was to

(A) preemptively enter the Second World War to avoid a surprise attack

(B) continue American isolationism by ending the Lend-Lease Program

(C) trade with both Axis and Allied nations to bolster the American economy

(D) stop the influx of Latin-American immigrants from entering the United States

(E) provide aid for the families of victims who died in Pearl Harbor

435. The Nazi Party was an extreme example of what political ideology?

(A) Communism

(B) Socialism

(C) Fascism

(D) Nationalism

(E) Democratic socialism

436. The main function of the Office of War Mobilization during the Second World War was to

(A) create a system of selective service

(B) coordinate government agencies involved in the war effort

(C) use the media to stir popular support for the war

(D) ration industrial materials that would be needed for the war effort

(E) fix prices and establish a system for rationing certain consumer goods

437. What was the main function of President Roosevelt's Executive Order 9066?

(A) To force Japanese-Americans into internment camps

(B) To make striking in a wartime industry a crime

(C) To institute a policy of lend lease with Allied powers

(D) To ban discriminatory hiring within the federal government

(E) To ban the sale or shipment of arms to belligerent nations

438. Which of the following battles is considered to be a turning point in the Pacific Campaign during World War II?

(A) Battle of Guadalcanal
(B) Battle of Iwo Jima
(C) Battle of Leyte Gulf
(D) Battle of Midway
(E) Battle of the Coral Sea

439. What was the Allied strategy in the Second World War?

(A) The Allies would focus on defeating the Axis powers in Europe and then the Pacific.
(B) The Allies would focus on defeating the Axis powers in the Pacific and then Europe.
(C) The Soviet Union would focus on Germany, and the United States would focus on Japan.
(D) The United States would focus on the Pacific, while the other Allies focused on Europe.
(E) The Allies would divide their forces, simultaneously attacking in Europe and the Pacific.

440. The Allied invasion of Normandy, France, was code-named

(A) Operation Barbarossa
(B) Operation Torch
(C) Operation Overlord
(D) Operation Cartwheel
(E) Operation Quicksilver

441. The purpose of the Manhattan Project was to

(A) assassinate Adolf Hitler to hasten the end of the war
(B) develop improved jet technology to gain superiority
(C) develop an atomic bomb
(D) destroy a German espionage ring located in New York City
(E) coordinate an Allied invasion of France

442. President Roosevelt attempted to address racial inequality in government jobs by creating the

(A) Congress of Racial Equality
(B) Fair Employment Practices Committee
(C) Women's Army Corps
(D) Office of War Mobilization
(E) braceros

443. During the Second World War, Tehran, Yalta, and Potsdam were

    (A) pivotal military victories for the Allied nations
    (B) decisive victories for the Axis powers
    (C) sites of Nazi concentration camps
    (D) sites of conferences held by the Big Three
    (E) key beaches during the invasion of Normandy

444. The Japanese officially surrendered by signing a treaty

    (A) on the battleship *Missouri*
    (B) on the island of Okinawa
    (C) in the city of Hiroshima
    (D) in the city of Tokyo
    (E) in the Japanese emperor's palace

CHAPTER 16

The Cold War and Postwar America

445. The coining of the term *iron curtain* is attributed to which leader?

(A) Harry Truman
(B) George Marshall
(C) Dwight Eisenhower
(D) Winston Churchill
(E) Douglas MacArthur

446. George F. Kennan most strongly supported which policy?

(A) Containment
(B) Massive retaliation
(C) Mutually assured destruction
(D) Bans on nuclear testing
(E) The creation of NATO

447. The Truman Doctrine and the Marshall Plan were similar in that they

(A) provided justification for military actions against authoritarian governments
(B) provided economic aid while containing Soviet influence
(C) returned the United States to its prewar isolationist policies
(D) focused on expanding American business interests in Latin America
(E) were used as the basis for creating the United Nations

448. What was the Berlin Airlift?

(A) The massive evacuations of diplomats following the Soviet takeover of West Berlin
(B) The aerial arrival of Soviet forces to capture the capital of Germany
(C) The delivery of goods and necessities after a Soviet blockade of West Berlin
(D) The evacuation of West German citizens following the construction of the Berlin Wall
(E) The delivery of Soviet propaganda to West Berlin in an attempt to fuel a revolution

449. The formation of NATO and the Warsaw Pact were similar in that they

(A) focused on economic security and development
(B) called for collective security against outside threats
(C) were used as an attempt to alleviate Cold War tensions
(D) illustrated international opposition to the United Nations
(E) effectively isolated Asia from the Western world

450. The communist revolution in China was led by

(A) Jiang Jieshi
(B) Kim Il Sung
(C) Ho Chi Minh
(D) Deng Xiaoping
(E) Mao Zedong

451. The major function of HUAC was to

(A) provide education funding for veterans
(B) stop domestic infiltration of communism
(C) contain the spread of communism in Europe
(D) demobilize the American economy from wartime production
(E) investigate the actions taken by Joseph McCarthy

452. *The Crucible* by Arthur Miller was an analogy of the Salem Witch Trials of New England and

(A) the events of the Holocaust
(B) racism in the southern states
(C) the acts of Joseph McCarthy's Senate committee
(D) the rise of Hitler in Nazi Germany
(E) the infiltration of communism in the United States

453. Julius and Ethel Rosenberg were executed for

(A) refusing to denounce the Communist Party
(B) giving nuclear weapons secrets to the Soviet Union
(C) serving as German spies during the Second World War
(D) giving nuclear weapons secrets to China
(E) attempting to assassinate President Eisenhower

454. During the decade following the Second World War, the U.S. national economy

(A) more than doubled
(B) fell back into depression
(C) suffered from a decade-long recession
(D) remained mostly unchanged
(E) relied mostly on European loans

455. Which of the following was *not* a result of the Korean War?

(A) Establishment of a military-industrial complex
(B) The racial integration of the armed forces
(C) Division of the Korean Peninsula at the 38th Parallel
(D) Passage of the Montgomery G.I. Bill
(E) A peace treaty between the United States and Japan

456. The Eisenhower Doctrine illustrated

(A) a more relaxed approach to the spread of communism
(B) the return of American isolationism
(C) a rejection of the Truman Doctrine and the Marshall Plan
(D) fears of the spread of communism in Asia
(E) the increased role of petroleum in American foreign policy

457. President Kennedy's policy of "flexible response" differed from Eisenhower's New Look Policy in that

(A) it restricted the use of nuclear weapons
(B) it allowed for a response to a wider spectrum of warfare
(C) it focused on securing American access to the Middle East
(D) it created an alliance of North Atlantic nations against the Soviet Union
(E) it promised military and economic support to nations fighting communism

458. President Harry Truman's domestic program was called the

(A) Fair Deal
(B) Great Society
(C) New Deal
(D) New Frontier
(E) Square Deal

459. Which of the following was an accomplishment of President Eisenhower's domestic policy?

- (A) Expansion of the Tennessee Valley Authority
- (B) Launch of the first satellite into space
- (C) Creation of a national interstate highway system
- (D) Creation of federally funded health care for the elderly
- (E) Creation of the Department of Housing and Urban Affairs

460. William J. Levitt helped the expansion of the American suburbs by

- (A) introducing mass-produced housing developments
- (B) creating the Federal Housing Administration
- (C) designing an interstate highway system
- (D) establishing the installment plan
- (E) creating an improved mass-transit system

461. Betty Friedan and Dr. Benjamin Spock differed in their views of women in that

- (A) Friedan supported the idea of the Cult of Domesticity, while Spock did not
- (B) Friedan rejected the notion of the feminine mystique advocated by Spock
- (C) Spock argued that women should focus on child rearing, while Friedan rejected this notion
- (D) Friedan argued that women should pursue traditional jobs in domestic services and child care while Spock did not
- (E) Spock strongly advocated a woman's use of birth control, while Friedan rejected the use of contraception

462. The 1950s literary and cultural movement that rejected the decade's social conformity was called the

- (A) Lost Generation
- (B) Beat Generation
- (C) hippies
- (D) Yippies
- (E) yuppies

463. Which pair of events best illustrates the incongruence of the domestic trends of the 1950s?
    (A) The emergence of rock and roll and of televangelists
    (B) The popularity of rock and roll and the decline in movie attendance
    (C) The work of Dr. Spock and the reemergence of the Cult of Domesticity
    (D) Suburban sprawl and the growth of the automotive industry
    (E) McCarthyism and the actions of HUAC

464. Which of the following was *not* a consequence of the 1962 Cuban Missile Crisis?
    (A) The Soviet Union agreed to remove its nuclear missiles from Cuba.
    (B) The United States agreed to remove its nuclear missiles from Turkey.
    (C) The Moscow-Washington hot line was created.
    (D) President Kennedy launched the Bay of Pigs invasion of Cuba.
    (E) Premier Khrushchev was forced out of power in the Soviet Union.

CHAPTER 17

Civil Rights, the 1960s, and Vietnam

465. The Supreme Court decision in *Brown v. Board of Education* overturned

(A) *Plessy v. Ferguson*
(B) *Dred Scott*
(C) The Taft-Hartley Act
(D) *Youngstown Sheet & Tube Co. v. Sawyer*
(E) The Civil Rights Act

466. CORE and the SCLC were similar in that both organizations

(A) believed in the use of militant protest
(B) were church-based organizations
(C) advocated change through nonviolence
(D) did not allow white membership
(E) rejected Martin Luther King Jr.'s passive resistance

467. The approaches of Dr. Martin Luther King Jr. and Malcolm X to the civil rights movement differed in that

(A) King was part of the SCLC, and Malcolm X created SNCC
(B) Malcolm X adopted a view of the "alleged inferiority of the Negro" while King did not
(C) King fought for desegregation, while Malcolm X supported a separate identity for African-Americans
(D) King, unlike Malcolm X, strongly promoted the ideals of black nationalism
(E) Malcolm X, unlike King, was a follower of Stokely Carmichael

468. The civil rights movement's Freedom Summer and the Selma March

(A) brought attention to the black-power movement
(B) directly increased membership within the Black Panthers
(C) illustrated the lack of African-American voting rights
(D) led to the creation of the Southern Manifesto
(E) led to the Civil Rights Act of 1964

469. Which of the following was *not* part of the 1964 Civil Rights Act?

(A) Banning of different voter registration practices based on race
(B) Banning of discrimination in public accommodations
(C) Allowing for federal funds to be withheld from programs that practice discrimination
(D) Creation of the Equal Employment Opportunity Commission
(E) Outlawing of poll taxes

470. Lyndon Johnson's Great Society ended primarily due to

(A) a lack of popular support within the nation
(B) the escalation of United States military involvement in Vietnam
(C) the emergence of another Red Scare
(D) the race riots that erupted after the assassination of Martin Luther King Jr.
(E) the moon landing

471. Which leader is *not* paired with the cause he or she is associated with?

(A) Betty Friedan—women's rights
(B) César Chávez—migrant workers' rights
(C) Dennis Banks—Native American rights
(D) Rachel Carson—Japanese-American rights
(E) Ralph Nader—consumer protections

472. President Kennedy tried to keep communism out of Vietnam by

(A) providing military assistance to Ho Chi Minh
(B) sending nearly 100,000 soldiers into the region
(C) providing the southern Vietnamese government with American military advisers
(D) allying with the Viet Cong against the Ngo Dinh Diem
(E) launching a bombing campaign against Cambodia

473. President Johnson escalated the Vietnam War in response to the

(A) My Lai Massacre
(B) Second Gulf of Tonkin incident
(C) establishment of the Viet Cong
(D) release of the Pentagon Papers
(E) French withdrawal from the region

474. During the Vietnam War, television influenced popular opinion of the conflict by

(A) allowing President Johnson to directly justify the war through public televised addresses

(B) being used to create propaganda to garner support for the conflict

(C) bringing images of the brutality of the conflict into people's homes

(D) giving the antiwar movement a platform to deliver its message

(E) showing national debates on the war, allowing viewers to make their own decisions

475. The Vietnam War finally ended when

(A) South Vietnam defeated the Viet Cong

(B) the United States led a successful invasion of Cambodia

(C) the United States withdrew its armed forces

(D) the North Vietnamese army successfully captured South Vietnam

(E) the United Nations divided the nation at the 17th Parallel

476. Four deaths resulted after a clash between antiwar student groups and National Guardsmen at which U.S. college?

(A) University of California, Berkeley

(B) Kent State University

(C) Ohio State University

(D) Columbia University

(E) Rutgers University

477. The major North Vietnamese and Viet Cong offensive launched on the Vietnamese New Year in 1968 is referred to as

(A) the My Lai Massacre

(B) Operation Rolling Thunder

(C) the Tet Offensive

(D) the Ho Chi Minh Trail

(E) the Khmer Rouge

478. Which of the following Americans was directly in charge of the soldiers involved in the My Lai Massacre?

(A) Eugene McCarthy

(B) Robert McNamara

(C) Robert Clark Clifford

(D) William Calley

(E) Robert Kennedy

479. Which of the following terms was *not* part of the 1973 Paris Peace Agreement signed between the United States and Vietnam?

    (A) Removal of all American military forces from the region

    (B) Release of all war prisoners

    (C) End of military actions in Cambodia and Laos

    (D) Division of North and South Vietnam at the 17th Parallel

    (E) Agreement by North and South Vietnam to hold free elections

480. Which of the following provisions was *not* part of the 1973 War Powers Act?

    (A) The president must notify Congress within 48 hours after deploying military abroad.

    (B) Only Congress has the power to declare war.

    (C) The president must provide Congress with justification for his actions after deploying the military abroad.

    (D) Troops cannot be deployed for more than 60 days without congressional approval.

    (E) Congress can demand that the president withdraw troops from overseas.

CHAPTER 18

End of the Cold War, the 1970s to the Present

481. During his presidency, Richard Nixon's "southern strategy" policy focused on

(A) cutting funding to southern schools that were still segregated
(B) making it easier to meet desegregation requirements
(C) furthering the implementation of the 1965 Voting Rights Act
(D) more strictly enforcing fair-housing laws
(E) gaining popular African-American support in the South

482. In foreign affairs, President Nixon's policy of détente was illustrated by

(A) relaxing Cold War tensions by engaging in talks with China and the Soviet Union
(B) rejecting the ideals of realpolitik
(C) his bombing campaign of Cambodia
(D) firing Henry Kissinger as secretary of state
(E) rejecting the SALT I agreement

483. The SALT I and SALT II agreements were created primarily to

(A) form a cartel controlling a majority of the world's petroleum resources
(B) create diplomatic ties between the United States and China
(C) negotiate arms control between the major superpowers
(D) further the U.S. policy of containment of communism
(E) reduce tensions within the Middle East

484. What was the primary reason behind the Watergate break-in in 1972?

(A) Nixon wanted to purge his administration of possible communist infiltration.
(B) CREEP wanted to spy on the Democratic Party.
(C) President Nixon wanted to recapture the leaked Pentagon Papers.
(D) The FBI was monitoring the Democratic Party's election campaign.
(E) Nixon wanted to fake a break-in of his campaign headquarters to gain public support.

485. The combination of inflation and economic recession faced in the United States in 1973 was caused in part by

(A) the opening of diplomatic relations with China and the Soviet Union
(B) OPEC's increasing the price of oil
(C) the North Vietnamese capture of Saigon
(D) the signing of the Camp David Accords
(E) the signing of the SALT I agreement

486. What action did Gerald Ford take to attempt to heal the nation following the Watergate Scandal?

(A) He asked citizens to wear WIN buttons.
(B) He pardoned Richard Nixon.
(C) He provided military support to the South Vietnamese government.
(D) He ordered a full investigation of the Nixon administration.
(E) He signed the Helsinki Accords.

487. Jimmy Carter won the 1976 presidential election by

(A) flaunting his knowledge of nuclear technology
(B) capturing the support of the Moral Majority
(C) promoting himself as a Washington outsider
(D) increasing government regulations on industries
(E) proposing a tax on gasoline

488. The 1978 peace agreement between Israel and Egypt was called the

(A) Helsinki Accords
(B) Geneva Accords
(C) Peace of Paris
(D) Camp David Accords
(E) SALT agreements

489. What international incident helped Ronald Reagan defeat Jimmy Carter in 1980?

(A) First Persian Gulf War
(B) Camp David Accords
(C) Iran hostage crisis
(D) Iran-Contra Affair
(E) Signing of SALT I

490. What were the two major areas of focus of Ronald Reagan's economic plan?

(A) Expanding federal assistance programs and increasing government
(B) Adopting Keynesian economics and cutting military spending
(C) Funding urban development and lowering taxes on the wealthy
(D) Lowering taxes and reducing government regulations
(E) Increasing taxes and expanding the Great Society

491. Who was appointed the first female Supreme Court justice?

(A) Ruth Joan Bader Ginsburg
(B) Sandra Day O'Connor
(C) Frances Perkins
(D) Sonia Sotomayor
(E) Margaret Thatcher

492. What was the overall impact of perestroika and glasnost on the Cold War?

(A) They strengthened the communist system in Eastern Europe.
(B) They brought an end to the strategic arms race between the United States and Soviet Union.
(C) They helped lead to the collapse of communist regimes in Eastern Europe.
(D) They led to the SALT I and II agreements.
(E) They resulted in the Iran-Contra Affair.

493. The First Persian Gulf War began when Saddam Hussein

(A) launched an attack on Israel
(B) overthrew the democratic Iraqi government
(C) attempted to assassinate George H. W. Bush
(D) launched an invasion of Kuwait
(E) began developing weapons of mass destruction

494. In attempting to reform the nation's health care system, President Clinton wanted to

(A) provide health insurance to all Americans
(B) provide health care coverage for the poor
(C) offer loans to students pursuing a career in medicine
(D) end Medicaid and Medicare
(E) provide health insurance to the elderly

495. The Republican Party's 1994 Contract with America pledged to

(A) fully fund the "Star Wars" program
(B) end the federal welfare system
(C) balance the federal budget
(D) pass universal health care
(E) tighten immigration laws

496. The 2000 presidential election was similar to the 1824 election in that

(A) the House of Representatives decided the election
(B) Republicans captured all three branches of government
(C) the candidate who received a majority of the popular vote lost the election
(D) neither candidate won enough electoral votes to win the presidency
(E) the Supreme Court had to decide the final outcome

497. The controversy in which members of President Reagan's administration illegally sold arms in violation of a congressional embargo has become known as

(A) the Iran-Contra Affair
(B) the S&L crisis
(C) Whitewater
(D) the HUD scandal
(E) the Inslaw Affair

498. Which of the following statements is true of the impeachments of both President Clinton and President Johnson?

(A) Both presidents were accused of illegally firing advisers.
(B) Both presidents were accused of committing perjury while under oath.
(C) Both presidents were found guilty by the Senate.
(D) Because of the impeachments, neither president sought reelection.
(E) Both presidents were found not guilty by the Senate.

499. Which of the following events is not associated with Al Qaeda?

    (A) the bombing of the USS *Cole*

    (B) the September 11 attacks

    (C) the 1998 bombings of U.S. embassies

    (D) the bombing of the Oklahoma City Federal Building

    (E) the Madrid train bombings

500. Which of the following legislation was passed in direct response to the events of September 11, 2001?

    (A) the USA PATRIOT Act

    (B) the FISA Act

    (C) the McCain-Feingold Act

    (D) the War Powers Resolution

    (E) the Brady Bill

ANSWERS

Chapter 1

1. (C) Throughout the last Ice Age, over the period of roughly 22,000 to 7,000 years ago, the climactic shift caused increased glaciations in both the Arctic and Antarctic, causing a global lowering of ocean levels. During this same period, other land bridges such as those connecting Australia to surrounding lands also appeared. Interestingly, D is incorrect because climatologists theorize that during this time period, there was a lack of precipitation caused by ocean currents and location of regional mountain ranges.

2. (E) Maize first appeared circa 5000 B.C. in the highland regions of Mexico. It reached North America in about 1200 B.C., though the spread of its cultivation in North America is believed to have been slower than in other parts of the Americas.

3. (E) With the exception of groups such as the Cahokia settlement in the present-day Mississippi Basin and the Ancestral Puebloan (Anasazis) culture in the Four Corners region of the Southwest, most Native American groups in North America lived in small, impermanent, matrilinear groups right up to the arrival of European explorers.

4. (A) The Native American Mississippian Valley culture is often associated with vast complexes of mound structures constructed around A.D. 1200. Archaeological evidence shows that this group illustrated a much higher level of political organization than was common among most indigenous populations in North America, though the civilization began to decline and vanish nearly a century prior to European arrival in North America.

5. (E) The Iroquois League founded around the 16th century initially consisted of the Mohawk, Oneida, Onondaga, Cayuga, and Seneca and spanned what is now southeastern Canada into New York. While initially consisting of five nations, the league expanded to six when the Tuscarora joined in the 1700s. The league began to decline after its allies, the British, were defeated in the American Revolution. The Powhatan were a tribe from eastern Virginia that controlled a confederacy of roughly 30 tributary tribes. They are associated with the early history of the Jamestown settlement. Pocahontas, the daughter of a Powhatan chief, is stated to have rescued John Smith. The confederation declined after the two Powhatan Wars in the 1600s.

6. (C) Though the Native Americans had developed high-yielding agriculture illustrated by the Three Sisters (maize, beans, and squash) cultivated by groups such as the Creek and Cherokee, they did not develop the intensive farming techniques commonplace in Europe. This could be partly due to the commonly held reverence for the natural world. However, many groups did use slash-and-burn clearing techniques to open forest and clear areas for agriculture on a limited basis.

7. (A) L'Anse aux Meadows, located in present-day Newfoundland, marks the location where Norse seafarers arrived around A.D. 1000. The settlement was short lived and soon forgotten except in Norse legend. Later archaeological finds rediscovered the settlement in the 1960s.

8. (B) The pre-Columbian Mesoamerican and Central American civilizations developed highly sophisticated societies, such as the Aztecs (containing by some estimates over 20,000 people at the time of European arrival), as well as highly complex trade networks. Also, the Mayans demonstrated advances in astronomy in their calendar. However, large, domesticated draft animals were not introduced until European arrival.

9. (A) The technique of growing beans, squash, and maize first appeared around A.D. 1000. The maize provided a structure for the beans, and the squash aided in maintaining moisture in the soil. This allowed populations' densities to increase within the Eastern Seaboard region of North America.

10. (C) Most Native Americans believed that while one had the right to use land for various purposes, it could not be owned outright. Therefore, while one person could grant permission to another to use land, it could not be sold outright.

11. (A) The Anasazi or Ancestral Puebloans established the cliff dwellings that now define areas such as Mesa Verde and Hovenweep on the Colorado Plateau. The civilization reached its high point around A.D. 900–1130. Archaeologists debate the reason for their disappearance, though many speculate it may have resulted from prolonged drought.

12. (A) Native American groups across the North American continent shared the trait of using kinship networks to define their clans. They consisted of a group of related families (aunts, uncles, cousins, etc.) connected through common ancestry.

13. (B) Maize, commonly referred to as corn, is a New World crop originating from the area that is now modern-day Mexico. Wheat, cattle, horses, and coffee are Old World crops. The introduction of American agricultural products to Europe and vice versa is part of what is called the Columbian Exchange.

14. (A) The Navajo occupied the area that is now Utah, Arizona, and Mexico. The Ojibwa are in the region of modern Minnesota. The Powhatan occupied the area around the Jamestown settlement in Virginia. The first Anglo-Powhattan War ended with the marriage of the Powhatan chief's daughter Pocahontas to settler John Rolfe. The Pequot occupied the region of modern-day Connecticut, and the Wampanoag were located in Massachusetts. The leader of the Wampanoag, Metacom, was known to the settlers as King Philip. In 1675, a war broke out between the settlers and the Wampanoag; it became known as King Philip's War.

15. (A) Wampum were belts made of beads usually constructed from shells. Wampum was used by Eastern Woodland tribes for multiple purposes including noting treaties and commemorating historical events. After the European arrival, wampum was also used as a type of currency with colonial traders.

Chapter 2

16. (D) While the crusaders were mostly unsuccessful in maintaining lands conquered in the Middle East, the returning soldiers introduced many new Eastern commodities, which created a strong market demand for them within Europe. To bypass the land routes traditionally used by traders and bypass Mediterranean nations such as the Italian states, many nations began to explore possible sea routes, ushering a new age of innovations in maritime travel.

17. (C) While the Black Death had a strong impact on European societies, the increase in trade and an emerging class of merchants played the leading role in ending feudalism. With trade, merchants and artisans moved away from the manor system, which was the basis of feudalism during the Middle Ages. Also, towns and cities became more dominant, as did the return of currency-based economies.

18. (B) The Magna Carta, which was signed by King John in 1215, ensured certain liberties to all free people, as well as protection of certain rights. Many of these rights can be seen in the present-day Bill of Rights. While the initial document attempted to check the absolute rule of the king, the notion of a true separation of powers did not truly originate with the 1215 signing, and while commoners did gain certain protections under the document, it was the aristocracy that forced the king to eventually agree to the charter.

19. (C) The Columbian Exchange refers to the transfer of European products in exchange for those in the Americas. While this exchange would become a cornerstone of trade, it was not limited to the exchange of agricultural or material goods. It also included diseases, ideas, and even humans through the form of slaves exported to Europe.

20. (C) Under the *encomienda* system, Spanish colonists were granted not only land but also the labor of the indigenous people to guarantee a profit. This was initially offered with the understanding that the Spanish would ensure protection and fair treatment, but most indigenous workers were exploited under this arrangement. This system would become a foundation of the economy for Spanish colonies in the Americas and also used later in the Philippines.

21. (A) In 1532, Francisco Pizarro conquered the Incan Empire located in present-day Peru. The Incan population had recently been inflicted with a wave of smallpox, which destabilized the political leadership within the region. The event happened roughly 11 years after Hernán Cortés subdued the Aztec Empire in the region that is modern-day Mexico. The Aztecs also were considerably weakened by an outbreak of smallpox.

22. (D) The 1494 agreement created a line that would divide the unclaimed land left in the Americas between the Spanish and the Portuguese. The line of demarcation established in the treaty was roughly halfway between the Portuguese-held Cape Verde Islands and Spanish-held Hispaniola. Spain gained lands west of the line, while Portugal gained lands to the east. The effects of this are illustrated to this day by the Portuguese-speaking nation of Brazil.

23. (A) In 1513, Balboa led his expedition across the Isthmus of Panama and became the first European explorer to see the Pacific Ocean. Its name was given by Ferdinand Magellan, who labeled it the "peaceful sea." Coronado notably explored the North American Southwest from the area ranging from modern-day Kansas to the Grand Canyon. Vespucci identified

South America as a continent by exploring its coastline. The Americas still serve as his namesake. Vasco da Gama was the first European explorer to reach India by sailing around Africa in 1498. Dias was the first European explorer to reach the southern tip of Africa in 1488.

24. (D) Sieur Robert Cavelier de La Salle explored the lower Mississippi River in 1682 and claimed the surrounding territory for France, naming it Louisiana in honor of his sovereign, Louis XIV. In 1535, Cartier explored the Saint Lawrence River. Louis Joliet, a priest, explored the Great Lakes and upper Mississippi River with Jacques Marquette, a French trader, setting up missions and trading posts in 1637. In 1608, Quebec, France's first permanent settlement, was established by Samuel de Champlain.

25. (D) While the Spanish and French made religious conversion a major goal of New World settlement, the Spanish were able to export vast amounts of wealth from the Americas in the form of precious metals. The early French explorers in North America pursued an intensive fur trade.

26. (C) El Camino Real, or royal road, was a system of trails that connected the various Spanish missions, forts, and outposts along northern Mexico and California's western coast. El Camino de Cruces refers to a path created through the Panamanian jungle after Francisco Pizarro conquered the Incan civilization in South America in 1531. The path was used to transport precious metals and other goods to eastern ports. The Old Spanish Trail is a system of routes initially used by the Spanish but named by John C. Fremont as he surveyed lands in the U.S. Southwest during the 1840s.

27. (C) Pueblos initially referred to communities established by Native Americans in the Southwest. They became centers of trade, though they also became sites of violence such as the Pueblo Revolt of 1680. Missions served as the primary location for religious conversion. They were established by the Catholic Church. Presidios were the names of the military outposts established throughout New Spain. *Ejiados* were the communal lands held by Native Americans within Mexico.

28. (D) Starting with Christopher Columbus's first expedition to the Americas, the spread of Christianity served as a major function of exploration. While the papacy did play a role within the New World, such as the establishment of the line of demarcation under the Treaty of Tordesillas, the Spanish monarchy retained sovereignty over its possessions in the Americas.

29. (B) Even though the Dutch Reformed Church was maintained as the official church of Dutch settlements in North America, such as that of New Amsterdam (present-day New York), the Dutch attempted to attract many of the populations displaced by conflicts following the Reformation. By the 1700s, nearly half of the population in Dutch possession was not Dutch and did not follow the Dutch Reformed Church.

30. (D) In 1519, Ferdinand Magellan and his crew of over 230 men and five ships left Spain to find a western route to Asia. In 1522, a single ship from the expedition and a small crew of 18 survivors returned, completing the first trip around the globe. Magellan himself did not survive the voyage. He was killed during a dispute between his crew and an indigenous population in the Philippines.

Chapter 3

31. (B) In a proprietary colony, the individuals who receive the charter to found the colony retain the rights to create laws for the colony and appoint the governor. Many colonies were founded in this manner, but the practice began to decline in the 1700s as the monarchy began to concentrate its control. By the outbreak of the American Revolution, only Delaware, Maryland, and Pennsylvania still held proprietary charters.

32. (A) The Middle Passage was part of the triangle of trade routes that defined Atlantic colonial trade and brought Africans to the Americas, where they were sold into slavery. The first African slaves arrived in the English North American colonies in 1619, brought by Dutch traders. The movement of African-Americans out of the southern United States during the early 20th century is referred to as the Great Migration. The removal of Cherokee Indians to Oklahoma in 1838, often referred to as the Trail of Tears, resulted from President Andrew Jackson's Indian Removal Act of 1830. The Northwest Passage was the proposed inter-oceanic passage sought by explorers such as Henry Hudson.

33. (E) Even though laws concerning African slaves made it difficult for them to travel or communicate freely, several slave uprisings occurred, including the Stono Rebellion in 1739. New York City had slave uprisings as early as 1712.

34. (A) Queen Elizabeth, also referred to as the Virgin Queen because she never married, granted Sir Walter Raleigh permission to explore the eastern coast of North America. He was granted permission by Queen Elizabeth to create a settlement on the coast north of the Spanish land claims in the region.

35. (E) The headright system established in 1619 was introduced by the Virginia Company and offered 50 acres of land to any man who paid his own way to the Virginia Colony. It furthermore offered an additional 50 acres for each additional person he brought with him.

36. (E) Through the middle of the 1700s, religious leaders such as Jonathan Edwards and George Whitefield led a religious revival in the colonies that focused on emotional experiences. It resulted in the emergence of new sects such as the Baptists and Methodists.

37. (D) During Bacon's Rebellion, poor whites (many former indentured servants) and blacks banded together against what was viewed as a ruling class. In response, the Virginia government moved to further institutionalize African slavery as a way to control one segment of the poor population.

38. (E) John Rolfe arrived at the end of the Starving Time, the winter of 1609–1610. He proceeded to cultivate a milder strain of tobacco, helping to introduce the colony's first major staple crop, as well as helping to popularize the dangerous habit of tobacco smoking. In 1614, Rolfe married Pocahontas, the daughter of the Powhatan chief. In 1616, Rolfe returned to England with Pocahontas, who became a popular guest in the English court.

39. (B) Mercantilism was a dominant economic philosophy during the 16th to the 18th centuries. Under this system, international commerce exists to increase a country's wealth especially in acquiring gold and foreign currency. Under mercantilism, exports were viewed as desirable and imports as undesirable unless they led to even greater exports. Colonies were useful in this system because countries could use them to acquire raw materials and had access to markets without having to trade with foreign nations.

40. (D) The Massachusetts Bay Company established Massachusetts as a chartered corporate colony in 1630. It became a royal colony in 1691, but its citizens retained the ability to elect representation in the colonial government. Learning from earlier attempts to establish colonies such as Jamestown, which suffered from a period of starvation that nearly destroyed the colony over the winter of 1609–1610, Massachusetts was well provisioned. While slavery was legal in the Massachusetts Bay Colony, there were fewer slaves than in the southern colonies, and the practice was ended in the 1780s.

41. (A) John Peter Zenger was a printer and journalist from New York who in 1735 was acquitted on charges of libel for an attack made on William Cosby, the colonial governor at the time. This established a precedent for freedom of the press, later included in the Bill of Rights. John Woolman was a Quaker preacher who traveled throughout the American colonies conducting sermons against slavery. Jonathan Edwards (most famous for his sermon "Sinners in the Hands of an Angry God," 1741), Gilbert Tennent, and George Whitefield are considered leaders of the Great Awakening religious revival that took place in the middle of the 18th century.

42. (E) In addition to being a successful printer and philosopher, Franklin is to be noted as one of the great inventors and scientists during the colonial period. Some of his inventions include bifocal glasses, the flexible catheter, a map of North Atlantic Ocean current patterns, the principle of conservation of charge, the lightning rod, and the Franklin stove. Interchangeable parts, however, are accredited to Eli Whitney after he obtained a federal contract to manufacture 10,000 muskets in 1798.

43. (C) Pennsylvania, which was established in 1681 by the Quaker William Penn and has been called one of the better-advertised colonies, attracted a diverse mix of artisans and craftsmen. Because of the Quaker faith, the Pennsylvania colony stressed fairer treatment of the Native Americans, though this effort was often undermined by others who joined the colony. While Pennsylvania did allow religious freedom and did not have a state tax-sponsored church, because of pressures from England the colony did deny political rights to certain groups such as Catholics and Jews. Also, while the Pennsylvania colony did practice capital punishment, it was at a much lower rate than practiced in England.

44. (B) Both Pennsylvania and Maryland were given charters or permission by the sovereign to be established in North America under proprietary charters. Proprietary colonies differed from royal colonies in that royal colonies were controlled by the king, who appointed a governor and council to the colony. In proprietary colonies, the colonies' founders, such as William Penn in Pennsylvania or George Calvert in Maryland, maintained control over the governorship and many of the laws directly. A corporate colony was a colony chartered for a specific corporation such as a joint stock company; examples were Rhode Island and Connecticut.

45. (C) In 1732, James Oglethorpe was granted a proprietary charter to establish Georgia, named after King George II. Oglethorpe, a social reformer, wanted to use the land as a place to send people who had been imprisoned as debtors. The colony also served the purpose of establishing a defensive buffer between the English North American colonies and Spanish-held Florida.

46. (D) While New England serves as an early example of publicly supported schools, the education provided to both males and females was to promote the Puritan religious beliefs. Over 50 percent of the New England population was literate, and this was in part because literacy was seen as important so the colonists would be able to read the Bible. Religious instruction was a major focus of the education offered. Only eight years after the Massachusetts Bay Colony was established, Harvard College was founded to train young men for the ministry.

47. (C) While the Spanish initially used the indigenous population as forced labor through policies such as the *encomienda* system, as did the Portuguese, these populations began to dwindle as a result of European disease and harsh labor conditions. In 1502, the Portuguese began trading slaves from West Africa to New World colonies. Nearly 11 million Africans became victims of this system of forced labor.

48. (D) The scattering of African people and their culture during the three centuries that followed Columbus's arrival in the Western Hemisphere has been referred to as the African diaspora. During this period, millions of Africans were forcibly relocated to the Americas. In some areas, such as the English West Indies and Haiti, they outnumbered European colonists. Slave codes were harsh laws put in place to maintain order within areas with slave populations. The African slaves were, however, able to hold onto many of their traditions and culture through creolized language and religious practice.

49. (E) In 1634, Lord Baltimore, who was a member of a prominent Catholic family in England, received a charter to establish Maryland. While profit was a main goal, the charter also was intended to provide a safe haven for his fellow Catholics who faced persecution in England under the Church of England—for example, not being allowed to marry in the Catholic Church.

50. (A) While many Puritans left England in the 1630s to escape religious persecution, when they arrived in North America, they did not practice religious tolerance. All members of the Massachusetts Bay Colony had to attend Puritan churches and pay taxes to support it.

51. (D) In 1630, John Winthrop described the Massachusetts Bay Colony as a city on the hill, stating, "The eyes of all people are upon us." The colony did not practice religious tolerance, however, and its treatment of Native Americans was similar to that of the colonists in Virginia. Conflicts such as King Philip's War resulted.

52. (C) In New England, women who were widowed could maintain property and contracts. When they remarried, however, these rights ended, and their husband would take control of the woman's estate. Women in New England were encouraged to read yet did not have the right to vote or hold public office.

53. (C) An initial reason Maryland was established was to provide refuge for Catholics who were persecuted in England. Lord Baltimore allowed freedom of worship from its founding, however, and many Protestants began to migrate into the region, threatening Catholic domination in the colony. The Toleration Act, while extending toleration to all Christians, was mainly to protect the rights of the Catholics settled there. It protected Christians, but non-Christians such as Jewish colonists did not receive any protections.

54. (D) The southern colonies' economy was dominated by the export of staple crops such as tobacco, rice, and indigo. Upland cotton was initially not a major cash crop but later dominated the southern economy after the cotton gin was invented by Eli Whitney in 1793, making the removal of seeds and processing of the fiber economically viable. Slaves and indentured servants initially worked side by side. This illustrated a potential danger, however, after Bacon's Rebellion, in which they banded together against the plantation owners in 1676.

55. (C) Roger Williams, though having separatist ideals, alienated himself from and was eventually exiled because of his rejection of Puritan practices in Boston. His belief in liberty of conscience called for individual freedom of religion and a separation of church and state. In 1636, he founded Providence, which stood apart from other North American colonies in that it practiced religious tolerance.

56. (B) Hutchinson left England for New England to escape religious persecution, but once she was in Boston, she began to speak out against Puritan authority within the colony. She rejected church authority if it in her opinion violated the authority of God. When she was placed on trial for her beliefs in 1638, she defended her beliefs concerning a personal relationship with religion over the authority of the church. For these beliefs she was banished from Massachusetts. Hutchinson and her followers left the Massachusetts Bay Colony and established Portsmouth in Rhode Island.

57. (A) While the soil and climate were not as accommodating for the production of crops as in the southern colonies, agricultural exports served as a major component of the middle colonies. The climate did not support the growth of high-profit crops such as tobacco and indigo, or the cultivation of rice. Instead, grains such as wheat, oats, and barley became the major agricultural exports of the region. While agriculture was a major component of the economy, the farms in the middle colonies tended to be smaller, and slavery did not flourish. Furthermore, much of the agricultural production was consumed internally within the colonies.

58. (B) During the 17th century, roughly half of the European settlers who arrived in North America were indentured servants. Indentured servants were laborers who contracted to work for a set period of time in exchange for passage to the Americas. Unlike a slave, an indentured servant was required to work only for a limited term specified in a signed contract. This practice slowed, however, after Bacon's Rebellion, when poor farmers, including many former indentured servants, rose up against the wealthy landed planters. Afterward, the use of African slaves became more common.

59. (D) New England, like many of the northern colonies, had generally thin, rocky soil; hilly land; and longer, more severe winters than in the South. This made intensive farming of staple crops difficult. Instead, New England diversified its economy. New England harnessed water power to establish mills and used the abundant timber for shipbuilding.

Furthermore, harbors within the region became a major source of prosperity, promoting trade and fishing.

60. (A) In 1676, Nathaniel Bacon led an uprising in Virginia, marking the first rebellion in the colonies. The event became known as Bacon's Rebellion. It was sparked by Native American raids on the outskirts of the colony but illustrated a rejection of Governor William Berkley's policies, which favored the wealthy planters over the poor. The uprising inspired a similar revolt in Maryland later that year.

61. (A) The Piedmont is a plateau of forests and hills in the western part of Virginia leading to the Appalachian Mountains. When the fertile land of the Tidewater was taken, many poorer farmers and former indentured servants moved into this region. The farms in the Piedmont tended to be smaller, and many farmers in this region faced economic hardships. The disparity between the Piedmont and Tidewater eventually led to uprisings such as Bacon's Rebellion.

62. (D) The Tidewater is the region that constitutes roughly 70 miles of the Atlantic Coast along the James, Potomac, York, and Rappahannock Rivers. This region was extremely fertile and became home to the larger and more successful plantations within the colonies. The poorer farmers and former indentured servants were often forced to move west to the hillier and less productive Piedmont.

63. (C) The House of Burgesses was created in 1619 and was the first representative body of its kind in the Americas. While it did have the power to make laws concerning the colony, those laws could be vetoed by the governor, who was initially selected by the officials within the joint stock company, and by the king after 1624, when Virginia became a royal colony. The House of Burgesses was allowed to remain even after Virginia became a royal colony.

64. (E) King Philip's War took place in the southern part of New England and lasted from 1675 to 1676. The Native Americans were led by Metacom (or Metacomet), the leader of the Wampanoag Confederacy. He was named King Philip by the New England colonists. The conflict resulted from colonial encroachment onto Native American lands and decline in the Native American trade economy. While the Native Americans initially succeeded in inflicting damage upon the colonial settlements, they eventually ran low on supplies and were faced with disease, which caused them to collapse.

65. (A) In 1735, John Peter Zenger was put on trial for criticizing New York governor William Cosby. Zenger was charged with libel after accusing the governor of corruption and taking bribes. Zenger's lawyer, Andrew Hamilton, proved that Zenger's accusations were not false, so he was innocent of libel. This became a basis for the notion of the freedom of the press.

Chapter 4

66. (A) Before the French and Indian War (ending in 1763), the English government had limited direct interference with the American colonists, treating them with a policy referred to as salutary neglect. As long as the colonies exported raw materials to Britain and imported finished goods from Britain, Britain left them alone. This policy came to an end after 1763 as Prime Minister George Grenville ordered the British navy to begin enforcing the Navigation Acts initially passed in 1651 to recoup funds and pay off debts accumulated during the French and Indian War.

67. (A) In 1758, Lord William Pitt replaced the Earl of Loundoun as the commander in chief of the British troops in America, after Loundoun proved himself as inept in the all-important areas of Indian policy and frontier battle strategy. Pitt pursued a policy that involved making peace with important Indian allies and changing the army's strategy to fit the territory and landscape of the frontier. He also began to plan attacks on French forts within the Ohio River Valley. While the British eventually received lands east of the Mississippi River, most of the fighting was concentrated in the Eastern Seaboard, Ohio River Valley, and Saint Lawrence River.

68. (C) Part of the 1774 Coercive Acts (known by the colonists as the Intolerable Acts) was the Massachusetts Government Act, which repealed the Massachusetts Bay Colony's right to elect its own legislature, in effect turning it into a royal colony. Thomas Gage was made the royal governor and instituted martial law within the colony. Also, under these acts, many of the provisions of the Quartering Act, which had been repealed earlier, were put back into place. The Administration of Justice Act allowed trials to be held in locations outside of the area where the crime took place. Furthermore, the Boston Harbor was closed until the damages caused by the Boston Tea Party were repaid.

69. (A) The Albany Congress was a meeting of Connecticut, Maryland, Massachusetts, New Hampshire, New York, Pennsylvania, and Rhode Island to arrange treaties with the Native Americans and develop a defensive plan to repel any attacks made by the French. Benjamin Franklin proposed a plan to create a union among the colonies under the British Crown. The plan ultimately was rejected but later inspired the Articles of Confederation, written in 1777, which served as the first U.S. government until 1787.

70. (A) In protest of such acts as the 1765 Stamp Act and the 1767 Townshend Acts, groups such as the Sons of Liberty organized colonial boycotts of British goods. These nonimportation societies attempted to use economic pressure to force Britain to acknowledge what colonists saw as their political rights.

71. (D) The Proclamation of 1763 was issued by the British government following the French and Indian War. The first purpose of the treaty was to separate the colonists from the Native Americans by creating a boundary between the two groups along the Appalachian Mountains in hopes of reducing conflicts between them as settlers began to push westward. Also, by not letting the colonists expand into the interior, the British government felt it could keep better control of the colonists and ensure their allegiance to the Crown. Furthermore, they could limit the creation of local industries that might undercut British trade. There was little discussion of religion within the proclamation.

72. (A) The Sugar Act of 1764 was in many ways a reissue of the Sugar and Molasses Act of 1733, which had imposed a tax on molasses to make English products cheaper than those from the French West Indies. The 1765 Quartering Act was put in place to alleviate the expense of stationing the large number of British troops needed to secure newly acquired lands following the French and Indian War by having the colonists supply the soldiers' room and board. The Quebec Act of 1774 gave much of the land in the Ohio River Valley to the colony of Quebec and was seen by the colonists as a punitive measure against the American colonies, since it was passed at the same time as the Coercive Acts, which were created in response to colonial protests, most notably the Boston Tea Party. The Currency Act was an attempt by the British government to stop the production of colonial scrip, or colonial currency that was used by the colonies to cover expenditures during the French and Indian War. The currency was often of little value and was seen to destabilize the colonial economy.

73. (A) The Albany Congress of 1754 was led in part by Benjamin Franklin. It was established to develop a strategic alliance with the Six Nations of the Iroquois people. Furthermore, Franklin believed it would allow the colonies to work for their own common defense against the French in the period leading up to the French and Indian War. The congress was to serve under appointments made by the Crown but contain a colonial representational body. The proposal was ultimately rejected by the colonists, but it served as a model for the later Articles of Confederation. The articles drafted by John Dickenson in 1777 were the first U.S. government after the American Revolution. The Committees of Correspondence were groups established by the local colonial governments in response to British actions leading up the American Revolution. They coordinated actions against the British government such as the colonial boycotts. The First Continental Congress formed in 1774 to respond to the passage of the Coercive Acts. The Second Continental Congress formed in the wake of the events at Lexington and Concord. It served as the ad hoc government throughout the revolution for the colonies.

74. (E) The Articles of Confederation were drafted in 1777 and went into effect at the conclusion of the American Revolution. This document created a loose confederation of the 13 states under a unicameral legislative body with representatives from each state. It illustrated the anti-monarchical sentiment within the colonies. The articles did not give the national government the ability to tax (they had to solicit funds from the states), raise an army (they had to ask the states to draw upon their militias), or regulate trade. The national government under the Articles of Confederation, however, was the only body that could declare war on a foreign power. The articles were replaced with the ratification of the U.S. Constitution.

75. (A) As early as the 1750s, colonists began to reject British taxes based on the notion "No taxation without representation." Boston lawyer James Otis argued that this taxation was "tyranny." Prime Minister George Grenville's rebuttal argument was that colonists were represented through virtual representation, meaning the government looked out for interests of all English subjects. This notion was further enforced with the 1766 Declaratory Act.

76. (D) When the Stamp Act was repealed in March 1766, the colonists were convinced that their boycotts and protests had resulted in a victory against Britain. The British government felt differently. With the repeal of the Stamp Act, Parliament put into place the Declaratory Act, affirming its right to tax and noting that the colonists were bound to the king "in all cases whatsoever." Colonists were required to provide housing for troops under the Quartering Act, the taxes on West Indies sugar came under the Sugar Act, the tax on household items came with the Townshend Acts, and the Currency Act ended the colonists' ability to produce their own currency.

77. (D) As a result of the December 16, 1773, "Tea Party" and the nearly £10,000 in damages, King George III believed harsh actions were necessary to force the colonists to submit to British authority. Four Coercive Acts were issued that closed the port of Boston until damages were paid, limited self-rule, allowed trials to take place in London, and reintroduced the policies of the Quartering Act.

78. (B) Crispus Attucks was a black dockworker and sailor in Boston. He was one of five people killed in the event that became known as the Boston Massacre in 1770 and is considered the first casualty of the American Revolution. In many ways, he became a martyr for the patriot cause, immortalized in Paul Revere's famous engraving of the event.

79. (C) Believing in all citizens' right to trial and the necessity of the rule of law, John Adams defended Captain Preston and other soldiers involved in the incident known as the Boston Massacre. During the event, five colonists were killed after an angry mob attacked the soldiers. It took place on March 5, 1770. In the end, Captain Preston and six other soldiers were acquitted. Two other soldiers were found guilty after evidence showed they had fired directly into the crowd. John Dickenson, author of "Letters from a Farmer in Pennsylvania" and the "Olive Branch Petition," was a lawyer from Pennsylvania. He also served in both the First and Second Continental Congresses, penning the Articles of Confederation in 1777. Samuel Adams, brother of John Adams, was a leader of the Sons of Liberty. His use of propaganda helped increase support for the patriot cause. Andrew Hamilton defended John Peter Zenger in the 1735 case establishing a precedent for the freedom of the press in the colonies.

80. (C) In the aftermath of the events of Lexington and Concord, John Dickenson authored the document to avoid the escalation of violence. It was ratified by the Second Continental Congress in 1775. The British king outright rejected the document, and the revolution began.

81. (C) On April 19, 1775, Massachusetts governor Thomas Gage ordered 700 British troops to destroy a store of arms being collected by the militias there. They were also to seek out the patriot leaders Samuel Adams and John Hancock. Colonial intelligence learned of the plan, however, and the arms were moved to another location. Regardless, a skirmish broke out between militiamen and British troops on the green of Lexington, sparking the American Revolution. The Second Continental Congress formed in response to the events of Lexington and Concord, which later created the Continental Army.

82. (A) Starting in the 1760s, the British government began issuing writs of assistance to help end smuggling within the colonies. The warrant allowed soldiers to search for items without noting a specific location and did not expire. The Boston attorney James Otis challenged the use of these general warrants in 1761. Though he lost, his case inspired other colonists such as John Adams. The requirement to house and feed soldiers was referred to as quartering. This action was also seen as a violation of colonial rights and helped inspire amendments in the Bill of Rights.

83. (A) The purpose of the 1765 Quartering Act was to alleviate the costs of keeping a high level of soldiers in North America at the conclusion of the French and Indian War. The colonial assemblies were required to provide for the needs of soldiers stationed within the colonies, including bedding and food. The law later included providing soldiers with living quarters in taverns and unoccupied houses. The Third Amendment in the Bill of Rights addresses this by stating, "No Soldier shall, in time of peace be quartered in any house, without the consent of the Owner, nor in time of war, but in a manner to be prescribed by law."

84. (C) Going into the war, the British possessed many advantages. They held the greatest navy in the world as well as the strongest army. The colonists had only a small, untrained group of volunteers, and their navy consisted of a few vessels. The British also had the manufacturing capability to make arms as well as a treasury that could support the war effort. They were unable, however, to fully utilize their loyalist support.

85. (D) The Battle of Saratoga, often considered the turning point of the American Revolution for the colonists, was led by Horatio Gates. At that time, General Washington was leading his troops at Brandywine. Here Washington was defeated, and Philadelphia fell to the British, forcing the Continental Congress to abandon the city.

86. (A) During the American Revolution, the British army often found itself outgunned. The British used muskets with unrifled barrels because these weapons were quicker to reload. The colonists, however, had muskets with rifled barrels, which greatly increased their accuracy, though they were slower to reload. The British maintained more Native American alliances, which would create troubles for the young United States as its people expanded west following the conclusion of the revolution.

87. (B) During the war, the British actively recruited slaves, especially those whose owners were patriots. During the war, a majority of African-Americans fought for Britain under the promise they would gain freedom. Though some African-Americans fought for the patriot cause, the colonists were reluctant to enlist black soldiers. At the end of the war, the British took thousands of slaves with them as they withdrew from the South. Some were given freedom in Canada, while others remained enslaved and were forced into labor in the West Indies.

88. (D) By 1778, the patriots gained control of the Ohio River Valley and halted the British attempt to isolate New England from the rest of the colonies. Starting in 1778, the British began to focus their strategy in the South, hoping to incite southern loyalist sympathizers and capture key ports such as Savannah and Charleston. General Cornwallis established a camp at Yorktown in Virginia. He found himself surrounded, however, and was forced to surrender after the patriots held siege on his position with the assistance of the French. The British government and Benedict Arnold did devise a plan to turn over West Point to the British in 1780, but the plan was foiled.

89. (C) After 1778, the British army began to focus on the South, successfully capturing key southern ports. General Cornwallis attempted to secure Yorktown, but the French navy took control of the Chesapeake Bay at the Battle of Hampton Roads, cutting off British supply lines and allowing American and French forces to besiege the British position. Cornwallis surrendered on October 19, 1781, marking the last major battle of the American Revolution.

90. (A) At the conclusion of the revolution, many Americans feared the reemergence of a monarchy or dictatorship. These fears of a strong central government are illustrated by the creation of the Articles of Confederation. In this government, most of the power was held by individual states. This arrangement proved ineffective, however, because the government lacked the power to tax or regulate commerce, leading to economic instability, inflation, and uprisings.

91. (C) The Enlightenment was an 18th-century intellectual movement with a strong focus on the individual, rationalism, and natural rights. Philosophers of this movement, such as John Locke and Jean-Jacques Rousseau, inspired Thomas Jefferson in his writing of the Declaration of Independence. The declaration's reference to "Life, Liberty, and the pursuit of Happiness" echoes the ideas from Locke's *Two Treatises on Government*, though Locke originally referred to life, liberty, and property.

92. (B) While the Declaration of Independence states, "All men are created equal," Jefferson implied that all free citizens are politically equal. Most scholars feel that this notion of equality did not apply to wealth. Furthermore, the statement did not apply to those not considered to be full citizens, such as women and slaves. The notion of equality has evolved over time, however, and it inspired abolitionists, suffragists, and other civil rights groups in later generations.

93. (D) Going into the winter of 1776, the Continental army under George Washington was unable to secure a large victory. The army was badly defeated at the Battle of Long Island and was forced to retreat through New Jersey to Pennsylvania. The victory at Trenton in December 1776 helped save the Continental army as well as George Washington's career. The loss at Brandywine allowed the British to take Philadelphia, and the Battle of Monmouth ended in a draw. Bunker Hill was seen as a moral victory for the colonists in that they held off the first two British attacks. However, in the end, they lost their position at Charlestown Peninsula, losing the battle.

94. (C) The Continental army consisted of many untrained militiamen and volunteers. A good number of them lacked knowledge of field drills and maneuvering, which put the army at a disadvantage against the well-trained British army. General Von Steuben trained Washington's army over the winter of 1778, instilling much-needed training in field drills. His practices became the foundation of the Continental army's field training manual.

95. (C) The Battle of Saratoga has been considered by many historians to be the turning point of the war for the colonists. This battle ended the British plan to sever New England from the rest of the American colonies. It also convinced the French to extend their support to the patriots more openly, and it convinced the Spanish to enter the conflict as an ally of the French.

96. (A) Mary Ludwig Hayes's husband fought in Washington's army at the Battle of Monmouth. During the battle, she brought pitchers of water to cannons, so the barrels could be washed out before reloading. After her husband was injured in the fighting, she took his place at the cannons. Washington made her an honorary sergeant after the battle, and the nickname "Molly Pitcher" has become a part of American folklore.

97. (B) Though certain slaves gained their freedom during the American Revolution, at the war's conclusion, the institution remained unchanged, and the freedoms granted by the revolution did not extend to most Africans living in the country. The Treaty of Paris indirectly referenced slavery in Article 7, stating that the British should leave American property, including slaves, unmolested as they withdrew.

98. (A) In 1786, Daniel Shays led an uprising of New England farmers and merchants against the government. It helped inspire the Philadelphia convention along with the creation of the U.S. Constitution. The Whiskey Rebellion took place in western Pennsylvania during President Washington's administration. It was a response to Alexander Hamilton's creation of an excise tax on spirits. Gabriel Prosser's Rebellion was an attempted slave uprising in Virginia in 1800.

99. (D) The Northwest Ordinance was a successful piece of legislation under the Articles of Confederation that dealt with the old West (the Ohio River Valley to the Mississippi River). It created a process through which territories could apply for statehood. The ordinance also outlawed slavery in the Northwest Territory, and it promised to respect land claims of the Native Americans within the region (a provision that was often ignored).

100. (B) As a result of anti-monarchical sentiments and fears of a strong central government, the Articles of Confederation gave the central government few powers, allowing the states to retain many powers, including the power to regulate trade. This resulted in myriad economic problems for the early independent United States, including commerce disputes between the states themselves. The U.S. Constitution gave Congress the ability to regulate trade and commerce between states and with foreign nations.

Chapter 5

101. (D) The American Revolution was officially ended with the 1783 Treaty of Paris. In treaty negotiations, the United States was represented by Benjamin Franklin, John Adams, and John Jay. With the treaty, Britain recognized the nation's independence, formalized U.S. borders, and arranged for the removal of British troops. The Treaty of Westphalia ended the European conflict known as the Thirty Years' War. The Treaty of Versailles ended World War I. The Treaty of Ghent ended the War of 1812, and the Treaty of Tordesillas divided lands in the Western Hemisphere between the Spanish and Portuguese.

102. (B) While the central government formed by the Articles of Confederation proved to be too weak, it did successfully implement several policies that carried over to the U.S. government under the Constitution. John Hanson under the articles designed the Great Seal of the United States, helped create a system for western territories to apply for statehood under the Northwest Ordinance of 1787, and created the U.S. Treasury and the postal service. The reservation system for Native Americans was created in 1851 under the Indian Appropriations Act.

103. (D) Rhode Island did not participate in the 1787 convention that produced the U.S. Constitution. At the time of the convention, Rhode Island had low taxes and modest economic security, and Rhode Islanders feared that the convention would overthrow the

Articles of Confederation, producing a government that would be less beneficial to the state. Rhode Island was also the last state to ratify the Constitution, not doing so until May 1780.

104. (B) The New Jersey Plan was created by William Patterson and gave each state one vote. It was created as a response to the Virginia Plan, in which representation was based on population. Patterson's plan had one legislative house, which was given the power to tax and regulate commerce.

105. (D) James Madison's Virginia Plan called for a bicameral legislature (one that contains two houses). Madison believed that the one-state, one-vote system under the Articles of Confederation was ineffective. He therefore called for representation based on population. In his plan, there would to be an upper and lower house that would choose the executive and judicial branch. The system also called for checks and balances.

106. (D) The Great Compromise was proposed by Roger Sherman of Connecticut. It took elements of both the New Jersey Plan and the Virginia Plan, creating a bicameral legislature. In the Senate, each state had equal representation, two senators per state. Representation in the House of Representatives was based on population, reflecting the Virginia Plan.

107. (A) James Madison is often considered the Father of the Constitution for several reasons. He researched government before the convention, especially works by Montesquieu. He also took the minutes of the convention, offering insights. His call for a bicameral legislature became the basis for the current House of Representatives and Senate.

108. (A) Judicial review is the power of the courts to strike down laws or actions that violate the Constitution. The only way to overrule judicial review by the legislative body is to amend the Constitution itself. The first use of judicial review was under the *Marbury v. Madison* ruling decided by Chief Justice John Marshall in 1803.

109. (B) The Three-Fifths Compromise was introduced by delegates James Wilson of Pennsylvania and Roger Sherman of Connecticut to deal with the debate over deciding representation in the House of Representatives and the distribution of taxes. If only free citizens were counted toward a state's total population, the South feared it would suffer an imbalance in federal representation, since it possessed a larger slave population, and slaves were not considered citizens. Without a clause taking the slave populations into account, many southern states would have refused to ratify the Constitution.

110. (A) The Three-Fifths Compromise was an agreement made between the northern and southern states at the 1787 Constitutional Convention to deal with the apportionment of seats in the House of Representatives and the distribution of taxes. While delegates who opposed slavery felt that only free citizens should be counted, pro-slavery delegates objected. Roger Sherman and James Wilson introduced the Three-Fifths Compromise to broaden support for the Constitution. Under the proposal, slave populations in each state would be based on three-fifths of the total slave population. The compromise was put in Article I, Section 2 of the Constitution. This was significant because later, in the events leading to the Civil War, it was used to illustrate the constitutionality of slavery. Though the compromise did increase the amount of representation southern states had in Congress, they still were in the minority with only 47 percent of the seats, and this number declined as the northern population rapidly expanded over the next 60 years.

111. (B) The Antifederalists illustrated the anti-monarchical sentiments held by many following the American Revolution. They feared the Constitution created in 1787 would give too much power to the federal government at the expense of the state governments and the individual. They were concerned about the possibility of the central government growing too strong with provisions for a strong executive branch, the elastic (or "necessary and proper") clause in the legislative branch, and the idea of the government keeping a standing army in times of peace. Most Antifederalists would agree to the Constitution only if provisions were made for the inclusion of a Bill of Rights.

112. (E) Many Federalists such as Alexander Hamilton disagreed with the inclusion of a Bill of Rights. They were concerned that a listing of rights could be dangerous: if the government were to protect specific rights, what would become of rights not listed? To persuade nine states to ratify the Constitution, the Federalists conceded to the Antifederalists, and a Bill of Rights was added to the document. The Ninth and Tenth Amendments addressed Hamilton's and the Federalists' concerns by giving all rights not noted in the Constitution to the states or to the individual.

113. (B) Article II of the Constitution defines the powers of the executive branch of the federal government, as well as the office of the president. Worried about the executive branch becoming too powerful, the framers developed a system of checks and balances among the executive branch, the legislative branch (outlined in Article I of the Constitution), and the judicial branch (outlined in Article III). This ensured that no single branch of the federal government could become too powerful. Article IV deals with the states, while Article V outlines the processes needed to amend the Constitution.

114. (C) John Marshall did serve as secretary of state, but under John Adams. He is best known for being the fourth chief justice of the U.S. Supreme Court as well as the longest-serving Supreme Court chief justice in U.S. history, serving for 34 years (1801 to 1835). In this period of time, he wrote many of the decisions in many of the cases that defined the powers of the federal government. Alexander Hamilton served as secretary of the treasury under President Washington; Jefferson was the secretary of state, Randolph was the first attorney general, and Henry Knox was the first secretary of war.

115. (B) Using the "necessary and proper" (elastic) clause, Congress created the federal court system beneath the Supreme Court. Many felt that this was an overreach of the federal government, but supporters believed there was a need for a system of federal courts with broader jurisdiction. The act also created the position of attorney general, who heads the U.S. Department of Justice. The attorney general is the top law enforcement official in the federal government, dealing with legal affairs at the national level.

116. (C) Alexander Hamilton's plan for paying off the war debt involved the federal government absorbing the state debts then reissuing bonds at the same value plus interest. Many southern states had already paid off their debts and felt the reissuing of bonds would benefit mostly northern investors.

117. (C) In 1796, President John Adams sent Charles Pinckney, John Marshall, and Elbridge Gerry to France to ease tensions in the wake of Jay's Treaty with Britain. Instead of being allowed to meet with the French foreign minister, they were greeted by French agents, who demanded a bribe. This created an outcry within the United States, leading to an undeclared naval war and helping the passage of the Alien and Sedition Acts.

118. (C) The Federalist-dominated Congress passed four laws in 1798 that were designed to protect the nation during an undeclared war with France following the XYZ Affair. The four parts of the acts consisted of the Naturalization Act, the Alien Act, the Alien Enemies Act, and the Sedition Act. The Sedition Act called for fines or imprisonment of people who criticized the government and the president. The Republicans under Jefferson saw this as a thinly veiled attempt to silence their party. While most of the provisions expired by 1800, the Alien Enemies Act is still in effect.

119. (A) Edmond-Charles Genêt was the ambassador to the United States during the French Revolution. He arrived in 1793. Upon arrival, he began to call on Americans to attack British vessels, as well as Spanish-held New Orleans. These actions were a violation of George Washington's Proclamation of Neutrality. Charles Talleyrand was the French foreign minister at the time of the XYZ Affair. Premier Georges Clemenceau was the leader of France during World War I. Ferdinand Maximilian was instated as the leader of Mexico by France after Mexico defaulted on debts owed to France. Maximilian Robespierre led France during the French Revolution.

120. (C) In 1794, Thomas Pinckney was sent to Spain and arranged a treaty that formalized the U.S. border with Spanish-held Florida. It also secured U.S. access to the Mississippi River and the port at New Orleans. This provision was vital to western farmers who needed the river to transport their goods to market. The Alien and Sedition Acts were widely unpopular among Republicans, many of whom made up the population in the western United States at the time. These western farmers also highly disapproved of Hamilton's economic program, which levied excise taxes on whiskey, which eventually incited the Whiskey Rebellion in 1794.

121. (C) The first national bank was part of Alexander Hamilton's economic program. The bank was given the power to issue paper money and to handle tax receipts and government money. It was intended to create fiscal order, establish credit, and address the currency problems facing the new nation. The bank provided a lucrative investment opportunity for northern bankers and merchants but offered little initial gain to the farmers in the South and West. Jeffersonian Republicans, many of them farmers, argued that the bank was unconstitutional. Nonetheless, the bank was approved in 1791.

122. (B) The Whiskey Rebellion was an uprising of western Pennsylvanian farmers in 1794. It was in response to an excise tax on whiskey, which was an important source of revenue to the farmers. Jay's Treaty (1794) with Britain set up two commissions to formalize the boundary between the United States and Canada. It also arranged for the removal of British troops still in the Northwest Territories. Pinckney's Treaty of 1795 clarified the U.S. border with Spanish-held Florida. The Louisiana Purchase added Louisiana territory to the United States, and the Adams-Onís Treaty of 1819 added Florida.

123. (D) The Kentucky and Virginia Resolutions were written by James Madison and Thomas Jefferson in response to the Alien and Sedition Acts of 1798, which they saw as a violation of the First Amendment and a violation of constitutional power. Madison also saw the creation of the first national bank as unconstitutional, as well as a way to benefit northern investors along with the issuing of bonds. James Madison, who like many Republicans supported revolutionary France in its war with Britain, objected to Jay's Treaty. He felt that it made too many concessions to the British, bringing the two nations closer.

124. (B) In response to the Alien and Sedition Acts of 1798, Virginia and Kentucky, led by Thomas Jefferson and James Madison, drafted the resolutions arguing that states could nullify laws if they were seen as unconstitutional.

125. (C) Alexander Hamilton favored a loose interpretation of the Constitution and a strong central government, mistrusting the common masses. His economic plan often benefited northern investors and favored manufacturing over agriculture. He also called for the national government to assume the war debts of the states, angering many of the southern states, which had already paid off their debts.

126. (E) The *Marbury v. Madison* case took place after Thomas Jefferson attempted to block John Adams's appointment of William Marbury to the Supreme Court. Marbury attempted to sue, but Chief Justice John Marshall denied his petition. The *Marbury v. Madison* decision established judicial review, allowing the Supreme Court to strike down laws and actions that violated the Constitution. It also further defined the powers of the executive branch.

127. (D) John Marshall was appointed chief justice of the Supreme Court as part of Adams's midnight appointments. The Federalists lost the executive branch with the election of Thomas Jefferson in 1800, along with the majority in both houses of Congress. Yet they were able to retain influence in the Supreme Court for many years, as Marshall became the longest-serving chief justice in U.S. history.

128. (B) Handsome Lake was a leader of the Alleghany Seneca during the early 19th century. He advocated the development of peaceful relations with white settlers and called for the adoption of sedentary agriculture. He was best known for his calls for Native Americans to completely reject alcohol, which he referred to as the "great engine" that introduced many "evils amongst Indians."

129. (E) The Embargo of 1807 was signed by Thomas Jefferson to avoid direct U.S. involvement in the Napoleonic Wars by ceasing trade with England and France. The act was mostly ineffective, because the British continued to smuggle goods into the United States though Canada and the Eastern Seaboard. The embargo did, however, hurt both the northern and southern economies. One area of the economy that did benefit was manufacturing. Northern manufacturing was able to expand and become less reliant on the British.

130. (C) Henry Clay of Kentucky became the speaker of the House of Representatives in 1810. He was part of a group of westerners known as the War Hawks. They were one of the first generations to be born within the United States after its independence. They supported war against Britain to stop impressments, end Native American attacks in the West, and remove the British presence in Canada, which they believed supported the attacks. They also supported western expansion. These factors would help steer the United States to war in 1812.

131. (D) The XYZ Affair was a diplomatic incident between the United States and France in which the French officials attempted to extract a bribe from U.S. ambassadors. Throughout the conflict between France and Britain during the Napoleonic Wars, the British navy would board American ships and conduct an act known as impressments, where they would force sailors to serve on their ships. The most notable instance of this act was the Chesapeake Incident, in which the British navy attacked an American naval ship in an attempt to impress American sailors. This event brought the United States to the brink of war with Britain. Furthermore, the British were accused of funding Native American uprisings in the West. This incensed the western states. In 1810, legislators from the South and West were elected, creating a powerful bloc known as the War Hawks, who called for war against Britain to stop this support and promote American expansion further into Spanish-held territories.

132. (A) The Hartford Convention took place in 1814 during the War of 1812. New Englanders were strongly against the war and threatened to secede from the Union. However, when the war ended, the Republicans gained even more influence, and the Federalists declined, eventually disappearing as a national party.

133. (B) Francis Scott Key wrote the lyrics to what is now the national anthem while aboard a British ship in Baltimore during a British attack on Fort McHenry. He was attempting to arrange for the release of an American taken prisoner by the British. The Battle of the Thames saw the death of the Shawnee leader Tecumseh. The loss of the American army at the Battle of Bladensburg resulted in the British torching Washington, D.C. Oliver Hazard Perry won a decisive victory for the United States in the Battle of Lake Erie, while Andrew Jackson won a decisive victory at the Battle of New Orleans, though the battle occurred after the Treaty of Ghent was signed, ending the war (though the treaty had yet to be ratified by the Senate).

134. (C) The War of 1812 concluded with the signing of a treaty in Ghent, which is located in modern-day Belgium, in August 1814. The treaty led to a cease in the fighting and to the restoration of territorial boundaries to where they were before the war.

135. (D) Following the War of 1812 and the signing of the Treaty of Ghent, relations between the United States and the British were mostly restored. Territorial borders were restored, and impressments by the British ceased, though mainly because the need for sailors lessened with the conclusion of the Napoleonic Wars. While the United States did not gain land in Canada, it did retain land in western Florida that it captured from Spain.

136. (B) In 1839, the African slaves forcibly overtook the ship on which they were being transported. The ship was eventually taken into custody by the United States. In 1841, John

Quincy Adams defended the right of the slaves to be returned to Africa. The Supreme Court agreed with Adams, and 35 of the slaves were returned to Africa.

137. (E) Though the idea for the Transcontinental Railroad was first debated in 1832, construction was not started until after gold was discovered in California. The project officially began when Abraham Lincoln signed the Pacific Railroad Act in 1862, and it was completed in 1869, when the Central Pacific and Union Pacific met at Promontory Point in Utah.

138. (A) The Erie Canal opened in 1825 and connected the Hudson River to Lake Erie. The canal ran for nearly 363 miles from Albany on the Hudson to Buffalo on Lake Erie. Over 50 locks were needed to overcome the nearly 600-foot change in elevation. The canal illustrated both the U.S. transportation revolution and Henry Clay's American System.

139. (C) Though the cotton gin made cotton the chief cash crop of the South during the antebellum period, Eli Whitney made little profit off the actual invention. The design of his invention was stolen before he could patent it. The invention did, however, change the economy of the South. Because the cotton gin could quickly remove seeds from the hardy upland cotton strain, the cultivation of cotton spread throughout the South and West. More land and labor were needed, so in many ways, the cotton gin helped inspire the 19th-century fervor of Manifest Destiny.

140. (A) At the conclusion of the American Revolution, the market price of tobacco plummeted. Former tobacco farmers began to sell off their slaves and switch to growing wheat and other grains. With the invention of the cotton gin, this trend was quickly reversed, and the number of slaves nearly doubled within 20 years after the gin's invention.

141. (A) The Seventh-Day Adventists are members of a religious movement that emerged in the United States during the middle of the 19th century. It was one of numerous religious revivals that defined the Second Great Awakening. This movement was characterized by widespread Christian evangelism and conversions. Other groups associated with the Second Great Awakening include the Mormons, the Anabaptists, and the Restoration Movement.

142. (D) In the summer of 1800, Gabriel Prosser attempted to lead a massive slave uprising with the goal of capturing Richmond, Virginia. The uprising was suppressed before it was able to take place, and 26 people were hanged. The rebellion, though thwarted, resulted in stricter slave laws within the state and throughout the South.

143. (A) The Twelfth Amendment to the Constitution was ratified in 1804 and was a response to irregularities during the presidential elections of 1796 and 1800. In 1796, John Adams won the presidency as a Federalist, but the Constitution provided that the candidate who received the second largest number of votes became vice president, and that person was Adams's political rival, Thomas Jefferson. Because of the development of sectionalism and parties, this arrangement became seemingly unworkable. In the presidential election of 1800, the vice presidential candidate, Aaron Burr, received more electoral votes than Thomas Jefferson, the presidential candidate. The House of Representatives was forced to decide the election, in part due to the support given by Alexander Hamilton, who openly disagreed with Jefferson's political views.

Chapter 6

144. (B) The Treaty of Ghent, signed in 1814, ended the War of 1812 between Britain and the United States. It restored borders to their prewar positions but failed to resolve major issues behind the start of the war, including impressments, freedom of the seas, and other major border concerns.

145. (D) The 1819 case of *McCulloch v. Maryland* concerned Maryland's attempt to challenge the second national bank by imposing a tax on all bank notes not chartered in Maryland. Chief Justice John Marshall wrote the Supreme Court's majority decision in the case, establishing two major principles for the American government: upholding the doctrine of implied powers for the federal government under the "necessary and proper" clause and asserting the power of the federal government over that of the state governments. Under these measures, the second national bank was deemed constitutional.

146. (B) The 1832 *Worcester v. Georgia* decision stated that Native Americans have federal protection from state governments that infringe on their tribal sovereignty. The case resulted from the state of Georgia attempting to seize Cherokee land for cotton production. While Chief Justice John Marshall wrote the majority decision deeming the action unconstitutional, the court had no power to enforce the decision. Both Georgia and the federal government under the Jackson administration ignored the ruling, and between 1837 and 1838, the U.S. Army forcibly removed around 15,000 Cherokees. The forced march became known as the Trail of Tears, as nearly one in four Cherokees died during this relocation.

147. (D) The 1824 *Gibbons v. Ogden* case settled a dispute over the state of New York charging a fee on out-of-state riverboats. The larger issue settled by the case was that commerce between states (interstate commerce) could be regulated by the federal government through Congress. *McCulloch v. Maryland* established the authority of the federal government over state governments. *Plessy v. Ferguson* (1896) allowed for the "separate but equal" doctrine. In *Dartmouth College v. Woodward* (1819), the Supreme Court held that state governments may not interfere with private contracts. *Schenck v. United States* (1919) established the notion that speech can be limited if it creates a clear and present danger.

148. (E) The 1823 Monroe Doctrine was issued by President Monroe as part of his annual address to Congress. The act closed the Western Hemisphere to further colonization by the European powers. It also was to be a deterrent to keep European nations from interfering with the political development of the newly independent Latin American states. In 1904, Theodore Roosevelt greatly expanded the scope of the doctrine by announcing that the United States could intervene in Western Hemisphere states if they became unstable. This has become known as the Roosevelt Corollary.

149. (C) The Missouri Compromise of 1820 outlawed slavery north of latitude 36°30′ north (Missouri's southern border) with the exception of Missouri. This upheld the early

Northwest Ordinance of 1787, which banned slavery in the old Northwest Territory, but allowed the expansion of slavery in the South. The struggle to maintain a balance of free and slave states helped create the tensions that led to the Civil War.

150. (A) The Missouri Compromise was signed into law in 1820. Missouri was admitted into the Union as a slave state, and Maine (formerly part of Massachusetts) entered as a free state. This preserved the balance between free and slave states. It also set the boundary of free and slave states at latitude 36°30′ north (Missouri's southern border). The Kansas-Nebraska Act of 1854 effectively repealed the act, and the *Dred Scott* decision of 1857 deemed the compromise unconstitutional, adding to the tensions that led to the Civil War.

151. (C) James Monroe signed the Missouri Compromise into law on March 6, 1820. Maine, formerly part of Massachusetts, was admitted as a free state in order to maintain a balance of free and slave states. The law was deemed unconstitutional with the *Dred Scott* decision. See the answers to questions 149 and 150 in this chapter for greater detail on the Missouri Compromise.

152. (B) The National Trades Union was established in 1834 and was the first national union of trades that combined unions from multiple states and boasted nearly 300,000 members. But because of the economic panic of 1839, the union collapsed. It is considered to be an important milestone for the creation of later unions such as the National Labor Union (established in 1866), which grew to nearly 600,000 members, and the Knights of Labor (established in 1869), which incorporated nearly a million diverse members. Both of those unions also eventually collapsed.

153. (B) In 1789, Samuel Slater moved from England to the United States, where he violated English law by constructing British textile machines. Amazingly, he committed this act of industrial espionage from memory. He created the nation's first water-powered spinning mill in Pawtucket, Rhode Island, bringing about the nation's Industrial Revolution.

154. (C) Because many immigrants entered the United States through northern ports, an abundance of unskilled labor was available to work in the emerging textile factories throughout the region. Furthermore, factories such as the Lowell textile mills in Massachusetts employed young, unmarried women from nearby farms to work in the factories. They were seen as ideal labor, since they worked for less money and were considered less likely to organize. They made up a majority of the labor in the New England region until the 1840s, when they were displaced by a large wave of Irish immigrants.

155. (A) In 1782, Evans created the first continually operating and fully automated flour mill. The mill produced flour that was finer, drier, and easier to store, helping to make flour production more efficient. Both the cotton gin and interchangeable parts were introduced by Eli Whitney. The cotton gin transformed the southern economy by making cotton its chief staple export. Interchangeable parts revolutionized production and became a keystone in America's industrialization, allowing tools and machines to be built and repaired more efficiently. Robert Fulton's *Claremont* was the first commercially successful steamboat. It revolutionized transportation in the United States and allowed farms and factories to trade their goods more efficiently.

156. (E) In 1843, Congress funded the first telegraph line connecting Washington, D.C., to Baltimore, Maryland. The system employed the telegraph designed by Samuel Morse (whom Morse code is named after). The system ran along the railway and was completed in May 1844. Later that year, the importance and popularity of the telegraph system materialized during the Whig Party's nominating convention. Nearly instantaneous updates of the convention's progress could be obtained in the nation's capital, though the convention was taking place in Baltimore. The importance of the telegraph would be illustrated again during the Civil War, when it allowed Abraham Lincoln to receive updated information of the war's progression.

157. (E) The American System was introduced following the War of 1812 and was supported by Henry Clay and others, including John Quincy Adams and John Calhoun. It called for high protective tariffs to protect the United States from Britain dumping cheaper goods in American markets and thus allowed for new enterprises and industries to emerge. It also called for investment in the nation's infrastructure, such as the construction of roads and canals to promote interstate commerce—for example, the Erie Canal and Cumberland Road. The American System also called for the continuation of the national bank to promote a single currency, establish nationally issued credit, and facilitate trade. It also advocated keeping the prices of public lands high to increase the federal government's revenue from land sales.

158. (E) When James Monroe was elected in 1816, the United States came under the control of a single party, the Republicans. The Federalist Party had met its demise as a national party in part because of the nation's success in the War of 1812 and the failure of the Hartford Convention. Because the nation was dominated by a single party, political cooperation was common, creating a unifying nationalist spirit.

159. (A) The Adams-Onís Treaty was signed in 1819 to ease tensions between the United States and Spain dealing with territorial concerns within the Western Hemisphere. In the treaty, Spain ceded Florida and formalized western claims through the Rocky Mountains to the Pacific Ocean, as well as borders along the Louisiana Territory. California was gained after the Treaty of Guadalupe Hidalgo (1848), following the Mexican-American War. The Philippines and Puerto Rico were gained with the Treaty of Paris in 1900 at the conclusion of the Spanish-American War.

160. (C) Construction of the Cumberland Road, also known as the National Road, began in 1811 in Cumberland, Maryland. Eventually it reached west through the Alleghany Mountains to Wheeling, Virginia, on the Ohio River. There were plans to extend the road to the Mississippi, but the project was never completed. The Cumberland Road was one of the first federally funded highway improvement projects within the United States. It was also part of Henry Clay's American System, which called for the improvement of internal systems of transportation to foster commerce.

161. (C) Jefferson in the Kentucky Resolution and John C. Calhoun's nullification theory both stated that the state governments could strike down federal laws that they saw as illegal. Both believed the Constitution was an agreement among sovereign states. Jefferson created the Kentucky Resolution in response to the Alien and Sedition Acts passed under John Adams's administration. Calhoun's nullification theory was in response to the increase in protective tariffs passed in 1824 and 1828, which hurt southern cotton exports.

162. (A) The Preemption Act passed in 1841 allowed squatters living on government land to purchase up to 160 acres of land at a discounted price. The offer was made to people who had lived on the land for at least a year and two months. It also mandated that new states such as Ohio and Missouri would give 10 percent of proceeds from future land sales to the federal government. This act helped fuel America's westward expansion and the belief in Manifest Destiny.

163. (E) James Albert Bonsack invented the first industrial cigarette-rolling machine in 1880, revolutionizing the tobacco industry in the second half of the 19th century. The cotton gin (1793), steel plow (1837), mechanical reaper (1831), and steamboat (1807) all helped create the agricultural boom that defined the American economy prior to the Civil War. The cotton gin, invented by Eli Whitney, quickly removed the seeds from upland cotton, and cotton became the United States' premier staple agricultural export. The steel plow invented by John Deere allowed farmers to till soil more effectively, which expanded farmable lands. The mechanical reaper invented by Cyrus McCormick lessened the labor needed to harvest grain. The steamboat expedited river travel, allowing western farmers to bring their goods to market faster.

164. (A) Alexis de Tocqueville traveled throughout the United States in the 1830s and published his most famous book, *Democracy in America*, in 1835. In this work, he describes his observations of American society. He notes the effects of a democratic society in providing equality and opportunity. De Tocqueville discusses the difference between land ownership in Europe and the United States and the impact that access to land ownership has on individual citizens of all classes. The ability to own land and move outward to find new opportunity made Americans unique as a people on the move, which allowed for greater social mobility, causing a break from European traditions of aristocracy. De Tocqueville also discusses other factors of American society, such as the deep role religion had within American society and the inequality found in the treatment of Native Americans and slaves.

165. (A) The Cult of Domesticity, also referred to as the doctrine of separate spheres, emphasized the role of women in preparing their children for adulthood by acting as a nurturing mother and dutiful wife who exemplified expectations of virtue and morality. The belief was popular in both the United States and Britain during the 19th century. Because women were seen as natural nurturers, opportunities as teachers did emerge, but overall, this view became an obstacle for women seeking rights and equality.

166. (C) In 1837, Mary Lyon established the first women's college in the United States, the Mount Holyoke Female Seminary. Oberlin College in Ohio admitted four female students in 1837, making it the first college in the nation to admit both male and female students.

167. (B) The American Colonization Society was created by Robert Finley in 1816. It had a dual mission: returning freed blacks to Africa in hopes of giving them greater access to freedom, while also alleviating slave owners' fears of an increase in free former slaves living in the United States. Thousands of freedmen and former slaves migrated to Africa through this program, many eventually establishing the independent state of Liberia.

168. (B) John C. Calhoun ran for vice president and, unlike the presidential candidates, won the needed majority to win the election. Adams, Clay, Crawford, and Jackson all failed to win the needed majority of electoral votes, as the race was divided among the four Republicans. The election was the first time since the passage of the Twelfth Amendment that an election had to be decided by the House of Representatives.

169. (B) In the election of 1824, four Republican candidates vied for the presidency, since the Federalist Party no longer had a major presence on the national political stage (with the exception of John Marshall in the Supreme Court). The Republican contenders included John Quincy Adams, Andrew Jackson, William Crawford, and Henry Clay. Andrew Jackson won the largest number of both popular and electoral votes but lacked the needed majority of electoral votes. (He won 99 electoral votes but needed 131 for the majority.) The election was then decided in the House of Representatives. In what Jackson called the corrupt bargain, John Quincy Adams was declared the winner of the election after Henry Clay put his support behind Adams.

170. (D) The Kitchen Cabinet was the nickname given to Andrew Jackson's close-knit group of unofficial advisers. During Jackson's first term, he had a political split with his vice president, John C. Calhoun, and fired five of his eight cabinet members. His Kitchen Cabinet included Martin Van Buren and two newspaper publishers, Amos Kendall and Francis Blair. The term has been used numerous times since Jackson to describe close, trusted advisers to the president, as in the Kennedy and Reagan administrations.

171. (D) The election of 1828 saw a rematch between Andrew Jackson and sitting president John Quincy Adams. In many ways, the election also introduced a more modern style of campaigning, employing slogans, songs, and massive rallies. Jackson played off his 1812 "Old Hickory" slogan and made hickory sticks a gimmick in his campaign. Jackson easily won the election, ushering in a period dominated by Jacksonian Republicans.

172. (B) Though Andrew Jackson had gained a reputation as an "Indian fighter" during his early career, as president he instead opted to remove Native Americans to reservations in the West. In 1830, Congress passed and Jackson signed the Indian Removal Act. This legislation forcibly relocated thousands of eastern tribes to lands in the West such as the area that is now Oklahoma. Many native people perished in the forced removal, including one in four Cherokees on what became known as the Trail of Tears.

173. (C) Andrew Jackson was nicknamed King Andy because of the way he increased the power and the influence of the presidency and executive branch. This was especially illustrated by his ending of the second national bank. At the same time, he served as a symbol of the common man, increasing the individual's access to the political process. Furthermore, his campaign is seen to have helped usher in a new era of elections with massive rallies and usage of the media.

174. (C) The Tariff of Abominations was a protectionist tariff passed during the Jackson administration to protect northern manufacturers from cheaper imports from other countries, most notably Britain. The South strongly opposed the series of protective tariffs that had been passed in the years following the War of 1812. John Calhoun, Jackson's vice president, strongly opposed this third addition to the tariff, calling it the Tariff of Abominations because it hurt the South's ability to sell cotton, its chief cash crop, to Britain. The tariff also made it harder to import cheap manufactured goods from Britain. Calhoun furthermore called upon his home state of South Carolina to nullify the act, in what became known as the nullification theory. See the answer for question 161 in this chapter for more information on the nullification theory.

175. (C) Andrew Jackson was the son of poor Scottish-Irish immigrants in the backwoods of the Carolinas. He was the first president since George Washington to lack a college education. Nevertheless, he was not a "common man" as often portrayed. Like many earlier presidents, he was a wealthy land and slave owner who had an extremely lucrative career in politics and law.

176. (B) After two terms, Andrew Jackson chose not to run for a third term. Instead, he chose his vice president, Martin Van Buren, to be his successor. In the election of 1836, Van Buren defeated the three Whig Party candidates: William Henry Harrison, Daniel Webster, and Hugh White.

177. (A) One of the driving issues of the election of 1832 was the national bank. Jackson strongly opposed its renewal, seeing it as an agent of the aristocracy, benefiting northern bankers and merchants and not southerners or common people. He also feared that the bank could use its power to corrupt democratic institutions by bribing officials and buying elections with its economic power.

178. (B) The Whig Party was created by people who feared the growth of the executive branch during Andrew Jackson's administration. They also were concerned about the ending of the national bank, which led to an economic panic from 1833 to 1834. States' rights groups also supported the Whig Party, especially after the Force Bill of 1833, which further asserted the power of the federal government.

179. (E) In 1836, Jackson allowed the second national bank to expire. Before the expiration of the national bank, Jackson moved the bank's funds to state banks often referred to as pet banks. Many of these banks were located in New York City, causing the financial capital of the United States to move there from Philadelphia. The Whig Party was created in reaction to the economic panic caused by the ending of the bank, as well as the furthering of executive power in destroying the bank.

180. (B) The Specie Circular was an executive order issued by Andrew Jackson and carried out by his successor, Martin Van Buren. It required that all future lands be purchased using silver and gold. This was done to stop land speculators from purchasing large tracts of land using bank notes that often had little real value, caused in part by the creation of pet banks—small state banks that received the funds of the former national bank.

181. (D) The Whig Party formed in 1834 in response to what party members saw as an overextension of presidential authority by Andrew Jackson. The ending of the national bank, as well as infringements upon states' rights, earned Jackson the nickname King Andy. Many supporters of the Whig Party strongly supported term limits to further check the power of the executive branch.

Chapter 7

182. (E) As American settlers began to push west of the Appalachian Mountains, native people grew concerned about the encroachment into places such as Kentucky, which had been considered a kind of "hunting reserve" and buffer zone between Native Americans and white settlers. Two Shawnee Indian leaders, Tecumseh and his brother Tenskwatawa (also referred to as the Prophet), felt that action needed to be taken to stop U.S. encroachment. They advocated the rejection of western society and argued that land treaties such as the Treaty of Fort Wayne were invalid. The also created a coalition to resist further encroachment onto their land.

183. (E) William Lloyd Garrison was a prominent leader of the abolitionist movement during the first half of the 19th century. Through his publication, the *Liberator*, and as a founding member of the American Anti-Slavery Society, he called for the immediate emancipation of slaves. He also later went on to be a leader in the women's suffrage movement.

184. (A) During the first part of the 19th century, women began to play a greater role within their households. This change is illustrated by trends such as the smaller size of American families and the greater primary role women played in child rearing. This new role is often credited with helping women establish greater independence while they were being limited by the societal expectations within the Cult of Domesticity. This domestic feminism was used in the late 19th and early 20th centuries by anti-suffragist movements to attempt to keep women from obtaining the right to vote.

185. (D) The number of births among most white females during the 19th century decreased by as much as half from the Revolutionary War era. While conception and birth control were still considered taboo topics of conversation, women began to take greater control of regulating family size. This new assertion of women within the household illustrated the notion of domestic feminism.

186. (A) In 1848, Lucretia Mott and Elizabeth Cady Stanton organized the first convention dealing with women's rights at Seneca Falls, New York. At this convention, they issued the Declaration of Sentiments, outlining the goals and demands they felt were needed for women to achieve equality, as well as the injustices faced by women. The convention lasted for two days and hosted lectures on law and discussions on women's roles in society.

187. (E) The temperance movement emerged in the 19th and early 20th centuries in order to reduce and in many cases outlaw the consumption of alcohol. Temperance societies appeared in the United States as early as the 1780s, but the temperance movement began to flourish during the early 1800s, and many leaders linked temperance to other prominent 19th-century movements such as women's rights and the abolitionist movement. The temperance societies would eventually inspire the Eighteenth Amendment, outlawing the sale of alcohol in 1918.

188. (B) During the 1840s, Dorothea Dix lobbied the Massachusetts state government to establish institutions for the mentally ill. Before then, people deemed mentally ill were often placed in prisons and offered little by way of treatment. Dix also lobbied her state for general prison reform. She eventually lobbied the federal government to reform the treatment of the mentally ill. Her efforts led the government to create land grants to establish more hospitals and provide greater funding. Though the legislation was vetoed by President Franklin Pierce, Dix blazed the trail for future reformers in this area.

189. (B) Horace Mann was a leader in reforming public schools in Massachusetts, and his reforms spread throughout the nation, helping establish the foundation for modern education. He supported the use of taxes to provide public education for all young people and felt education should prepare students to be responsible members of American society. By the 1850s, most northern states provided free public elementary schools, and the number of free high schools increased, but at a much slower rate. John Dewey also was a noted reformer in public education, helping to bring about a modern approach to schools in the 20th century.

190. (B) Educational reformers of the 1800s, such as Horace Mann, felt that schools should move beyond providing simply training in reading, writing, and math. They believed schools should also teach children to be good citizens with self-discipline. Reformers supported taxation to support schools, as well as compulsory attendance until a certain age. Also, many reformers pushed to remove religion from the classrooms. Opposition to this led to an increase in the number of religiously based private schools, especially in the northeastern United States.

191. (D) During the first half of the 19th century, employment opportunities for women were extremely limited. While many young women found employment in textile mills, most worked only until they were married and took on the role of homemakers, as expressed by the Cult of Domesticity. Other jobs, such as teaching, nursing, and domestic services, were available because they fit into the pattern of what was believed to be the natural sphere of women: nurturers and caregivers with the ability to raise children. Women did not truly begin to enter the field of secretarial work until the invention of the typewriter in the 1880s, and even then, their access was limited. It was not until the First World War that large numbers of females found employment in this area. However, by the 1930s, fewer men entered the field, and women grew to be a majority.

192. (B) Horace Mann, considered one of the founders of modern public education reform, advocated that schools accept students from diverse backgrounds. See questions 189 and 190 in this chapter for more information on Horace Mann.

193. (D) Partly in response to the aftereffects of industrialism and the new era of economic capitalism, many reformers of the early 1800s began to question the rapid changes taking place in society. Over the first part of the 1800s, nearly a hundred utopian communities emerged and battled these new trends of societal evils in an effort to create perfect communities. Examples of these communities included the Shakers in Oneida, New York, and New Harmony in Indiana, which was founded by the industrialist Robert Owen.

194. (A) In 1825, the Scottish industrialist Robert Owen established New Harmony in Indiana. It was to be a utopian community of hardworking, well-educated individuals who would work together for the common good. See the answers for questions 193 and 195 in this chapter for more information on utopian communities.

195. (B) John Humphrey Noyes established the Oneida Community in New York in 1848. Noyes rejected the traditional rigid religious beliefs held by the Puritans. His beliefs rejected the notion of private property and were also against monogamous marriages. This belief led to persecution from the surrounding communities, so the group relocated itself to Oneida. The Icarians were a French utopian movement that established itself throughout the frontier of the United States, including Texas. The Spring Farm Colony was a utopian community established in 1846 in Wisconsin. The Brook Farm Community was a utopian community that practiced communal living and was founded in Massachusetts during the 1840s. See the answer for question 194 for information on New Harmony.

196. (A) Harriet Tubman, born into slavery in Maryland, escaped to freedom in the North in 1849. She returned to the South more than 13 times to lead groups of other slaves to freedom on what has become known as the Underground Railroad. Later, Harriet Tubman would assist the abolitionist John Brown in recruiting members for his intended uprising, and she would serve as a Union spy during the Civil War.

197. (D) As the abolitionist movement grew in the United States, divisions began to appear. One major source of contention was the role that women should be allowed to serve. William Lloyd Garrison allowed women to participate actively in his organization, the American Anti-Slavery Society. This alienated some members, including Arthur and Lewis Tappan, who left the organization and formed their own society, the Liberty Party, in 1840. They felt that female participation went against the appropriate role of women at the time.

198. (C) Many workers in the North feared that if slavery were abolished, they would have to compete with African-American workers for factory jobs. It was assumed that the former slaves would be willing to work for lower wages. Many Northern states that outlawed slavery continued to pass laws limiting African-American rights. In some cases, some states would not allow freedmen to take up residency within the state.

199. (C) The transcendentalist movement emerged as a rejection of what was perceived as the intellectualist doctrine of the institutions of higher learning at the time. Participants in the movement sought understanding beyond empiricism and established ideas, instead trying to rise to a greater level of emotional understanding at a personal and instinctual awareness. Leaders of this movement included Ralph Waldo Emerson and Henry David Thoreau. *Walden*, written by Henry David Thoreau in 1854, serves as a famous example of both transcendentalist and early-American literature.

200. (B) Nathaniel Hawthorne was a critic of the transcendentalist movement, parodying it in his 1852 work *The Blithedale Romance*. Edgar Allan Poe was also known for his criticism and satire of transcendentalism. Ralph Waldo Emerson and Frederick Henry Hedge founded the movement in Massachusetts with the creation of the Transcendental Club in 1836. Thoreau's *Walden* is considered by many to be a hallmark of literature within the movement, as is Fuller's *Woman in the Nineteenth Century*, which also was an early product of the 19th-century feminist movement.

201. (A) While the transcendentalist movement rejected many notions of the prominent religious beliefs of the early 19th century, Emerson believed strongly in creating an individual connection to spirituality that transcended established doctrine. His religious views illustrated a connection to many Eastern religions but also strongly supported the notion of divinity within one's life.

Chapter 8

202. (D) As the population of slaves in the South increased, especially after the invention of the cotton gin in 1793, slave owners felt that the mixing of free and enslaved blacks could create instability within the region, increasing the likelihood of revolts. To avoid uprisings, state legislatures enacted Black Codes, such as those instituted after Gabriel Prosser's attempted revolt in 1800, Denmark Vesey's rebellion in 1820, and Nat Turner's rebellion in 1831. Many of these codes required free blacks to have special work licenses to reside in the state, while others banned free blacks from working in certain fields. Many Northern states had similar laws to prevent free blacks from settling within their borders as well.

203. (B) In the wake of the Mexican-American War, the United States gained vast territories in the West. This raised concerns over the expansion of slavery. To find a middle ground between those who supported slavery and those who were opposed, Congress opted to leave the decision to the individual territory as each applied for statehood. This, however, often led to bitter struggles within the territories, as illustrated in Kansas. As Kansas applied for statehood, violence between abolitionists and supporters of slavery broke out, leading to an event described as Bleeding Kansas.

204. (C) The early 19th century was noted for its wide variety of social reform movements, but at the same time, it was also marked by strong religious revival movements such as the Second Great Awakening. Because of this, religion played a greater role in the individual's life while it also served as the basis of many of the reform movements.

205. (A) With the waves of migrants coming to the United States during the 1800s, most migrants established themselves in areas where they had family connections, depending on relatives for support until they could establish themselves. Many German and Scandinavian immigrants established farming communities in the Midwest, while poorer Irish immigrants created communities within the cities of the Northeast. In reaction to the large waves of immigrants coming into the United States, nativist societies began to emerge as early as the 1830s and held their first national conventions in 1845.

206. (E) During the 1820s through the 1850s, Ireland experienced a massive crop failure. To escape the harsh economic conditions and poverty, many Irish fled their native land for hopes of prosperity in the New World. This led to the rise of nativism, the belief that native-born individuals should be favored over immigrants, within the United States. Also, in response to the Irish, many anti-Catholic leagues formed over fears that the Irish would be more loyal to the pope than to their new country.

207. (D) During the 1850s, many of the nativist groups and anti-Catholic organizations banded together to protect the United States from the perceived threat of Catholics migrating into the country. Originally forming in New York in 1843, the American Republican Party, later called the Know-Nothing Party, emerged. The name Know-Nothing was derived from the various groups' secrecy: when asked about their organization, they would deny knowledge. In 1855, the party officially changed its name to the American Party. The group's anti-Irish and anti-German platform yielded notable support during the 1840s and 1850s, influencing elections as a third party. The party dissolved by 1856, however, after it became divided over the issue of slavery.

208. (B) The Hudson River School emerged in the mid-19th century and began with landscape painters such as Thomas Cole and Fredric Church, who reflected themes of Romanticism. Many of the paintings depicted pastoral settings of the Hudson River Valley as it was being rapidly developed. They often presented ideal notions of the harmony between humans and their natural surroundings, reflecting the works of transcendentalist authors such as Emerson and Thoreau. The movement illustrated a break with a reliance on the need for European training in artistic development.

209. (D) *Leaves of Grass* was written by Walt Whitman and first published in 1855, though he continually revised it throughout his life. It is considered to be one of the greatest influences on American poetry, as well as a breakthrough in the free-verse style of poetry. It was extremely controversial at the time of its publication because of its sexual and homoerotic imagery. Samuel Clemens, better known as Mark Twain, was one of America's most famous authors and satirists in the late 19th century, producing works such as *Tom Sawyer* and *Huckleberry Finn*. Henry David Thoreau helped define the transcendentalist movement with his works, which included *Walden*. Herman Melville is often classified defining the literary genre of dark Romanticism, with which Edgar Allan Poe also is often associated. Emily Dickinson was an influential American female poet who furthered the notions of feminist literature in the 19th century.

210. (D) James Fennimore Cooper was one of the first American authors to use the American frontier as a distinct setting in literature. His works, which included *Last of the Mohicans*, illustrate the encroachment of civilization upon the American frontier and, with it, the conflicts that inevitably result between nature and progress. In many ways, Cooper's works illustrate a first truly American literary movement, breaking away from Europe, celebrating the American pioneer spirit.

211. (A) Edgar Allan Poe's work often depicts a dark and pessimistic view of human nature and is often linked to the dark Romanticism. His works rejected the themes found in the transcendentalist movement. He is remembered for such works as *The Tell-Tale Heart*, *The Raven*, and also the first true detective novel, *The Murders in the Rue Morgue*.

212. (B) In 1853, under orders from Millard Fillmore, Commodore Matthew Perry arrived in Japan with a fleet of ships. He demanded that he be allowed to deliver to the emperor a letter calling on Japan to open trade. Realizing that it could not defend itself against Perry's modern navy, Japan agreed. A year later, Perry returned with an even larger fleet, and the Japanese agreed to U.S. trade terms in the Convention of Kanagawa on March 31, 1854.

213. (D) John L. O'Sullivan is generally credited with being the first to use the expression *Manifest Destiny* in print. In 1839, he alluded to the ideal in a short essay, but he used the exact phrase in his famous essay "Annexation" in 1845. The term *Manifest Destiny* was used by the loyal Democratic journalist to justify the annexation of Texas and Oregon Territory.

214. (A) President Polk cited the Monroe Doctrine, initially delivered by James Monroe as part of his seventh State of the Union Address in 1823, in terms of the prevailing spirit of Manifest Destiny. He used it to justify the annexation of both Texas and Oregon Country, to keep other European powers, especially Britain, from laying claims to further lands in

North America. Furthermore, Polk extended the doctrine to justify American intervention in the Western Hemisphere, not only against an existing threat, but also against actions that could be perceived as threats.

215. (D) Throughout the 1840s and 1850s, the Democrats used "Manifest Destiny." Democratic president James K. Polk, Democratic journalist John L. O'Sullivan, and many others used the concept to justify America's westward expansion, tapping into the nationalistic and religious sentiments of the period. Whigs and manufacturers often resisted the notion of westward expansion, instead wanting the nation's focus to be on economic development. They also saw western expansion as eroding the power and influence of northeastern states. Abolitionists also resisted the concept, fearing that it would increase the number of slave states within the Union. Native Americans feared the expansion would further threaten their traditional land claims.

216. (C) "Manifest Destiny" expressed the belief that the United States had a mission to expand, spreading its form of democracy and freedom. Inspired in part by the Second Great Awakening, America was once again viewed as a "city on the hill," or a beacon of democracy that had the divine duty of expanding its culture, values, government, and religion across the North American continent. President Polk tied the belief to the Monroe Doctrine, which states that any attempt made by a European power to establish itself in North America would be seen as a threat to U.S. security. The notion of Manifest Destiny was rejected by the Whig Party of the 1830s and 1840s. The Whigs felt that the focus of the United States should continue to be on the ideals of the American system, which stressed development of the economy and internal improvements in existing regions.

217. (C) During the late 1820s and the 1830s, Joseph Smith created the foundations of the modern Church of Jesus Christ of Latter Day Saints in western New York. According to Smith, he had received a new book of the Bible, which became the foundation of the new Mormon church. He began to develop a large following, but his organization faced increasing persecution for many of its beliefs and practices. The group was forcibly chased from Ohio and Missouri, and eventually Smith was killed by an angry mob in Illinois. The subsequent leader, Brigham Young, led the group to Utah, where they established themselves in what is now Salt Lake City and expanded throughout Utah. The Mormons still continually faced challenges from citizens as well as the U.S. government. President James Buchanan even sent the U.S. Army into Utah against the Mormon settlers in 1857 to quell what he saw as political dissonance. The expedition was plagued by misfortune, however, and many historians feel this hurt Buchanan's ability to address much of the violence that preceded the Civil War.

218. (A) The Oregon Trail is probably one of the most famous western trails, because thousands of Americans traveled in the period before the Civil War to reach the area that is now Washington, Oregon, and Idaho. The trail ran from Saint Louis, Missouri, along the Platte River to the fertile Willamette Valley of the Pacific Northwest. It is estimated that roughly 400,000 settlers used the trail and the other trails that branched off. The Mormon Trail led to Utah, the Santa Fe into Mexico, and the California Trail to San Francisco. The many farmers who reached the Oregon Territory were important because they altered the balance of population to an American majority. This helped lay the case for ending the joint American-British occupation of the region in the 1840s.

219. (B) The slogan "Fifty-Four Forty or Fight!" originated in the 1840s concerning the border dispute between the United States and Britain. The two countries had occupied the territory jointly until 1828. At that time, Britain had offered the United States land south of the 49th Parallel, but Democrats believed the U.S. land claim extended to the southern tip of the Russian claim in America, which is modern-day Alaska. The issue was eventually resolved under President James K. Polk with the 1846 Oregon Treaty, in which the formal boundary was set at the British-proposed 49th Parallel. The final border dispute, dealing with control of San Juan Island, was not settled until 1872.

220. (D) The issue of Texas annexation divided the country throughout the 1830s and 1840s. The South quickly supported its annexation for nationalistic reasons (Texas's independence was won by the Americans), as well as the South's desire to incorporate new lands where slavery had already been established. The issue was finalized in 1845, when Texas was admitted into the Union as the 28th state. The battle between pro- and anti-slavery groups was exacerbated by the addition of new slave states. Congress attempted to rectify the issue later with the 1850 compromise introduced by Henry Clay.

221. (C) Pancho Villa led a raid on the New Mexico border town in 1916, which caused General John Pershing to lead an expedition into Mexico in a failed attempt to capture him. This occurred over half a century after Texas gained its independence in 1836. In 1829, Mexico outlawed the practice of slavery. By this time, American planters owned roughly 1,500 slaves on their cotton and sugar plantations. Worried about the growth in population of English-speaking, non-Catholic settlers in the region, as well as the inability to fully enforce Mexican law, the government, led by Santa Anna, closed the borders to new immigrants and imposed taxes on American imports. Furthermore, the government increased the number of troops within the region after abolishing regional government. Stephen Austin attempted to protest these developments and advocated for Texas becoming a separate state. His demands were denied, and he was imprisoned for treason. This led to large protests, fueling the calls for independence.

222. (E) The Battle of the Alamo was a siege of a San Antonio chapel and fort held by Americans seeking independence from Mexico. Six thousand Mexican soldiers led by Antonio Lopez Santa Anna held the American position under siege from February 23 to March 6, 1836. In spite of suffering heavy casualties, the Mexican army eventually took the position, slaughtering all 187 American soldiers within the Alamo. This act of aggression and harsh tactics angered the Americans. The call "Remember the Alamo" inspired more Americans to join up and participate in the fight for Texas independence. Six months after the siege, the Texans soundly defeated the Mexicans at the San Jacinto River, securing Texas's separation from Mexico.

223. (B) The war of Texas's independence ended with the Battle of San Jacinto, on April 21, 1836. Sam Houston led an army of Texans to victory over the forces of Santa Anna. The Mexican forces were soundly defeated in a battle that lasted only 18 minutes. Santa Anna was captured shortly after the battle and forced to sign the Treaties of Velasco (see question 224). The 1848 Treaty of Guadalupe Hidalgo concluded the Mexican-American War (see question 230). The Texans' army was defeated at both the Alamo and Goliad. However, the two battles and the brutal actions committed by the Mexican army following each helped the Texans gain dramatic support for the cause and became a rallying cry for the Texan army.

224. (A) After the Battle of San Jacinto, President Santa Anna was forced to sign the Treaties of Velasco, recognizing the independence of Mexico and allowing Santa Anna and his army to go free. The treaty called for the end of hostilities between Mexico and Texas, as well as the removal of all Mexican troops in Texas. It also called for the release of prisoners on both sides. The treaty, while signed by Santa Anna, was never ratified by the Mexican government. The major fighting ended with the treaty, but Mexico did not fully recognize Texas independence until the end of the Mexican-American War and the signing of the Treaty of Guadalupe Hidalgo in 1848.

225. (B) While the debate over the annexation of Texas raged on in the U.S. Congress, Britain began to take an interest in the region. Though Britain opposed slavery, the British saw annexing Texas as an opportunity to curb U.S. expansion in North America as well as to reduce American authority. Furthermore, they saw it as an economic opportunity, where they could reduce their dependence on U.S. cotton while creating an outlet for manufactured goods without having to deal with high U.S. tariffs. When Britain's plans were discovered, many Americans became outraged. James K. Polk cited this action as a clear violation of the Monroe Doctrine. Furthermore, it ultimately helped President Tyler push through the annexation of Texas on December 29, 1845.

226. (D) Though Texas desired to ultimately be annexed by the United States, sectionalism greatly delayed the process. Whigs felt the addition of a new Southern state would further erode their political power. Abolitionists feared that annexing Texas would increase the influence of pro-slavery states. Furthermore, the United States had created a treaty with Mexico, and the annexation of the former Mexican Territory would create grounds for war between the two nations. Ultimately, when British plans to turn Texas into a colony were discovered, Americans became outraged. This eventually helped end the stalemate and allow for congressional approval of the annexation of Texas in December 1845.

227. (B) Because tensions between Mexico and America were high over the annexation of Texas by the United States in 1845, as well as a border dispute between the two nations, President James K. Polk ordered General Zachary Taylor to the Rio Grande. This eventually sparked the Mexican-American War in 1846. The war was strongly supported by southern and western states, as well as most Democrats, including John C. Calhoun. Whigs, including Daniel Webster, strongly opposed the war. Many saw the declaration of war as a misuse of executive power. Many also felt that the war was immoral, since it would further extend the practice of slavery. Henry David Thoreau even expressed his opposition by not paying his taxes. He was arrested for this, leading him to write his famous essay "The Duty of Civil Disobedience." Despite the objections, militarily the United States was extremely successful. Stephen Kearny took control of Mexico, and Taylor successfully captured lands as far south as Mexico City.

228. (C) The Mormon church was founded by Joseph Smith in 1830 in western New York. The Mormon leader, Brigham Young, led church followers to the frontier in Utah, where they established themselves in 1847. Because the Mormon practices and beliefs were seen by some as un-American, many felt that the Utah Mormons might attempt to break away from the United States; President Buchanan ordered a military expedition into the region in 1857. See the answer to question 217 for more information on Smith and the Church of Jesus Christ of Latter Day Saints.

229. (D) During the presidential election of 1844, the Whig Party nominated the well-known Henry Clay as their candidate. The Democrats, however, chose a "dark horse" (relatively unknown candidate) named James K. Polk from Tennessee. Polk made the issue of expansion a focal point of his platform, calling for the annexation of Texas as well as all of the Oregon Territory. While Polk showed certainty on these issues, Clay seemed to waver. In the end, however, the election was decided by the emergence of a spoiler third party called the Liberty Party. This small abolitionist group split Clay's support, allowing Polk to win the election.

230. (A) After a successful campaign in Mexico, in which American forces were led by Zachary Taylor and Winfield Scott, most of the larger Mexican cities came under American control. Following the Battle of Chapultepec in September 1847, Winfield Scott occupied the Mexican capital of Mexico City. At this point, Mexico was no longer able to defend itself further and was forced to negotiate peace with the United States with the Treaty of Guadalupe Hidalgo on February 2, 1848. In addition to ending the conflict, the treaty established the U.S.-Mexican border of the Rio Grande, forcing Mexico to cede the land now occupied by the present-day states of California, Nevada, Utah, and parts of Colorado, Arizona, and New Mexico. The treaty also gave the United States undisputed control of Texas, which Mexico refused to officially recognize as independent.

231. (E) In response to the territorial gains made as a result of the Mexican-American War, concerns over the balance between free and slave states once again stirred within the United States. In 1846 and again in 1847, Pennsylvania Democratic Congressman David Wilmot introduced the Wilmot Proviso in an attempt to ban the practice of slavery in all territories acquired after the Mexican-American War. The measure was ultimately rejected, and concerns over the expansion of slavery into these new territories continued until the passage of the Compromise of 1850.

232. (C) President James K. Polk's ordering of Zachary Taylor to the Rio Grande led to the start of the Mexican-American War in 1845. Taylor, nicknamed "Old Rough and Ready" by his troops, led American forces into northern Mexico. He became a national hero after he soundly defeated the Mexican forces under the command of Santa Anna at the Battle of Buena Vista. This helped him secure the presidency in 1848, becoming the first president never to have held any previous elected office.

233. (A) The Gadsden Purchase by President Franklin Pierce on June 24, 1853, was the last major territorial purchase of the contiguous continental United States. The land was purchased from Mexico and now makes up the southern borders of New Mexico and Arizona. One of the main reasons for the purchase, besides settling border disputes remaining from the Mexican-American War, was for a planned route of a transcontinental railroad. The purchase sparked further debates over the issue of slavery, and the plans for the railroad were suspended with the outbreak of the Civil War.

234. (B) Historian Frederick Jackson Turner released his Frontier Thesis in 1893, as the western frontier was deemed closed after the completion of the Transcontinental Railroad and the increase of population in the western states. He argued the West and expansionism during the 19th century positively affected American government and society. He noted that the frontier made Americans different from Europeans by helping them to develop a truly unique culture.

235. (A) Stephen Kearny, nicknamed "the Long Marcher," led his troops from Fort Leavenworth in Kansas to Santa Fe, New Mexico. After capturing Santa Fe, he led his troops to southern California, where he met up with a naval expedition and captured California as well. The Mexican-American War began when Zachary Taylor led American forces to the Mexican border under the orders of President Polk. Winfield Scott led the U.S. Army into Mexico, capturing Mexico City.

Chapter 9

236. (C) The 1823 Monroe Doctrine was issued as part of James Monroe's seventh State of the Union Address. John Quincy Adams, Monroe's secretary of state, was one of the main authors. The doctrine was partly a response to the creation of the Holy Alliance in Europe, which consisted of Spain, France, and Russia. At the conclusion of the Napoleonic Wars, Spain and France wished to reclaim lost lands in the Western Hemisphere, and Russia sought to increase its holdings in the Pacific Northwest extending into Oregon Country. Prior to this, the United States had already recognized the independence of many of the former colonies. Hoping to retain the United States' position as the leading power within the Western Hemisphere, Monroe issued the doctrine as a symbolic closing of the Americas to future European colonization or control. The Monroe Doctrine would be cited by James K. Polk as a reason to annex Texas over 20 years later, after it was discovered Britain might be interested in incorporating the territory. This widened the Monroe Doctrine to allow preemptive measures against perceived threats of European involvement in the Western Hemisphere.

237. (D) Starting in the early 1800s, immigrants to the United States began leaving Europe in hopes of better opportunity and wages. Furthermore, crop failures throughout Europe, especially in Ireland, and politically repressive governments increased the number of people coming into the United States. The Industrial Revolution offered many factory jobs. Since the new arrivals to the country were often willing to work for lower wages, tensions began to grow with established workers. Nativist groups began to form and eventually formed a national party called the Know-Nothings.

238. (C) While it is a commonly held myth that baseball was invented by Abner Doubleday in New York, the sport actually can be traced back to an earlier English sport called rounders. The sport had been played in America since colonial times but evolved over time into new incarnations such as town ball. Alexander Cartwright further adjusted the rules to create the basis for what is now the modern game. Sports such as baseball became increasingly popular during the antebellum period as more people had access to leisure time. The popularity of sporting events was also increased by innovations such as the telegraph, which allowed newspapers to report on events from around the nation more quickly.

239. (A) Internal improvements following the War of 1812 helped promote commerce among the various regions of the United States. The National or Cumberland Road connected the Ohio River Valley to the Eastern Seaboard. Canals and riverboats allowed western goods to reach eastern markets more efficiently. Furthermore, agricultural goods could make it to cities, allowing urban areas to keep up with their growing size, while the northern cities could sell their manufactured goods to the West and South. Also, more raw materials could be supplied to northern factories.

240. (A) Transcendentalism emerged during the early 19th century as an intellectual, philosophical, and literary movement (see chapter 7 question 199). Pragmatism was an intellectual movement that focused on practical approaches to understanding of knowledge. It was introduced by C. S. Peirce and William James during the late 19th century. The social gospel, an intellectual movement of the late 19th and early 20th centuries, applied Christian ideals to address social problems of the time period. "The Gospel of Wealth" was an essay written by Andrew Carnegie in 1889 describing the role of philanthropy within the new American upper class. Social Darwinism was a theory developed by philosophers such as Herbert Spencer in the late 19th century. It applied Darwinian theories to human society.

241. (D) When Brigham Young and his followers first arrived in the area that is now Salt Lake City, it was a desolate region surrounded by mountains. The Great Salt Lake was useless as a water supply for drinking or irrigation. The Mormons had to build massive systems of irrigation from the surrounding mountains to be able to establish agriculture in the region. This made the area unlikely to attract future settlers, which was positive, since the Mormons had been chased from numerous locations in the East and the church's founder had been killed by an angry mob when the church attempted to establish itself in Illinois.

242. (B) The personal-liberty laws were established by several Northern states to help free blacks in the face of the Fugitive Slave Act, which was passed as part of the Compromise of 1850. The laws limited use of prisons to hold accused fugitives, forcing bounty hunters to provide evidence that their captives were in fact fugitives, as well as providing for the rights of the accused. This was done so the Northern states would not have to invoke the notion of nullification.

243. (C) The Compromise of 1850 was introduced by Henry Clay after tensions arose with the acquisition of new territories from Mexico. Under the Compromise of 1850, Texas gave up its claims to the land that is now New Mexico. The state was compensated with $10 million, which it could use to pay off debts it still owed from its separation from Mexico. Furthermore, the territories of New Mexico, Nevada, Arizona, and Utah would decide on slavery through popular sovereignty. The compromise also outlawed the slave trade in the District of Colombia, and California was admitted into the Union as a free state. The Fugitive Slave Act was also enacted as part of the legislation forcing citizens to assist in the return of runaway slaves seeking freedom in the North.

244. (C) In 1846, a slave named Dred Scott attempted to sue his owner for freedom. He argued that his master took him to Wisconsin Territory, where slavery was illegal; Scott maintained that if he lived in a free state, he should gain the status of a free man. The court had to consider two key points: whether Scott was a citizen in the first place and whether residence in a free territory would gain Scott his freedom. The decision, written by Chief Justice Roger Taney, stated that blacks were not considered citizens and therefore did not have legal protection, including the right to sue. The ruling also stated that being in a free territory did not make a slave free, because it would violate the owner's right to property, causing the Missouri Compromise to be deemed unconstitutional.

245. (D) The *Dred Scott* decision, which was handed down in 1857 by Chief Justice Roger Taney, stated that African-Americans were not considered citizens under the Constitution and therefore did not have legal protection. See the asnwer to question 244 for more information on this case.

246. (D) In 1857, the United States was hit with a massive economic crash that furthered the divisions within the United States. The influx of gold from the California Gold Rush, which began in 1849, led to currency inflation, and grain production was overextended in response to demand caused by the Crimean War. Because of this, the crash hit the North and West hardest. The South was relatively untouched by the financial crash, because the price of cotton continued to be high in overseas markets. The South used this situation to justify its slave-based economy over the wage-based economy of the North.

247. (C) Harriet Beecher Stowe authored *Uncle Tom's Cabin* as a magazine series and then published it as a novel in 1852. Stowe, an ardent abolitionist, was the sister of the well-known minister Henry Ward Beecher. Stowe was, in many ways, inspired to write the novel after a fellow abolitionist, Elijah Lovejoy, was murdered by a pro-slavery mob. Emily Dickinson was a famous American poet of the late 19th century. Henry David Thoreau was an influential author and part of the transcendentalist movement of the early to mid-19th century.

248. (D) *Uncle Tom's Cabin* by Harriet Beecher Stowe describes the dehumanizing nature of slavery. The work reflected Stowe's own views of Christianity as well as the role of Christianity within the abolitionist movement. The work furthermore challenged the contemporary views of women's role in society held within the Cult of Domesticity. The novel did not, however, offer a path to the end of slavery, but only described the horrors of the institution.

249. (C) *Uncle Tom's Cabin*, written by Harriet Beecher Stowe, was well received in the Northern states, selling an estimated three hundred thousand copies in its first year published. In the South, however, it did not receive such a warm welcome. Many declared it slanderous. The author and bookstores that attempted to sell the novel received numerous threats. Authors of the South began to produce works to counter Stowe's attacks. These works included *The Sword and the Distaff* by the famous southern novelist William Gilmore Simms and Mary Henderson Eastman's *Aunt Phillis's Cabin*. John Brown led his famous uprising at Harpers Ferry almost seven years later, and the Know-Nothing Party represented the views of the nativist groups, taking a platform on restricting the influx of immigrants.

250. (B) The *Dred Scott* decision of 1857 declared that blacks were not guaranteed citizenship under the Constitution and therefore did not have political or legal rights. It also stipulated that an African-American's residence in a state or territory where slavery was illegal did not in any way grant emancipation. Combined, these principles further guaranteed the protection of slave owners' property rights while stripping even freedmen of any legal protection. This made the Fugitive Slave Act even more repressive, since those charged as fugitives had little legal protection or recourse. In essence, this made it easier to kidnap freedmen and allowed for cruel treatment of slaves who were captured.

251. (E) In August 1831, Nat Turner led a slave rebellion in Virginia. It resulted in 56 deaths, the largest number in such an uprising during the antebellum period. Southern states responded with stricter slave laws and Black Codes. Harriet Beecher Stowe published *Uncle Tom's Cabin* in 1852 (see questions 247, 248, and 249). "Bleeding Kansas" was the name given to the outbreak of violence in the Kansas Territory in 1854 as pro- and anti-slavery groups (including the abolitionist John Brown) battled over the issue of slavery. "Bleeding Sumner" refers to the assault on the abolitionist senator Charles Sumner from Massachusetts, who was severely beaten by Congressman Preston S. Brooks of South Carolina in 1856. Brooks attacked Sumner after Sumner made an anti-slavery speech, "The Crime Against Kansas," which directly insulted Senator Andrew Butler of South Carolina. John Brown, a militant abolitionist, led a raid on the military arsenal at Harpers Ferry in 1859, hoping to use the weapons stored there to arm future slave uprisings.

252. (B) The Kansas-Nebraska Act was introduced by Senator Stephen Douglas of Illinois in 1854. Its proposed purpose was to admit Kansas and Nebraska as states in order to build a connecting railroad from Chicago to the West. However, the act repealed the Missouri Compromise of 1820, which prohibited slavery north of Missouri, and allowed settlers in those territories to instead decide the issue through popular sovereignty. This led to a series of events in 1854 known as Bleeding Kansas, in which pro-slavery groups and abolitionists gathered in Kansas to influence the territories' stance on the issue. John Brown gained national attention during this time by killing multiple pro-slavery supporters with a sword, and this period in its entirety caused further political separation between the North and South.

253. (A) In the 1856 election, the American Party emerged from the Know-Nothing Parties that had been popular earlier and had limited success in areas such as New York and Pennsylvania. The party nominated former president Millard Fillmore as its candidate and had some success, winning roughly 22 percent of the popular vote. Part of the party's success was rooted in the popular anti-immigrant sentiment that existed at the time, but it was also influenced by the collapse of the Whig Party prior to the election. The Whigs split over the issue of slavery, and many of the anti-slavery Whigs in that election helped form the Republican Party, which was able to win 33 percent of the popular vote. James Buchanan of the Democratic Party won the election with 45 percent of the popular vote.

254. (C) The Freeport Doctrine was part of the Lincoln-Douglas debates during the 1858 Illinois Senate race. In the debates, Abraham Lincoln tried to make Stephen Douglas look like a defender of slavery, while Douglas attempted to defend himself by citing the notion of popular sovereignty. The earlier *Dred Scott* decision stated that territories were not allowed to outlaw slavery, making Douglas's position look weak. Douglas developed a position, which became known as the Freeport Doctrine, that while states could not outlaw the practice of slavery, they could still pass laws unfriendly to the practice that would prevent slavery from taking hold. Douglas's position was well received by the people of Illinois, and Douglas went on to win the Senate seat. At the same time, it alienated much of his southern support, hurting his future presidential bid. At the same time, the Lincoln-Douglas debates gave Lincoln nation recognition, enabling him to become the Republican candidate in 1860.

255. (A) The *Dred Scott* decision was the first time since the *Marbury v. Madison* case that the Supreme Court struck down a law passed by Congress. In *Dred Scott*, the court deemed that the Missouri Compromise was unconstitutional because it violated slave owners' rights to property. This upheld Stephen Douglas's proposed Kansas-Nebraska Act of 1854 insofar as slavery could not be automatically outlawed in the territories, but at the same time, it also made it illegal to outlaw the practice outright through popular sovereignty. Instead, the state would have to practice the Freeport Doctrine, also introduced by Douglas, which would involve creating laws that were so unfriendly to slavery that they would in effect keep the practice out of the state.

256. (E) Senator John J. Crittenden of Kentucky introduced the Crittenden Compromise on December 18, 1860, as an attempt to resolve the U.S. secession crisis, which began in 1860 with South Carolina seceding from the United States. Six other states—Mississippi, Florida, Texas, Alabama, Georgia, and Louisiana—soon followed. The compromise called for several Constitutional amendments that were well received by Southern Senators but quickly rejected by senators from the North, especially Abraham Lincoln, because they allowed for the expansion of slavery. The amendments within the compromise called for the reestablishment of the line created by the Missouri Compromise, banned federal restrictions of the slave trade, including within Washington, D.C., and strengthened Fugitive Slave Laws. The measure was introduced at the 1861 peace conference, but an agreement was not reached, and the Civil War began on April 12, 1861, with the Confederacy's attack on Fort Sumter.

257. (A) After leading the 1856 Pottawatomie Massacre in Kansas, the abolitionist John Brown in 1859 led an attempted attack on the federal arsenal at Harpers Ferry, Virginia. His goal was to capture the weapons held at the arsenal and use them to start an armed slave revolt. Initially, he asked Harriet Tubman to join him, though she had fallen ill prior. Brown's raid was defeated by a military detachment led by Colonel Robert E. Lee. John Brown's actions in Bleeding Kansas and Harpers Ferry represented a militant approach within the abolitionist movement. They furthermore illustrated the growing division and increasing tensions concerning slavery. Some saw Brown as a brave martyr, while many others viewed him as a terrorist. The raid itself furthered the tensions between the North and South, helping to usher in the Civil War.

258. (A) The Free-Soil Party mostly consisted of former members of the Whig Party and Democratic Party who strongly opposed the expansion of slavery. They existed as a third party during the 1848 and 1852 elections, with their strongest support being in New York. By 1854, most of the Free-Soil Party was absorbed into the newly emerging Republican Party.

259. (D) The Republican Party emerged in 1854, with membership including former Free-Soil Party members, Whigs, and anti-slavery Democrats. The party's platform was diverse, including economic policies and the development of a transcontinental railroad. However, the major unifying focus was the party's opposition to slavery. While the Republicans were unsuccessful in winning the presidential race in 1856 (their candidate, John C. Fremont, achieved 33 percent of the electoral vote, losing to Democratic candidate James Buchanan), they realized that if they could gain the support of the American Party, which was a single-platform party focused on limiting immigration, they might be able to win in the following election.

260. (B) The presidency of James Buchanan is difficult to summarize fully and has been debated by historians since his presidency. He is often blamed for his inaction as Southern states began to secede from the Union, limited in his actions by his strict constitutionalist views. He was also a supporter of slavery and strongly opposed the abolitionist movement embodied by the Republican Party. He has also been criticized for his dealings with the financial crisis of 1857, which in part resulted from the Democratic Party's push for lower tariffs that led to deficit spending under his administration. He also vetoed bills that would have led to the expansion of colleges. During the 1860 election, the Democratic Party split between the North and South.

Chapter 10

261. (E) Franklin Pierce, a Democrat from New England, was elected president in 1852. He was a dark-horse candidate, in many ways like Polk. This election also marked the end of the Whig Party, which became divided over slavery. Pierce supported both expansion, presiding over the Gadsden Purchase in 1853, and slavery, with the signing of the Kansas-Nebraska Act in 1854. This act enraged abolitionists and Free-Soilers because it nullified the earlier Missouri Compromise by leaving the issue of slavery in the two territories to popular sovereignty. The Gadsden Purchase also enraged northerners because it was set in place to build a transcontinental railroad across the South instead of the North. The 1854 Ostend Manifesto further angered abolitionists and illustrated his administration's expansionist intentions. It provided a plan for purchasing Cuba from Spain and called for the United States to use force if Spain refused to cooperate. In the end, Pierce was unable to maintain support from either the North or the South. He was not renominated for the presidency in 1856 but was instead replaced by James Buchanan.

262. (A) The Southern Confederacy, called the Confederate States of America, was established in 1861 and consisted of the 11 states that seceded from the Union. Its constitution was similar to that of the Union but protected the institution of slavery and reflected the Southern views of states' rights. This created a weaker federal government, like that created by the Articles of Confederation, which established the first official U.S. government. The lack of a strong central government caused many challenges similar to those of the United States under the Articles of Confederation, including difficulty in funding and maintaining a unified army. This hampered the South's ability to fully maintain its efforts during the Civil War.

263. (D) Fort Sumter was a costal fortification built at the entrance of the harbor at Charleston, South Carolina. Its construction started in 1816, following the War of 1812, but at the outbreak of the Civil War, it was still incomplete. On April 10, 1861, Confederate forces at Charleston demanded that the Union Army stationed at Fort Sumter surrender the fort. The fort's commander refused, and on April 12, Confederate artillery opened fire. This is considered to be the first armed engagement of the Civil War. The Union fort was unprepared for the engagement, and reinforcements could not arrive in time, so the fort was surrendered to the Confederacy on April 14.

264. (D) The First Battle of Bull Run took place on July 21, 1861. It is considered to be the first major land battle of the Civil War. The battle took place near the town of Manassas in Virginia, so it is also referred to as the First Battle of Manassas. (The Union often labeled battles based on physical features, such as the Bull Run River, while the Confederates named the battles after nearby towns.) The Union army, numbering roughly 28,000, was led by Brigadier General McDowell, while the Confederate army, consisting of roughly 32,000 men, was led by Brigadier General Johnston. The Union army, which was ill trained and inexperienced, failed to resist a Confederate counterattack and was forced to retreat, marking a Confederate victory. The Union suffered nearly 3,000 casualties, while the Confederate army suffered roughly 2,000. The battle foreshadowed that the Civil War was going to be long and hard-fought for both sides. McDowell was removed from command and replaced by George B. McClellan. Meanwhile, because of his stoic nature during the conflict, a previously unknown colonel by the name of Thomas Jackson earned the nickname "Stonewall" after he refused to yield during a Union advance. The Battle of Shiloh took place in Tennessee from April 6 to 7, 1862. The Battle of Fredericksburg occurred in December 1862 near Fredericksburg, Virginia. The Battle of Chancellorsville was fought from April 30 to May 6, 1863, near Spotsylvania, Virginia, and the Battle of Antietam took place on September 17, 1862, near Sharpsburg on the Antietam Creek in Maryland.

265. (A) During the Civil War, the border states consisted of Delaware, Kentucky, Maryland, Missouri, and West Virginia. These states allowed slavery but were aligned with and bordered free Union states. They also (with the exception of Delaware) bordered the Confederacy. The states were very valuable to the Union, so they were heavily considered in nearly all of Lincoln's actions during the war. Even in the Emancipation Proclamation of 1863, Lincoln made it clear that the border states would be exempt. The border states were important as a buffer zone, and if Maryland joined the Confederacy, Washington, D.C., would be engulfed by the Confederacy. These states were far from impenetrable; they became the sites of many of the war's most notorious battles and were crossed on numerous occasions by the Confederate army. Moreover, they were home to numerous factories, especially in Maryland and Delaware, which would have greatly benefited the industry-weak Confederacy.

266. (C) Going into the war, the Union had several clear advantages over the Confederacy. It had a larger population with a more industrialized base, so it could create a larger and better-supplied military. It also had a more balanced economy containing both factories and farms. It furthermore had more money in its treasury and banks. The Confederacy also had advantages. Seven of the eight military colleges in the United States were located in the South, giving the Confederacy more experienced leadership. Also, many Confederates considered this a war to save their way of life, boosting Southern morale early in the conflict.

267. (C) The Emancipation Proclamation was issued by President Lincoln in 1863 following the Battle of Antietam. While it was meant to emancipate (free) the slaves, it was applied only to the Confederate States. This was done to maintain the support of the border states, and it limited the proclamation's immediate impact, since the Confederate States saw themselves as not bound to the Union or Lincoln. But the proclamation did directly tie the issue of slavery to the war, making the conflict about something beyond simply reunifying the United States. While many Northern Democrats were upset by the action, it proved to be successful politically, and President Lincoln was able to win the election in the following year. The proclamation also helped increase black enlistment in the Union army.

268. (A) In 1861, President Lincoln suspended the writ of habeas corpus in Maryland and several other border states. This was done in response to riots and the rise of militias, which might have resulted in Maryland and other regions leaving the Union. Habeas corpus gives people accused of a crime the right to defend themselves. This right is listed in Article I of the Constitution. The Constitution, under the suspension clause, does allow the practice to be suspended "in cases of rebellion or invasion when the public safety may require it." Beyond the actions in Maryland, Lincoln also used the suspension to suppress the actions of Northern Democrats who sympathized with the Confederacy. These people were labeled "Copperheads" by their opposition in the North.

269. (B) During the Civil War, "Copperheads" referred to Northern Democrats and others who openly expressed their sympathies with and support for the Confederacy. They were given the label by Republicans who saw their actions as poisonous to the Union—dangerous as the venomous copperhead snake. Lincoln suspended the writ of habeas corpus to suppress the Copperheads during the Civil War. Copperheads were also referred to as Peace Democrats. The groups created several large societies, including the Knights of the Golden Circle in Ohio, which was led by Harrison H. Dodd. The organization called for armed uprisings in several Northern states. Copperheads also supported former general George B. McClellan in the 1864 election, but because of the negative press surrounding the organizations and recent Union military success, McClellan lost the election.

270. (D) After his failed Peninsula Campaign, which culminated with the bloody Battle of Antietam, George McClellan was removed from command in 1862. In 1864, however, Northern Democrats nominated him in the presidential election against President Lincoln. He tried to appeal to a war-weary Union public with an antiwar platform that called for ending the conflict and negotiating with the Confederacy. The Democrats found themselves split, while the Republicans, calling themselves the National Union Party, stayed strongly united. Furthermore, a series of successful military successes bolstered support for Lincoln, who easily won the election with 55 percent of the popular vote.

271. (C) The March to the Sea refers the Union movement of troops from Atlanta, Georgia, in November 1864 to Savannah in December of that year. The troops were led by Major General William Tecumseh Sherman and employed what is called the doctrine of total warfare. As the troops moved through the region, they destroyed all the infrastructure in their path, including roads, towns, and plantations, inflicting both military and psychological damage on the Confederacy. The naval blockade under Winfield Scott became known as the Anaconda Plan because it would put a stranglehold on the South's ability to trade. Both McClellan's Peninsula Campaign and Burnside's Charge at the Battle of Fredricksburg were Union failures. While Antietam, the last battle of the Peninsula Campaign, was a Union victory, it was costly, and McClellan failed to follow up, allowing Lee's army to regroup. General Ambrose Burnside's charge at Fredericksburg in 1862 against entrenched Confederate forces was a demoralizing loss that cost Burnside his command. Pickett's Charge was a failed offensive during the Battle of Gettysburg that nearly cost General Lee his army and served as a turning point in the war for the Union.

272. (D) The Battle of Shiloh is also called Battle of Pittsburg Landing. It took place from April 6 to 7, 1862, in southwestern Tennessee. Shiloh was a major battle in the Western Campaign of the Civil War. Though the battle began with a surprise attack by Confederate forces on the Union, General Grant received reinforcements and was able to launch a successful counteroffensive, winning the battle on the second day. In the end, it was one of the bloodiest battles up to that time, but the Union victory ended the Confederacy's ability to block the Union advance down the Mississippi River. The First Battle of Bull Run took place on July 12, 1861 (see answer to question 264). The Union demonstrated its inexperience and was forced to retreat, giving the Confederacy an early win. The Battle of Fredericksburg took place in 1862. The Union army was led by Ambrose Burnside. Prior to battle, Lee's Confederate forces entrenched themselves in the heights behind the town. Burnside's Charge cost the Union nearly 13,000 men and Burnside his command. The Battle of Chancellorsville was fought from April 30 to May 6, 1863, in Virginia. The Union was led by General Hooker. Lee divided his forces, taking Hooker by surprise. It was a dramatic victory for the Confederacy, illustrating Robert E. Lee's brilliance in military tactics. He did, however, lose General Jackson, his most trusted soldier, to friendly fire. The Battle of Cold Harbor took place from late May to early June in 1864. It marked one of the last battles of Grant's overland campaign. During the battle, Grant's troops were decimated by the fortified Confederate army. This loss forced Grant to give up his initial plans to take Richmond, Virginia, and instead head to the Confederate rail center of Petersburg.

273. (E) While the Confederacy suffered disadvantages such as a smaller population than the North and lacked the level of developed infrastructure of railroads found in the North, it was prepared in military leadership. A majority of the United States' military colleges were located in the South, and many of the United States' most experienced military leaders, such as Robert E. Lee, chose to fight for their home states in the South instead of staying with the Union army. The South's insistence on state independence hurt its cause, however, because the independence of each state limited the power of the Confederate government. Furthermore, the South failed to receive the support of the powerful industrial European states of Britain and France, giving it little recourse against the North's industrial might.

274. (B) Initially, the Confederate government planned to set up defensive positions and wait. They hoped that by using a war of attrition, they would be able to inflict heavy Union casualties with limited losses on their own side. By consistently repelling Union offensive strikes, they hoped to wear down their opponents' morale and will. This strategy failed because the Union had tremendous advantages by way of resources and in many ways was able to conduct a war of attrition of its own, despite its continual heavy losses. The South also failed to achieve the support of European powers such as Britain and France, although the two nations relied on Southern cotton. Instead of supporting the South, they found sources elsewhere, such as in India and Egypt.

275. (A) While General McClellan was viewed as a brilliant organizer and strategist, President Lincoln criticized him for being overly cautious. After the First Battle of Bull Run, Lincoln chose him to replace McDowell and create the Army of the Potomac.

276. (C) The Battle of Gettysburg was a three-day battle that took place in July 1863. More men died in this battle than any other battle on American soil. After the failed attack at Antietam, General Lee once again attempted to win a battle in the North. The Army of the Potomac, this time led by General Meade, engaged the Confederate Army of Northern Virginia at Gettysburg. On the third day, following heavy Confederate artillery assaults on Union lines, Lee ordered a massive Confederate charge to be led by General George E. Pickett. Because of the failure of the earlier artillery strikes, the charge was met by a strong Union defense, crushing the Confederate forces. Lee was forced to retreat, and his army was never able to recover from the losses or stage another Northern offensive. At almost the same time, Grant successfully laid siege to Vicksburg, ending with a Union victory on July 4. By taking this Confederate position, the Union was able to take control of the Mississippi River, dividing the Confederacy in half.

277. (B) The Gettysburg Address was delivered by Abraham Lincoln on November 19, 1863, at a dedication of a national cemetery at the site of the Gettysburg battlefield. The speech, which was considered short and was often overlooked at the time, has become one of the most important speeches in American history. In only roughly two minutes, Lincoln restated the purpose of the war as being not only to preserve the Union but also to defend the notions of human equality that defined the American Revolution.

278. (A) The Anaconda Plan, devised by General Winfield Scott, called for a naval blockade of Southern ports while leading a military force down the Mississippi River, cutting the Confederacy in half. Scott felt that cutting off the Southern economy through the blockade and then dividing the Confederacy would leave the South little choice but to seek peace, avoiding the need for the Union to engage in a bloody war.

279. (C) The *Merrimac*, constructed by the Confederacy, and the *Monitor*, constructed by the Union, illustrated an advancement of naval technology: the creation of ironclad ships. Ironclad ships were wooden steamships plated with iron. The traditional wooden ships were no match for these new vessels. The Confederacy was the first to employ this invention in naval warfare, but the Union quickly responded. The *Merrimac* and *Monitor* finally met in battle at Hampton Roads, off the coast of Virginia in March 1862. The battle itself was indecisive, with both sides declaring victory, but at the same time, the battle received much attention from the world's naval powers. The era of wooden navies had come to an end because ironclad ships had made them obsolete.

280. (B) The Civil War opened several opportunities to women, including factory and office work as well as nursing. Many women on both sides volunteered to help care for the immense number of wounded men that mounted from the intensive fighting. Dorothea Dix is probably one of the best-remembered nurses of the Civil War. Early in her career, she led the reform of mental hospitals, but during the Civil War, she became the superintendent of nurses for the Union. As superintendent of nurses, she helped open the field to future women. Furthermore, her insistence on providing care for both Union and Confederate soldiers has left her with an enduring legacy in both the North and South.

281. (B) Abraham Lincoln and Jefferson Davis were in many ways opposites. When Davis became president of the Confederacy in 1861, he had much more political experience than Lincoln. He had served as a U.S. senator and as secretary of war under Franklin Pierce. He also was a West Point graduate with military experience in the Mexican-American War. As president, however, he was ineffective. Lincoln, while lacking in political and military experience, better understood the importance of public opinion. This allowed him to connect better with voters and maintain the support of the various leaders in Congress and the states. Moreover, Lincoln surrounded himself with skilled advisers, while Davis often refused to delegate authority, causing tensions within his cabinet and with other officials.

282. (C) The Force Bill was issued in 1833 in response to the Nullification Crisis, when South Carolina, under the leadership of John Calhoun, threatened to not honor the Tariff of 1832. The Force Bill stated that the federal government could use all force necessary to enforce federal laws. The Morrill Tariff was passed in 1861 and, without representatives from the South to block it, doubled the prewar protective tariffs. The tariff won more support from Northern manufacturers and helped maintain the economy of the North throughout the war. The Legal Tender Act of 1862 allowed the federal government to produce a paper currency, which became known as greenbacks. The currency could not be redeemed for gold or silver, so its value fluctuated, but at the same time, it helped commerce and production to continue in the North. The National Bank Act did away with state banks, which were replaced by a series of national banks. This allowed the nation to produce a uniform currency. Together these acts helped the Northern economy expand, giving the North a strong advantage over the South.

283. **(D)** During the Civil War, life for many slaves remained relatively unchanged. Many were taken from fieldwork to do manual labor for the Confederate army. As the Union began to penetrate the South, many slaves did attempt to escape or seek refuge with the Union army. Others remained in their homes and on their master's plantations through the war. Slave uprisings did not drastically increase during the period. The South did suffer from a lack of industrial development compared with its Northern counterpart. The North had factories for the production of clothing, rifles, and ammunition. Much of the war materials were produced through cottage industries or through smuggling. Food shortages also plagued the South, as evidenced by the bread riots that occurred in Richmond, Virginia, in 1863. Furthermore, the Confederate government printed currency in such large quantities that it was devalued, making it hard for Southerners to purchase the few necessities that were available.

284. **(E)** Initially the Union army refused to enlist African-American volunteers. Congress eventually opened the military to African-Americans in 1862 after McClellan's defeats in Virginia. After the issuance of the Emancipation Proclamation, the number of African-Americans increased rapidly, though volunteers served in segregated units under mostly white supervision. Regardless, by war's end, they made up roughly 10 percent of the Union army. They were not initially placed in combat units but instead were forced to perform menial jobs and manual labor. Also, until 1864, they received less pay. Over time, black regiments such as the 54th of Massachusetts gained recognition for their abilities in combat. After 1863, the Confederacy also began to create African-American units. The black soldiers faced strong racism and harsh treatment, however, and were often given insufficient supplies and arms.

285. **(C)** A zeppelin is a type of rigid airship invented by a German named Ferdinand von Zeppelin at the end of the 19th century. He came to the United States as a military observer during the Civil War and noticed the use of hot-air balloons for reconnaissance. This and his earlier observations of balloons being used in the Franco-Prussian War inspired him to develop a new type of airship. Zeppelins were used during the First World War as bombers and for reconnaissance, and later they became a widely used form of transportation up through the 1930s. Shipping food in tin cans became a vital method of provisioning the Union army. The Gatling gun was an early rapid-fire weapon and a forerunner of the modern machine gun. It was introduced in the later part of the Civil War with deadly results. Primitive submarines were used by both the Union and the Confederate militaries. When the Confederate submarine *H. L. Hunley* sank the USS *Housatonic* in 1864, it marked the first time a submarine had sunk another vessel. Torpedoes also were used during the war, especially by the South. They operated more like mines, however.

286. **(A)** While Gettysburg and Vicksburg were important turning points in the war for the Union, the war ended officially with Lee's surrender at Appomattox Court House. By April 1865, the Confederacy was in a weakened state both militarily and morally. Desertion rates were ever increasing, and supplies were few. Grant's army pushed Lee's forces back and eventually on April 9 surrounded them at the Virginian town of Appomattox Court House. At that point, Lee and Grant met and worked out the conditions of the Confederacy's surrender, ending the war.

Chapter 11

287. (B) Lincoln's plan for Reconstruction was considered lenient by many Radical Republicans. Many felt that the South needed to be punished for seceding from the Union and starting the war. Lincoln, however, felt it was more important to reunify the nation, and his plan illustrated this in many ways. He required only 10 percent of the voting populations in each state to take an oath of allegiance. Each state was required to establish a new state government that swore to uphold the Thirteenth Amendment and emancipation. After this was completed, states would be allowed to hold elections and resume participation in the Union. Lincoln also offered pardons to any Confederate who took a loyalty oath, though military and government officials were denied this. He also did not require any state to give former slaves the right to vote. Lincoln's leniency was also illustrated by his rejection of the 1864 Wade-Davis Bill. Fearing that Southern states would reinstitute slavery after being readmitted to the Union, Radical Republicans introduced the legislation to increase the percentage of voters required to take a pledge from 10 percent to 50 percent. This illustrated the clashing of opposing viewpoints that would define the Reconstruction Era.

288. (C) On April 14, 1865, President Lincoln attended a performance of *Our American Cousin* at Ford's Theatre in Washington, D.C. During the performance, the acclaimed actor and former Confederate spy John Wilkes Booth shot the president. Lincoln died the following morning. This event left the nation in mourning but also created tensions within the government. Upon Lincoln's death, the vice president, Andrew Johnson, assumed the office. He was a southern Democrat who believed in an even more lenient Reconstruction plan than Lincoln's. This put him at odds with the Radical Republican–controlled government. The tensions continued to grow, eventually resulting in the first impeachment of a president in American history.

289. (D) Both Lincoln and Johnson supported what Radical Republicans saw as lenient plans for Reconstruction. But both insisted on what became known as the Ten Percent Plan. Once 10 percent of a Southern state's 1860 voters had taken an oath of loyalty, the state could rejoin the Union. This was after it had established a new state government that would ratify and adhere to the Thirteenth Amendment, which outlawed the practice of slavery. Neither plan called for the redistribution of land, an act supported by many former slaves as well as Radical Republicans. Lincoln's plan for states to reenter the Union, which was in many ways similar to Johnson's, was relatively simple. This was because Lincoln believed that the Southern states had never legally seceded in the first place. After Lincoln's death, Johnson initiated his own Reconstruction plan. It continued Lincoln's pardons of former Confederates. It also called on Southern states to repudiate their war debts. A major difference was that it did not require the 10 percent loyalty oath to hold a constitutional convention.

290. (D) After the Civil War, many southern leaders called for the creation of a "New South," which would be the home of cities and new industries. One area of focus was rebuilding and expanding the southern railroad networks. By the 1870s, much of the initial railroad infrastructure was rebuilt, and nearly 4,000 miles of new track were laid. This allowed for southern commerce to increase, and towns and cities began to expand. While the South never rose to the level of northern industrialism, new cotton, lumber, and iron mills allowed the economies of southern states to expand.

291. (D) The Freedman's Bureau, or the Bureau of Refugees, Freedmen and Abandoned Lands, was created in 1865 to provide aid to freed people and help them make the adjustment to freedom. It was created under the U.S. Department of War and headed by General Oliver O. Howard. While the bureau was short-lived (it was dismantled by 1869), it played an important role in providing for the basic needs of millions of war refugees. It, along with other programs established using Reconstruction funds, created a public school system similar to the ones found in the North in 1872. The Freedman's Bureau further addressed the educational needs of African-Americans. In its short existence, it created nearly 4,000 schools, including Howard University near Washington, D.C., in 1867.

292. (B) In 1866, a group of former Confederate soldiers in Tennessee created a secret society they called the Ku Klux Klan. Membership in the society spread throughout the South, encouraged by Southern whites' fears of African-Americans' newly found rights and freedoms. Much of the membership consisted of former Confederate leaders, who were excluded from pardons and therefore politics. As Reconstruction progressed, the violent acts of the Klan increased. Raids were conducted on black communities as well as on those who supported Republican reforms. Fear and intimidation were used to keep black communities from voting, as well as to force African-Americans into a subordinate role in society. Congress responded by passing the Enforcement Acts in 1870 and 1871. These acts outlawed the use of terror and force to keep people from exercising their right to vote. The military was also used to suppress the Klan's activities, helping to wipe out the Klan. The organization later reemerged in the post-Reconstruction years, however, and began to play a major role in politics in various regions throughout the nation.

293. (A) During the 1866 congressional elections, Radical Republicans were elected in large numbers. This was, in part, a response to Andrew Johnson's resistance to the Fourteenth Amendment, which would give African-Americans citizenship and, with it, legal status and constitutional protections. The Radical Republicans began to institute their own plans for Reconstruction. In 1867, they passed the Reconstruction Act, which implanted six sweeping provisions. One measure divided the South into five districts and put it under military rule. It also forced states to create new constitutions and allow both white and African-American males to vote. It also called on all Southern states to guarantee equal rights to all citizens and ratify the Fourteenth Amendment.

294. (A) In response to the emergence of the Ku Klux Klan during the years following the Civil War, the federal government instituted laws to protect the rights of freedmen. One of these laws was the Force Acts of 1870. The Tenure of Office Act of 1867 required the president to seek the approval of the Senate to remove officials they appointed. The act became the basis of Andrew Johnson's impeachment in 1868. The Reconstruction Act of 1867 divided the South into military districts.

295. (C) The Thirteenth Amendment, adopted on December 6, 1865, was the first of the Reconstruction Amendments. It officially abolished slavery and involuntary servitude, except as punishment for a crime. While the Emancipation Proclamation, announced by Lincoln in 1863, was intended to free slaves, it did so only in areas controlled by the Confederacy and did not address the border states. The Twelfth Amendment, ratified in 1804, did not deal with slavery or the rights of African-Americans at all. Its intention was to correct problems within the presidential electoral process. See answers to questions 297 and 299 for descriptions of the Fourteenth and Fifteenth Amendments.

296. (C) As Southern states met the demands of the Reconstruction Plans and were restored into the Union, many began to pass laws that restricted African-Americans' rights. These laws were known as Black Codes. These codes were intended to keep newly freed slaves in their subordinate positions, deny them political empowerment, and keep them out of certain sectors of the economy. Black Codes took the form of strict curfews, vagrancy laws, forced-labor contracts, and restrictions of property ownership. The Radical Republicans attempted to combat these actions through stricter Reconstruction measures, passage of equal-rights laws, and the use of the military. When Reconstruction ended, these codes continued and grew even more severe.

297. (D) The Fourteenth Amendment was created as part of the Reconstruction amendments. It was ratified on July 9, 1868. The amendment, which had five parts, opened citizenship to all people regardless of race or color and guaranteed due process and equal protection to all citizens. It also extended protections under the Bill of Rights to the state government. Before the Fourteenth Amendment, it was deemed that these protections applied only to the federal government. The amendment overturned the 1857 *Dred Scott* decision, which declared that African-Americans were not citizens and therefore were not protected under the Constitution. Furthermore, the equal-protection clause was later used as grounds for the 1954 *Brown v. Board of Education* decision, which helped end segregation.

298. (A) Following the Civil War, many Southerners saw whites who supported the actions of Reconstruction or became members of the Republican Party as traitors. They were given the nickname "scalawag." The term was derived from a Scottish word referring to a small or sickly cow. Many who fell into this category were poor farmers who resented the wealthy plantation class that had controlled the South prior to the war. Northern Republicans who moved South following the war to make a profit were nicknamed "carpetbaggers" by many Southerners. They were criticized for being profiteers and stealing jobs and industry from Southerners.

299. (D) The Fifteenth Amendment was ratified in February 1869 and stated that no citizen could be denied the right to vote because of race or color. Furthermore, citizens could not be denied the right to vote because they had been slaves. Even though the Fifteenth Amendment was not ratified until 1869, as early as 1867 the military had begun to register African-Americans in the South following the passage of the Reconstruction Act. The Freedman's Bureau was created to provide aid to the millions of displaced people, black and white, following the end of the war. The Sixteenth Amendment did not deal with Reconstruction but instead with Congress's ability to levy an income tax. See answers to questions 295 and 297 for discussion of the Thirteenth and Fourteenth Amendments.

300. (B) American political history was made in February 1868 when Andrew Johnson became the first president to be officially impeached. In an impeachment, the House of

Representatives officially charges an official with committing an illegal act. Though the main reason Congress moved to impeach Johnson was political and partisan disagreements, the main justification was that he had violated the Tenure of Office Act, which was passed in 1867 (see answer to question 294). In 1868, President Johnson attempted to fire Secretary of War Edwin Stanton, who had been appointed under Lincoln. This action violated the 1867 act. Ten other charges were made against Johnson, but after his trial in the Senate, Johnson escaped removal from office by one vote.

301. (E) The 1869 *Texas v. White* decision strengthened the federal government's actions during Reconstruction. It announced that states did not possess the legal right to secede and that attempts to separate from the Union were in fact illegal. It also upheld the federal government's right to restructure southern states' governments. This act further affirmed the power of the national government over the state governments. The notion of "separate but equal" was upheld by the Supreme Court decision in the 1896 case of *Plessy v. Ferguson*. The 1969 decision in *Brandenburg v. Ohio* protected the First Amendment right of the Ku Klux Klan and other inflammatory groups to hold rallies. The Fourteenth Amendment protected citizens' rights regardless of race or color.

302. (D) Ulysses S. Grant became a national hero because of his leadership during the Civil War. In 1868, he received an overwhelming majority of the electoral votes, though the popular vote remained relatively close against his Democratic opponent, Horatio Seymour. Many credit Grant's win to the support of African-Americans who were exercising their newly established suffrage for the very first time. While Grant's administration is often remembered for being marred by corruption, he did oversee several important actions under Reconstruction. He passed legislation promoting black voting rights and oversaw the passage of the Fifteenth Amendment. He also signed the Civil Rights Act of 1875, giving African-Americans equal treatment in jury selection and public accommodations. He also oversaw legislation including the Ku Klux Klan Act and the Enforcement Act to weaken the Klan, effectively wiping it out of existence until it reemerged in the 20th century. He wanted to better unify the nation. This was illustrated by his signing of the Amnesty Act of 1872, which provided pardons to former Confederates. He favored limiting the number of troops to be stationed in the South, worried that too large of a number would create resentment. At the same time, he tried to maintain enough to protect African-Americans and suppress groups such as the Ku Klux Klan.

303. (B) The 1864 Wade-Davis Bill was introduced by Radical Republicans in response to President Lincoln's Reconstruction plan, which the Republicans saw as too lenient. In Lincoln's plan, only 10 percent of the voting population needed to take a loyalty pledge to the Union before the state could reenter the Union politically. The Wade-Davis Bill attempted to increase this number to 50 percent. Lincoln ultimately rejected the bill through a pocket veto. He felt that it would be too difficult to mend the nation if the Wade-Davis Bill were enacted. The insistence that Southern states ratify the Fourteenth Amendment was an integral part of the Radical Republican's Reconstruction Act of 1867. The Fifteenth Amendment was ratified in 1869 during the Grant administration.

304. (B) While Reconstruction did extend many new rights and freedoms to former slaves, the idea of redistributing land was never put into action. Private property was seen as a vital right, so provisions for giving land to former slaves never were carried out. In the South, many plantation owners found themselves with their land but without labor and a means to pay hired hands. Meanwhile, former slaves and poor farmers found themselves with no land to support themselves. This led to the arrangement of sharecropping and tenant farming in the South. The plantation owners divided their land and gave it to the landless farmers to grow crops. At the end of the season, the sharecroppers would give a portion of the harvest to the landowner. This system often became corrupt. After failed harvests, the farmers often found themselves in debt to the landowners and would have to borrow against the following year's harvest. This cycle of debt often led to situations similar to that under slavery, creating a cycle of poverty for many poor planters.

305. (C) In 1873, a major northern banking firm went bankrupt, triggering a long series of financial failures that included banks, railroads, and numerous other companies. As a result, millions of people lost their jobs. This depression lasted for five years, and many began to blame the Grant administration, which was plagued with charges of corruption during the two terms of Grant's presidency. Though the Republicans retained control of the presidency with the election of Rutherford B. Hayes, through what is often called a corrupt bargain, and maintained the Senate, they lost control of the House of Representatives.

306. (A) The 1875 Whiskey Ring Scandal was one of several scandals to plague the Grant administration. In 1875, it was discovered that officials in the administration were pocketing money collected from whiskey taxes. This was one of several corruption cases that emerged during the Grant administration. In 1872, it was discovered that shares of stock in the Crédit Mobilier, a railroad construction company, were being sold to members of Congress at a discounted rate well below market value. It was also discovered that congressmen accepted numerous bribes from both the Union Pacific Railroad and the Crédit Mobilier. Grant's administration was also found to be connected with the 1869 Black Friday Scandal, which involved illegal gold speculation. The Star Route Scandal of 1881 plagued the Garfield administration and involved corruption within the postal service. The Teapot Dome Scandal was one of multiple scandals to plague the Harding administration, while Whitewater marred the Clinton administration during the 1990s.

307. (D) During the Civil War, the federal government began to offer grants and subsidies to railroad companies. The railroads continued to expand during Reconstruction, reaching nearly 200,000 miles by the start of the 20th century. The growth of the railroads sparked the expansion of industry throughout the country and opened new markets in once-distant corners of the country. This expansion was furthered by the completion of the Transcontinental Railroad. During this same time, prices for the once-dominant staple crops of cotton and tobacco declined.

308. (C) In the 1876 election, the Republicans nominated Rutherford B. Hayes, while the Democrats nominated Samuel Tilden of New York. In the election, Tilden won the popular vote, but neither candidate received the necessary electoral votes after the elections were contested in four states, including three in the South: Florida, Louisiana, and South Carolina. The election was placed in the hands of bipartisan committees consisting of members from both houses as well as members of the Supreme Court. See answer to question 309 for more information.

309. (C) The Compromise of 1877 was the deal struck within the bipartisan electoral committee created to decide the outcome of the 1876 election. The Democrats agreed to give the presidency to the Republican candidate, Rutherford B. Hayes. Meanwhile, the Republicans agreed to remove federal troops from the South, construct another transcontinental railroad through Southern states, and end Reconstruction. With the removal of federal troops, many Southern states introduced various codes that greatly limited the rights and freedoms of African-Americans, as well as institutionalizing segregationist policies. While laws such as the Force Acts continued, the army was no longer there to offer protection, and the decision of *United States v. Cruikshank* stated that the federal government could not enforce acts of discrimination made by individuals, further disenfranchising African-Americans.

310. (D) The 1876 decision of *United States v. Cruikshank* was rooted in an 1873 conflict between a white militia and freedmen gathered in front of a Louisiana courthouse. The event became known as the Colfax Massacre. In the aftermath, several of the white militia members were tried under the Enforcement Act of 1870, which made it a felony for a group to conspire to deprive anyone of his or her constitutional rights. The *Cruikshank* decision found, however, that only the state governments, not the federal government, could try individuals under the act. This decision, as well as the 1873 Slaughterhouse Cases and the Civil Rights Cases of 1883, ruled that the Fourteenth Amendment protects citizens from rights infringements only on a federal level, not to the states. These actions effectively ended Reconstruction reforms intended to bring about equality and let the states begin to create further Black Codes and institute Jim Crow laws.

311. (B) After decisions such as the *Cruikshank* decision, Slaughterhouse Cases, and Civil Right Cases, states began to create laws segregating facilities and public accommodations. This notion of "separate but equal" was upheld by the 1896 *Plessy v. Ferguson* decision. This allowed segregated conditions to continue constitutionally until they were eventually overturned in the 1954 *Brown v. Board of Education* decision. The remaining Jim Crow laws were overruled by the Civil Rights Act of 1964 and the 1965 Voting Rights Act under the Lyndon B. Johnson administration.

Chapter 12

312. (E) The Pendleton Act was passed on January 16, 1883, under the administration of Chester A. Arthur, in response to the assassination of President James Garfield by Charles Guiteau in 1881. Guiteau was a disgruntled Stalwart (member of the political faction within the Republican Party against civil service reform) who was hoping to receive a political appointment under the spoils system. The spoils system, also known as the patronage system, involved elected officials rewarding supporters with jobs or promoting public employees for political support. While the practice existed long before his administration, Andrew Jackson's administration is most associated with the term. It was derived in 1828 from the saying "To the victor belong the spoils." The Pendleton Civil Service Reform Act ended the spoils system and instituted a merit-based system. This law initially applied only to the federal government, allowing political machines to thrive at the state and local levels.

313. (B) The Civil Service Commission was created by the Pendleton Civil Service Reform Act in 1883 in the wake of James Garfield's assassination. It ended the spoils system by instituting a merit-based system, which required those seeking certain government jobs to take the civil service exam. It furthermore kept elected officials and appointees from firing public employees. This helped remove patronage from federal public employment.

314. (B) The Populist Party emerged out of the earlier farmers' alliances of the 1870s and 1880s. It first appeared in 1887 as a national third party. It was created in response to industrialism and the concentration of wealth in the hands of large banks and big business. The party called for banking reform, blaming the Panic of 1873 and the following economic downturn on unfair banking practices. The Populists called for the end of the national banking system, which never happened; instead, the Federal Reserve was created in 1913. Furthermore, they called for the nationalization of the railroads. This platform emerged mainly from the farmers who made up a major constituency of the party. They were against the unfair rate and rebate systems, which hurt small farms. These ideas led to accusations of socialism within the party. Rejecting the concentration of wealth, the Populists also called for a graduated income tax. This meant one's tax rates would increase as his or her income increased. Steps to institute this policy began in 1894 with the Wilson-Gorman Tariff, which imposed a uniform tax. The Populists' major focus was ending the gold standard and instead opting for "free coinage of silver." The Populists' 1896 presidential nominee, William Jennings Bryan, gave his famous "Cross of Gold" speech calling upon the nation to move away from the gold standard (see answer to question 345).

315. (D) The post–Civil War period saw rapid mechanization of agriculture. Improved plows, seed spreaders, and mechanical reapers, as well as steam-powered threshers and bailers, helped farmers cultivate larger amounts of land and reap larger harvests. This increased the supply of agricultural goods, lowering prices, and buying the new equipment often caused the smaller farmers to accumulate debt. Often these smaller farms were absorbed by larger farms, increasing the average size of farms. Also, many poorer farmers called for the coinage of silver and the removal from the gold standard. This action would cause inflation, which would benefit farmers burdened with debt. Though farming was hard on the Great Plains, the continuation of homestead acts continued to draw settlers to the open lands of the West through the late 19th century.

316. (C) As the mechanization of farming began to increase following the Civil War, more land in the West was tilled, and production of agricultural goods increased rapidly. This drove down the price of these goods. To maintain a profit, farmers were forced to produce even more. This constant production of excessive surplus continually kept prices lower. Following the Panic of 1873, many farmers found themselves in severe debt from low prices as well as the cost of new equipment. This, in part, led to the emergence of the Grange and Farmers' Alliances.

317. (A) As the American railroad systems expanded following the Civil War, previously inaccessible regions throughout the United States became easily reached. This made farming in the West more profitable, and many people began to move to the West to become private landowners and farmers. Furthermore, homestead acts made land affordable to poor people from the United States as well as immigrants. This resulted in the forced removal of Native American tribes who occupied these western lands. The increase of farming and the introduction of new mechanized tools led to greater surpluses of agricultural goods, driving down their prices. The prices were further lowered as the European demand for American agricultural goods declined.

318. (B) Cattle raising had been an important industry in the American Southwest since Spanish colonial times. However, following the Civil War, the American diet began to switch from pork to beef, and the price of beef began to rapidly rise with the increased demand. This trend was furthered by the introduction of the refrigerated railway car in the 1870s. While profits were made by wealthy ranchers, most of the cowboys who led the famous cattle drives saw little of the profit. Small ranchers often could not maintain a profit and were absorbed by larger ones. Also, life on the range was often full of hardships. Natural obstacles such as weather and a rough terrain challenged these cowboys, as did stiff competition for land, especially after more farmers began to establish permanent farms on once-open grazing spaces.

319. (A) "Robber baron" was the nickname given by critics to the heads of industry during the period following the Civil War. Also known as captains of industry, these men dominated their particular areas of business and amassed enormous fortunes. Examples include Andrew Carnegie in the steel industry, Cornelius Vanderbilt in railroads, and J. P. Morgan in banking and investment. By the 1890s, 10 percent of the nation's wealth was held by less than 10 percent of the population. The term *robber baron* was derived from what was seen by many as nefarious business practices, such as the use of monopolies and trusts, ill treatment of labor, and price-fixing.

320. (C) The Sherman Antitrust Act, passed in 1890, marked the federal government's first true attempt to limit trusts, cartels, and monopolies. A trust is a business formed with intent to control an area of commerce. A cartel is a group of independent businesses formed to regulate production and prices of goods among members. A monopoly is a business with such dominant control over a product or service that it can limit competition or make itself nearly a sole provider. While the law was intended to create a fairer playing field for businesses and industry, it was not truly pursued until Theodore Roosevelt's administration. In fact, one of its earliest direct applications was against unions involved in the 1894 Pullman strike (see answer to question 321).

321. (D) The Pullman strike of 1894 occurred after George Pullman cut wages in response to the depression in 1893. A union leader of the American Railway Union named Eugene V. Debs responded by organizing more than 120,000 workers to strike. It was announced that railroad workers would not run any trains that used Pullman cars. Though the strike was based in Chicago, the strike shut down rail lines across the nation. Eventually, the federal government intervened by passing an injunction against the union, making the boycott illegal, and by employing federal troops to break up the striking workers. The injunction, which was upheld in the courts, served as a major setback for labor, though the strike did lead to investigations of Pullman's business practices.

322. (A) On May 10, 1869, the construction workers of the Union Pacific Railroad met with workers of the Central Pacific at Promontory Point in Utah. The joining of these two lines marked the completion of the nation's first transcontinental railway system. Construction of the railroad began in 1862 with the passage of the Pacific Railroad Act during the early years of the Civil War. With the completion of the railroad, the first transcontinental telegraph line also was completed. Now people, goods, and information could be sent from the Atlantic to Pacific more efficiently and reliably. It furthermore helped open the Great Plains for settlement.

323. (C) The Gilded Age refers to the period from the end of the Civil War to the turn of the century. It was a time in American history marked with rapid economic expansion; the United States grew from being the world's fourth-largest industrial nation to the largest.

The term *Gilded Age* was derived from the 1873 novel *The Gilded Age: A Tale of Today*, authored by Samuel Clemens (better known as Mark Twain) and Charles Dudley Warner. Gilding refers to the decorative practice of covering a surface with gold leaf to give an illusion of value. This reference was used to reflect the large amount of capital being earned by the captains of industry (so-called robber barons) of the time, as well as the lavish lifestyles they often lived, while corrupt systems were found underneath the surface. Edward Bellamy, Ida Tarbell, Upton Sinclair, and Lincoln Steffens were all part of a later journalistic movement during the Progressive Era known as muckraking. Bellamy's *Looking Backwards* also looked at societal problems through the eyes of one who falls asleep and wakes up years later in a workers' utopia. See question 373 for information on Ida Tarbell, Upton Sinclair, and Lincoln Steffens.

324. (A) In a monopoly, a business has dominant control over a product or service so it can limit competition or make itself a nearly sole provider. Early legislation such as the 1890 Sherman Antitrust Act attempted to limit this practice and promote fairer competition, though the law was rarely used against business until the early 20th century under Theodore Roosevelt's administration. Monopolies that defined the post–Civil War period included John D. Rockefeller's Standard Oil Company (see answer to question 326). Another example of an early American monopoly was U.S. Steel. It was created by investor J. P. Morgan when he combined Andrew Carnegie's steel company with two other steel companies. The end result was the world's first billion-dollar industry.

325. (B) Vertical integration is a management strategy where a business controls all aspects of a commodity's production from start to finish. In the case of Andrew Carnegie, his steel company controlled the mines that produced the ore as well as the coal needed to process it, the mills that produced the steel, and the ships and trains needed for transportation. By controlling every aspect of production, the company could manage prices better and beat out competition, allowing Carnegie to obtain a near monopoly on American steel production.

326. (B) John D. Rockefeller's Standard Oil serves as an example of horizontal integration as a business practice. Beginning as a corporation in Ohio in 1870, the company acquired or put out of business almost all competing refineries. It soon expanded internationally, becoming one of the world's first international companies, controlling a majority of the world's refineries. This allowed it to control production as well as prices. Rockefeller's monopoly was eventually broken up into 34 separate companies in 1911 under U.S. antitrust laws.

327. (C) Gustavus Swift is remembered for creating a midwestern meatpacking empire in the late 19th century. The growth of his company was aided by his development of the first refrigerated railroad car. This allowed him to ship meat throughout the nation without worries of spoilage. He also developed methods to use animal by-products in the production of goods such as soaps and glue, creating further products. He is often remembered for his philanthropy, especially large donations to the University of Chicago. However, he has also been vilified for the dismal conditions found in his meatpacking plants as they were depicted by Upton Sinclair in his novel *The Jungle*.

328. (B) The Knights of Labor was established in 1869, and unlike the earlier National Labor Union, it organized individuals instead of just unions. It allowed a diverse membership of skilled and unskilled labor, with the exception of professional gamblers, lawyers, bankers, and people who sold liquor. Besides these exceptions, it did not discriminate, making it one of the first labor organizations that allowed membership regardless of gender, race, or ethnicity. The union collapsed in response to the Haymarket riot, and the American Federation of Labor (AFL) emerged in its place. Led by Samuel Gompers, the AFL initially allowed only white, male, skilled laborers to join.

329. (B) In May 1886, workers at the McCormick Harvester plant in Chicago and other protesters gathered outside to argue for an eight-hour workday. Tensions between protest-ers and law enforcement officers were high after four workers were killed by police on a previous day. At one point, someone in the crowd threw a bomb at the police, who then opened fire. In the resulting chaos, seven police officers and four protesters were killed, and more than 60 others were injured. Ultimately, the Knights of Labor, which was heav-ily involved with the strike, became associated with anarchists and soon collapsed. Public opinion became critical of unions, and the movement for an eight-hour workday was greatly delayed.

330. (C) Thomas Edison earned the nickname the Wizard of Menlo Park for the seemingly endless number of inventions he and his scientists produced from his New Jersey lab. He revolutionized entertainment with the motion-picture camera and phonograph. He revolu-tionized business with the creation of the universal stock ticker and cities with his develop-ment of the first practical incandescent lightbulb. By the 1880s, several major cities began to switch from gas street lamps to electric lighting. Edison was a strong advocate for direct-current electricity, but his chief rival for bringing electricity to homes was Westinghouse, which used Tesla's alternating-current (AC) electricity. After a struggle that is now often called the "current wars," Westinghouse won, and AC is standard for electrical supplies.

331. (D) Oliver Kelley, a former employee of the U.S. Department of Agriculture, estab-lished the National Grange of the Patrons of Husbandry in 1867. The Grange, as it became known, spread rapidly through the midwestern farm belts following the economic Panic of 1873. Because of the panic, farmers began to suffer from the low prices of crops, increased amounts of debt, and unfair railroad shipping practices. The Grange soon evolved from a social fraternity into a political organization. During the 1870s, the Grange helped farmers establish cooperatives to bring down the price of farm equipment and supplies, coopera-tively run grain elevators, and cooperatively run credit unions and banks. Eventually, the political wing of the movement was absorbed into the Farmers' Alliances of the 1880s and later the Populist Party in the 1890s.

332. (A) The Morrill Land-Grant Act was passed in 1862 during the Lincoln administra-tion, though an earlier version of the bill was passed by Congress in 1859 but vetoed by President Buchanan. The legislation was created to increase the number of colleges in the newly forming states in the West. It reflected the intentions described in the earlier Ordi-nance of 1785 and Northwest Ordinance of 1787, which called for land to be set aside for education purposes. Each state was given a certain amount of federal land, which the state would sell, using the profits to set up an endowment to create an institute of higher learning—a major boost for higher learning in the United States. Michigan State Univer-sity, which was established in 1855 through a state-run land-grant program, became the model for the Morrill Land-Grant Act.

333. (E) The Homestead Act of 1862 was signed into law by President Abraham Lincoln. Several subsequent homestead laws were created following this initial act. The act gave 160 acres of land to any citizen for free after payment of a registration fee. The homesteader then had to live on the land for five years, cultivating it and building a permanent dwelling. Initially, the act was open to all white citizens as well as immigrants who intended to become citizens. After the passage of the Fourteenth Amendment, African-Americans also became eligible under the act. The system had many critics, and many complained that the best lands were often taken by land speculators, who would later sell the land for a profit.

334. (C) The Interstate Commerce Act, which was passed in 1887 under the administration of Grover Cleveland, created the Interstate Commerce Commission (ICC). The ICC was a federal agency created to address public concerns over unfair railroad practices such as rate fixing and rebate programs that hurt small farmers and interfered with fair business competition. It also was to address railroad companies' influence over politics, especially in railroad towns. The government was to have the power to determine maximum rates and to stop discriminatory practices. The act and the agency were initially unsuccessful, since the ICC was not given any real enforcement powers. This was later addressed under Theodore Roosevelt's administration with the passage of the Elkins and Hepburn Acts of 1903, which increased the agency's regulatory power.

335. (D) The McKinley Tariff, which was passed in 1890, harmed farmers because it increased the prices of farm equipment and failed to address the falling prices of agricultural goods. Furthermore, it helped lead to the Panic of 1893. Interestingly, the economic panic caused by the tariff in many ways helped its author, William McKinley, get elected to the presidency over William Jennings Bryan in 1896, after many voters blamed the Democrats for the continuing economic downturn. The Grange, Farmers' Alliances, and the Populist Party were political organizations that strongly represented the interests of farmers, especially in the Midwest. The Homestead Acts helped people obtain free public land in the West.

336. (D) The U.S. Supreme Court's 1886 decision in the case of *Wabash, St. Louis and Pacific Railway Company v. Illinois* ruled that only the federal government can regulate commerce that extends beyond state boundaries. The decision led to the creation of the Interstate Commerce Commission in 1887. The Hepburn and Elkins Acts of 1903 were passed during Theodore Roosevelt's administration. The acts strengthened the Interstate Commerce Commission by increasing the agency's enforcement powers. The Comstock Law, enacted in 1873, banned the shipment of obscene or lewd mail through the postal service. While the law was originally used to limit pornography, it was later used to limit the shipment of contraceptives.

337. (A) The Battle of Wounded Knee, also referred to as the Massacre at Wounded Knee, took place on December 29, 1890, on the Pine Ridge Reservation in South Dakota. It marked the end of the Pine Ridge Campaign of the U.S. Army against the Sioux Nation. During the event, the U.S. Cavalry killed nearly 200 Native Americans. The event began after the Sioux Nation was forced onto a reservation in 1889. In response to harsh treatment and rejection of life on the reservation, many Sioux began to take part in a ritual practice known as the Ghost Dance. This practice was a purifying ritual that was to bring back dead relatives and restore the world as it was before the arrival of white people. The Bureau of

Indian Affairs looked upon this practice as a disturbance and outlawed the ritual. When the Sioux continued the Ghost Dance, the U.S. Army was sent in to deal with the "restless" tribe and arrest Chief Sitting Bull, who was encouraging the act. An altercation resulted, and the cavalry opened fire on the unarmed Sioux. This event marked the last major episode of violence during the Indian wars.

338. (D) The Dawes Severalty Act was passed in 1887 to deal with the distribution of Native American lands in what is now Oklahoma. The act divided the lands in the reservations into individual, privately owned plots in hopes of forcing the Native Americans to adopt Western cultural practices of farming and the nuclear family, forcing them to abandon communal ownership. This action also interfered with traditional religious and tribal government practices. In addition, the size of the land parcels distributed was often not large enough to sustain a living, furthering poverty on the reservations. In 1936, Congress issued the Meriam Report, which illustrated the fraud and mismanagement of Native Americans by the Department of Indian Affairs, which enforced the Dawes Act. The report also found that the Dawes Act illegally deprived Native Americans of their land rights, and further use of the act was ended.

339. (B) Bonanza farms were large farms that operated large-scale agricultural production. They emerged in the later part of the 19th century and were mainly used in wheat production. Most bonanza farms were owned by companies rather than by a single farmer. They were often run like factories by professional managers. New agricultural technologies and machinery, as well as the completion of the post–Civil War railroad networks, made bonanza farms possible. Furthermore, the availability of cheap land and the growth of eastern markets further inspired their expansion.

340. (C) In the wake of the ending of Reconstruction in the late 1870s, many southern states began to impose severe Jim Crow laws, which institutionalized racism and discrimination. Furthermore, with the withdrawal of federal troops, the African-American population had little protection from supremacy groups, such as the White League, which could freely terrorize black communities. With the passage of the Fourteenth Amendment, African-Americans became eligible for free lands under the Homestead Act. Many families took advantage of this and began to move to the open lands of the Great Plains, especially after the 1879 Louisiana Constitutional Convention declared the right to vote could be decided only by the states and not the federal government. Nearly 6,000 African-Americans moved to Kansas in what has been called the Kansas Exodus or Exoduster Movement.

341. (D) In 1874, General Oliver Howard, who earlier served as commissioner of the Freedman's Bureau, was sent to Idaho to fight in what are now called the Indian Wars. In 1877, he ordered that the Nez Percé tribe be relocated to a reservation despite an earlier treaty negotiated by Chief Joseph that ensured their right to the Wallowa Valley. When the Nez Percé resisted removal, Howard's troops used force, declaring their disobedience an act of war. After the American forces began to attack the Nez Percé, Joseph began to lead his tribe to Canada. Before they could reach the border, however, they were stopped by the army and were forced to surrender and relocate to Oklahoma.

342. (A) While historians debate the true origins of the Ghost Dance, it became prominent among numerous Native American groups in the 1880s. The ritual called for the peaceful end of the violence inflicted by the white settlers that continually stripped the Native Americans of their land. It also was believed that it would bring the tribes back to their traditional roots. After 1890, the Sioux Nation was forced onto reservations. In response to the hardships, the Sioux began to practice the Ghost Dance, even though it was outlawed by the Bureau of Indian Affairs (BIA). The BIA blamed Chief Sitting Bull for letting his people continue the ritual and sent federal troops to the reservation to arrest him, leading to the Battle of Wounded Knee, or the Wounded Knee Massacre (see answer to question 337 for more information). This event marked the end of the Indian Wars.

343. (B) Frederick Jackson Turner published what has become known as the Frontier Thesis in 1893. He argued that the United States' continual expansion into its westward frontier was important in defining the growth of the American character as well as American democracy. He stated that the harshness of the wilderness stripped settlers of many of their European elements and allowed for more truly American traits such as individualism and egalitarianism to take root.

344. (D) In the election of 1896, the Republicans recaptured the White House with William McKinley's defeat of the Democratic candidate, William Jennings Bryan. Bryan was able to capture the support of both the Populist Party and Democrats. He also earned the support of western farmers through his support of bimetallism. Though he met previous elections with limited success, he was praised as a master orator and was seen as the spokesman of the western farmers still suffering from the Panic of 1893. However, Bryan failed to win the support of the pro-business wing of the Democratic Party, which occupied many of the eastern states. The eastern states were also wary of Bryan's mostly Populist platform, which was seen as anti-business and anti-railroad. Furthermore, McKinley's campaign outspent Bryan's by a considerable margin. The election was close; McKinley sealed the election with 51 percent of the popular vote.

345. (B) The quotation is an excerpt from William Jennings Bryan's "Cross of Gold" speech given in 1896 at the Democratic nominating convention in Chicago. The speech was extremely well received at the time; Bryan was reportedly carried out on the shoulders of cheering supporters after he completed it. Election historians still consider it to be a quintessential piece of American oration. The speech was given in response to the debate of bimetallism, after the Coinage Act of 1873 placed the nation on a strictly gold standard. This directly hurt western farmers, and a push for a return of bimetallism or the silver standard became a focus of the Populist Party, which supported Bryan in the 1896 election.

346. (E) Tammany Hall was the Democratic political machine that dominated New York City politics through the mid-20th century. The machine gained most of its strength by providing services such as finding jobs and housing for the numerous immigrants who flooded into the city. In return for these services, the machine obtained the ability to control the immigrants' votes and get its candidates into elected offices. The machine then used these elected officials to provide it with services and sometimes just illegal public funds. One of the most notable leaders of Tammany Hall was William Marcy Tweed, better known as Boss Tweed. Tweed's ring became notorious for municipal graft and overcharging for services and contracts. The famous American cartoonist Thomas Nast began to use his political cartoons to bring attention to the illegal actions of the Tweed Ring, and it was eventually brought down in 1871. Tammany, however, continued into the next century.

Chapter 13

347. (B) In 1890, Alfred T. Mahan published *The Influence of Sea Power upon History*, arguing the importance of a strong, modern navy to maintain national strength. He argued that history illustrated that a highly developed modern navy and use of blockades could overpower a well-established land army. He also argued that the United States needed to accomplish several goals to maintain a modern navy, as illustrated by Britain throughout the 19th century. He argued for a canal through the isthmus of Central America, as well as numerous bases and coaling stations throughout the Pacific to promote trade with Asia. Mahan's work directly influenced the foreign policy of President Theodore Roosevelt, as illustrated by his leadership in the construction of the Great White Fleet, the completion of the Panama Canal, and his support for the Open Door Policy in China. Even the Roosevelt Corollary to the Monroe Doctrine can be seen as an extension of Mahan's arguments for importance of naval power.

348. (C) Seward's Folly refers to the United States' purchase of Alaska from Russia in 1867. The purchase was engineered by Secretary of State William H. Seward and Tsar Alexander II for the cost of $7.2 million. At the time, Alaska was seen as a barren wasteland, and the purchase of the nearly 600,000 square miles of northern land was called Seward's Folly or Seward's Ice Box. Later, Alaska was found to possess mineral resources of gold and oil that were worth many times what the United States had spent on the purchase. This action was one of several taken by Seward that greatly expanded the international influence of the United States. In 1865, Seward reaffirmed the Monroe Doctrine by arranging to have 50,000 American troops sent to the Texas-Mexico border to resolve the Maximilian Affair, where France tried to instate its own puppet regime in Mexico. Furthermore, in 1867, the year in which the Alaska Territory was purchased, he arranged for the annexation of the Midway Islands. This new territory in the Pacific provided an important military base and coaling station, further fostering trade with Asia.

349. (B) The Roosevelt Corollary was issued in 1904 by President Theodore Roosevelt. It was announced in response to the Dominican Republic's government going bankrupt earlier that year. Attempting to keep European powers, such as Germany, from interfering with Latin American and Caribbean nations that had fallen into debt, Roosevelt created this addition to the Monroe Doctrine. In the corollary, the United States asserted the right to intervene within these states to "stabilize" their economic affairs. This notion was extended to include not only economic instability but also political unrest. In addition to justifying involvement in the Dominican Republic, the corollary was cited as justification for the United States to act in Cuba, Nicaragua, Mexico, and Haiti. In this manner, the doctrine is often said to have allowed the United States to act as an international police force in the Western Hemisphere.

350. (D) Vice President Theodore Roosevelt stated the now-famous words "Speak softly and carry a big stick" at the Minnesota State Fair in September 1901, 12 days before the assassination of President William McKinley put him into the presidency. He also had used the slogan earlier in personal correspondence. Roosevelt borrowed the expression from an African proverb, implying that power was available to retaliate if necessary. He felt that the United States should actively pursue a policy of peace while at the same time brandishing military might. This sentiment became the basis of President Theodore Roosevelt's foreign policy, often referred to as Big Stick Diplomacy, which placed a strong focus on the United States's commercial interests in Latin America. It was also further illustrated in his issuing of the Roosevelt Corollary to the Monroe Doctrine, asserting the right of the United States to intervene in troubled states in the Western Hemisphere to promote stability. Some illustrations of Big Stick Diplomacy can be seen in the creation of the Great White Fleet (a modern navy that traveled the globe to display American naval might), Roosevelt's involvement in the Venezuelan dispute with Great Britain, and the construction of the Panama Canal. Roosevelt's diplomacy is further illustrated by his use of military force as justification for U.S. intervention in Cuba and Nicaragua. Many of the focuses of Big Stick Diplomacy were continued by Taft through Dollar Diplomacy (see answer to question 353). In contrast, Wilson's Moral Diplomacy (Missionary Diplomacy) attempted to shift away from the use of military force (see answer to question 354).

351. (A) While the concept of an isthmus canal dated back to the 16th century with the Holy Roman Emperor Charles V and the King of Spain, the French were the first to attempt its construction in the 1880s. Shortly after, however, they abandoned the project because of costs in terms of money and workers' lives. Alfred Mahan identified a U.S. need to possess such a canal in his work as a naval historian, and Theodore Roosevelt successfully pursued the engineering feat during his administration. Two locations were considered for the project: Nicaragua and Colombia. Philippe Bunau-Varilla eventually convinced the United States to choose Colombia, and the United States signed and ratified the Hay-Herrán Treaty in 1903. Colombia rejected the treaty, however, so Roosevelt backed a revolt in the Isthmus of Panama, which was then part of Colombia, and quickly recognized the region as an independent state. The United States then negotiated a new treaty, the Hay-Bunau Treaty, in 1903, allowing for the canal. Construction began in May 1904 and was completed in August 1914. The SS *Ancon* became the first ship to pass through the 48-mile canal.

352. (C) The Hay-Bunau Treaty was signed on November 18, 1903, by John Hay, the secretary of state under Theodore Roosevelt, and Philippe Bunau-Varilla, who was serving as minister to the United States for the new nation of Panama. The treaty gave the United States complete control of the 10-mile-wide Canal Zone, allowing for the construction of the Panama Canal to begin in May 1904. Philippe Bunau-Varilla, who was born in France, was the chief engineer of France's attempt to construct a canal through the Isthmus of Panama in the 1880s. He also convinced the United States to choose Panama (which at the time was part of Colombia) as the location for its attempt to build a canal linking the Atlantic and Pacific.

353. (C) Dollar Diplomacy is associated with the foreign policy of William Howard Taft. It described the efforts under President Taft to further the United States' policy aims in Latin America and East Asia through economic power. Unlike McKinley's Gun Boat Diplomacy or Theodore Roosevelt's Big Stick Diplomacy, Taft's approach advocated exchanging "dollars for bullets." In other words, his administration encouraged U.S. bankers to invest in foreign areas of strategic concern to the United States, such as East Asia and Latin America. Much of this effort was led by Secretary of State Philander C. Knox, who regarded the State Department as effectively an agent of the corporate community. This policy was clearly illustrated in Costa Rica and Honduras, where the United Fruit Company had a tight grip on just about every sector of the economy, so these nations came to be referred to as "banana republics." Taft's Dollar Diplomacy is also illustrated by the 1909 revolt in Nicaragua. The United States quickly backed the insurgents, who were supported by U.S. mining interests. Following this, Knox encouraged U.S. bankers to invest in Nicaragua and offer substantial loans to the new regime, giving the United States increased financial leverage over the country. President Wilson attempted to move away from both Big Stick Diplomacy and Dollar Diplomacy with his Moral or Missionary Diplomacy (see answer to question 354). Later, Hoover would introduce the Good Neighbor Policy in Latin America, though the policy itself is generally credited to Franklin Roosevelt. This policy called for the withdrawal of American troops and treatment of Latin American nations more as equals.

354. (D) Unlike Theodore Roosevelt's Big Stick Diplomacy and Taft's Dollar Diplomacy, Wilson's policy was based on a belief that the United States needed to use the promotion of American values and democratic institutions to promote international security. The practice became known as Moral or Missionary Diplomacy. Wilson moved from an era of diplomacy focused on force or finance to a policy committed to justice, democracy, and Christian values. This policy was illustrated when Victoriano Huerta seized power in Mexico, killing the elected president, Francisco Madero. Despite the urging from many in the United States, Wilson refused to recognize the government, calling it a "government of Butchers." Wilson's policy of Moral Diplomacy was not always successful. In 1914, he ordered the U.S. Marines to invade Veracruz after American sailors had been detained in what was called the Tampico Incident. William Taft's urging of U.S. banks to refinance Haiti's national debt serves as an example of Dollar Diplomacy, and Herbert Hoover's removal of troops from Nicaragua illustrates the later Good Neighbor Policy.

355. (E) The goal of the 1907 Gentlemen's Agreement was to reduce tensions between the United States and Japan, the two most powerful nations of the Pacific. The agreement was made between President Theodore Roosevelt and the emperor of Japan. In the agreement, the United States agreed not to place restrictions on Japanese immigrants or students, provided Japan limited further emigration to the United States. The policy was based on the nativist and anti-Japanese sentiments emerging in California during the late 19th and early 20th centuries. As a result of the policy, the number of Japanese coming to the United States was reduced, and in return, California allowed Japanese students to attend public schools.

356. (D) The "insular cases" were the subject of a Supreme Court decision in response to the acquisition of Hawaii and the land gained after the Spanish-American War. With these new lands, people began to debate whether new territories received full constitutional protections and rights. From 1901 to 1905, the Supreme Court made a series of rulings stating that the Constitution fully applied only in incorporated territories (Alaska and Hawaii) but not in unincorporated territories (Guam and the Philippines). This allowed Congress to make the final call on whether new U.S. possessions gained constitutional privileges or not.

357. (A) Because of improved technologies in the post–Civil War period, U.S. industry and agriculture had grown beyond the nation's rate of consumption. Business and political leaders believed that foreign markets were essential to further economic growth, so they promoted a more proactive foreign policy. This was one of numerous factors that promoted American overseas expansion. Other factors included ideas such as social Darwinism and Rudyard Kipling's "White Man's Burden," which promoted the idea that the superiority of Western culture should be spread to underdeveloped regions. Frederick Jackson Turner's Frontier Thesis, which stated the American frontier was the source of culture, further inspired expansion into new frontiers to maintain the American spirit. Naval strategist Alfred T. Mahan's *The Influence of Sea Power upon History* (1890) advocated expansion as crucial for the United States to become a world power.

358. (E) In 1895, Richard Olney, the secretary of state under President Cleveland, ordered Britain to settle a boundary dispute it had with Venezuela through U.S. arbitration. This expanded the Monroe Doctrine beyond merely closing the Western Hemisphere to Europe and established the United States as the lead arbitrator in the Western Hemisphere. While Perry's opening of trade with Japan in 1854, as well as John Hay's 1899 Open Door Policy, were important expansions of American foreign policy, they dealt more with Asia, which is beyond the Monroe Doctrine's focus on the Western Hemisphere. This was also the case with Hawaii. Polk's usage of the Monroe Doctrine under "Manifest Destiny," while important in increasing the doctrine's scope, took place in the first half of the 19th century.

359. (C) In 1899, Secretary of State John Hay sent notes to France, Germany, Britain, Italy, Japan, and Russia stating no country would extend its sphere of influence over China that would close Chinese markets to other Western powers. This would keep Chinese markets open to all of the major powers, especially the United States. While none of the nations agreed to the Open Door Policy, Hay announced in March 1900 that all of the countries had accepted the terms. The Open Door Policy showed little success early on, but the principles were reasserted in the Nine Powers Treaty signed in February 1922. The policy officially ended with the Japanese invasion of China during World War II. Still, the foreign policies of Theodore Roosevelt, William Taft, and Woodrow Wilson focused on maintaining an open door to trade with the abundant Chinese markets.

360. (D) Valeriano Weyler was sent to Cuba in 1888 to quell the disorder caused by the *insurrectos*, revolutionaries fighting for Cuban independence under the leadership of José Martí. Weyler set up concentration camps to crush the rebellions. Conditions in the camps were extremely harsh; prisoners lacked proper food, water, and other necessities. Nearly 30 percent of those interred within the camps died because of this. Reports of these actions were sent back to the United States, and American newspapers nicknamed Weyler "Butcher Weyler." Stories of atrocities at the camps and other sensationalized reports, known as yellow journalism, helped convince the United States to declare war on Spain in 1898. Porfirio Diaz and Victoriano Huerta were dictators during the Mexican Revolution. Wilson attempted to overthrow Huerta after he staged a coup and murdered Mexico's elected president, Francisco Madero, in 1912.

361. (B) On February 15, 1898, the USS *Maine* exploded in Havana Harbor, Cuba. While the actual cause of the explosion was debated, the United States blamed the Spanish military and used the action as a pretense for war. On April 25, 1898, President McKinley formally issued a declaration of war. In 1976, nearly a century after the fact, another investigation found that the cause of the explosion was most likely not a Spanish mine. The USS *Constitution* is one the United States' oldest naval vessels, commissioned in 1797. The USS *Maddox* was the U.S. ship involved in the Gulf of Tonkin incident that led to the escalation of the Vietnam War. The *USS Chesapeake* helped spark the War of 1812 after it was attacked by the British ship *Leopard* and four members of its crew were impressed. The USS *Olympia* was the flagship of Commodore Dewey in the Philippines during the Spanish-American War; it successfully led the total defeat of the Spanish fleet in that theater of the war.

362. (B) Publisher and newspaper tycoon William Randolph Hearst issued the famous quote to artist Fredric Remington, who was stationed in Cuba with the goal of reporting on atrocities taking place there. This served as an example of yellow journalism, sensationalized news reporting used by the major newspapers to compete for readers. Hearst and Joseph Pulitzer, who controlled the press at the time, attempted to outdo each other's papers as a part of the fierce competition to attract each other's readers. The stories concerning Cuba helped the revolutionaries in Cuba gain American sympathies and eventually push for war to free Cuba from Spanish control. Muckraking journalism was another prominent form of journalism during the period (see answer to question 373).

363. (E) On April 19, 1898, both houses of Congress adopted the Teller Amendment to the declaration of war issued against Spain. The amendment stated that the United States would not annex the island nation of Cuba but would instead leave it in the hands of the Cuban people. The Teller Amendment was replaced in 1901 by the Platt Amendment, which extended the United States' sphere of influence over Cuba. Under the Platt Amendment, the United States had the right to override decisions made by the Cuban government and directly intervene if Cuba became unstable. It also granted the United States territorial rights in the Guantanamo Bay Naval Base. The 1898 Treaty of Paris ended the Spanish-American War, causing Spain to relinquish its claims to most of its remaining colonial possessions. It gave Cuba its independence and gave the United States control of the Philippines, Puerto Rico, and Guam. The Hay-Bunau Treaty gave the United States control over the Panama Canal Zone.

364. (D) While Guam, the Philippines, and Puerto Rico were all acquired with the 1898 signing of the Treaty of Paris, Hawaii was annexed several years after a coup overthrew the ruling monarchy of Hawaii. American missionaries began to arrive in Hawaii in the 1820s, and by the 1850s, American sugar plantations began to dominate the islands' economy. By 1872, native Hawaiians were only a minority population on the island, and American business interests began to dominate the island's government. In 1893, the American business interests staged a revolution backed by the U.S. military, forcing Hawaii's last queen, Liliuokalani, to relinquish control and recognize the new government. While calls for the United States to formally annex the island began as early as 1894, they were rejected until 1898, when the administration of William McKinley formally annexed the territory.

365. (B) The Anti-Imperialist League began in New England following the start of the Spanish-American War in 1898. The league grew in size and included prominent Americans such as Mark Twain and William Jennings Bryan. The league's views were mixed between pragmatism (belief that an overseas empire would be too costly to maintain and require an expensive, enlarged military) and racism (worries that an overseas empire would lead to an influx of nonwhite immigrants). Other beliefs of anti-imperialists reflected more sentimental notions that American imperialism violated the self-determination of distant lands. In the end, however, America's business interests, with their need for new raw materials and expanded markets, won out, and the United States continued to expand its overseas possessions.

366. (B) Andrew Carnegie in 1901 authored the essay "The Gospel of Wealth," in which he argued that it is the responsibility of the rich to use their wealth to benefit society. He stated, "The man who dies rich dies disgraced," believing that it is wrong both to horde one's wealth and to squander it on frivolous things. He did not support distributing the money directly to charity organizations but instead favored directly controlling the use of the funds. He rejected the idea that money should be given directly to the poor, arguing instead that it should be for larger projects that would continue to benefit society. Carnegie's notion of this new type of charity can be seen in the nearly 2,800 libraries he funded.

367. (A) Booker T. Washington and W. E. B. DuBois were two influential leaders of the fight to obtain social equality for America's disenfranchised African-American policies. While they shared the same fight, they differed greatly in their envisioned methods. Washington called for accommodation, where African-Americans would "cast their bucket where they stood." While assimilation both socially and economically was his eventual goal, he focused first on social equality earned through the hard work of African-Americans. He believed that their primary focus should be in vocational education, and over time, future generations would rise up politically and economically. DuBois rejected this notion, which he referred to as the acceptance of "alleged inferiority of the Negro." He instead believed African-Americans should obtain a liberal arts education and pursue skilled professions, seeking immediate political and economic equality alongside social equality. This belief would later lead DuBois in his role in founding the Niagara Movement in 1905, when he stated, "We want to pull down nothing but we don't propose to be pulled down." He also later joined the NAACP and worked as the editor of its chief publication, *The Crisis*.

368. (C) W. E. B. DuBois and William Monroe Trotter began the Niagara Movement in 1905 to push for the end of the racial segregation and disenfranchisement of African-Americans. The organization also rejected the calls for accommodation made by black leaders such as Booker T. Washington. The Niagara Movement was eventually absorbed by the National Association for the Advancement of Colored People (NAACP) in 1911.

369. (A) The establishment of the NAACP in 1909 was probably the greatest achievement by African-Americans during the Progressive Era. Consisting of African-American leaders and white social justice reformers, it was created in response to the 1908 race riots in Springfield, Illinois. The organization established the mission to fight racial segregation and disenfranchisement of African-Americans in the courts. As the organization grew, it directly fought against Jim Crow laws. The NAACP's success was highlighted by the 1915 Supreme Court ruling in *Guinn v. United States*, which overturned practices that had kept African-Americans from being eligible to vote because of the Grandfather Clause, as well as the 1954 Supreme Court decision in *Brown v. Board of Education*, which helped overturn *Plessy v. Ferguson*, which had legalized the notion of "separate but equal."

370. (B) The 1896 Supreme Court decision in *Plessy v. Ferguson* upheld the constitutionality of racial segregation in public accommodations in what became known as the doctrine of "separate but equal." This allowed southern state governments to pass Jim Crow laws, which further disenfranchised African-Americans. The basis of *Plessy v. Ferguson* began when Homer Plessy, who was one-eighth black, challenged a Louisiana law that segregated railroad cars. Plessy argued that the segregated railroad cars violated his Thirteenth and

Fourteenth Amendment rights. The Supreme Court disagreed, stating that segregation was acceptable as long as equal accommodations were provided.

371. (D) During the 1836 presidential election, the Anti-Mason Party held the first nominating convention. Party supporters elected delegates who would attend the party convention and vote for the party candidate the electors supported. Soon after, the other major parties adopted the practice. During the Progressive Era, numerous additional reforms were made to the political system, giving the common person more access to government. Many states began to instate the initiative, which allowed average citizens to put bills before state legislatures. Furthermore, referendums, which gave citizens the right to vote directly on bills, became more common within state governments. Citizens were also given the power to remove elected officials from office with the recall. Finally, in 1904, Oregon began to elect its senators directly rather than having them chosen by the state legislature. In 1913, this practice became constitutional law with the ratification of the Seventeenth Amendment, which required all states to choose their senators through direct elections.

372. (C) Florence Kelley, the daughter of an influential Pennsylvania congressman, gained her own prominence as a leading reformer for workplace safety and against unsafe working conditions and child labor. In 1893, the governor of Illinois made Kelley the chief factory inspector for the state of Illinois, where she fought against child labor. In 1899, she joined the National Consumers' League, which fought to address the harsh conditions found in sweatshops. Furthermore, in 1907, she worked to sway opinion in the Supreme Court case *Muller v. Oregon*, which limited the maximum workday for female employees.

373. (A) The term *muckraking* was coined by President Theodore Roosevelt to describe the activity of investigative journalists who exposed corruption and inspired calls for reform during the Progressive Era. The term was derived from a character in the novel *Pilgrim's Progress* who spent his time mucking, or raking the filth from the floor, and never bothered to see the positive things around him. One example of a muckraking journalist was Ida Tarbell, whose *History of the Standard Oil Company* (1904) exposed the cutthroat business practices used by the Standard Oil Company to eliminate competition. Lincoln Steffens wrote *The Shame of Our Cities* (1904), which exposed municipal corruption and the ties between government and big business. Upton Sinclair's *The Jungle* (1906), besides being in part a manifesto for socialism, helped inspire the Food and Drug Act by illustrating the dangerous and unsanitary conditions in the meatpacking industry. Samuel Hopkins Adams's work "Drugs That Make Victims," published in *Collier's Weekly* in 1905, was an exposé on fraudulent medicines that often contained dangerous and addictive chemicals. His work helped inspire stricter regulation of pharmaceuticals.

374. (E) The 1908 case of *Muller v. Oregon* led to a landmark decision in labor history because it upheld the right of states to enforce limits on the hours a woman was required to work because of health-related reasons. The case was argued by future Supreme Court justice Louis Brandeis. Interestingly, a state law limiting working hours in New York was struck down in the 1905 *Lochner v. New York* decision. The 1917 *Bunting v. Oregon* decision extended *Muller v. Oregon* by allowing the state to limit the hours men worked as well.

375. (B) The Clayton Antitrust Act was passed in 1914 during the Wilson administration. The act gave the federal government greater strength in regulating business and controlling the formation of monopolies and trusts. The act directly defined illegal business conduct and practices such as companies issuing noncompetitive rebates and directors sitting on multiple boards of competing companies. It also gave the federal government the power to regulate mergers. Furthermore, unlike the earlier Sherman Antitrust Act, this law did not make labor unions and farm organizations subject to antitrust laws, so workers' rights to strike, boycott, and picket were made legal. Furthermore, injunctions were deemed illegal. This law marked a major step forward for organized labor, though World War I limited unions' further progress.

376. (C) Robert La Follette served as the governor of Wisconsin from 1901 to 1906. He was nicknamed "Fighting Bob" and was an advocate of progressive reform within his state. He fought against railroad trusts and corrupt political machines within his state. He later became a progressive leader in the Senate. Eugene V. Debs started as a labor organizer and later became a perennial presidential candidate for the Socialist Party. Samuel "Golden Rule" Jones was a progressive business leader who eventually became the mayor of Toledo, Ohio. As mayor, he fought to improve living conditions for working-class people within the city. He opened parks, reformed the municipal government, and instituted an eight-hour workday. Gifford Pinchot was the first head of the U.S. Forest Service. He helped President Theodore Roosevelt pursue his conservation policies, protecting the nation's natural resources.

377. (D) While Roosevelt did expand America's international influence through his corollary to the Monroe Doctrine and his mediation of the conflict between Russia and Japan, the Square Deal dealt only with his domestic program. Theodore Roosevelt announced his Square Deal in 1904. In the Square Deal, Roosevelt would pursue antitrust suits. Over the course of his presidency, he broke up nearly 44 trusts and monopolies. At the same time, Roosevelt wanted to protect business from extreme union demands. This was illustrated by his dealings with the United Mine Workers strike, where he addressed both the miners' and owners' concerns. By way of promoting consumer protection, Congress passed the Pure Food and Drug Act, creating the Food and Drug Administration (FDA), which allowed for the government to inspect meat products and outlawed the production, sale, or shipment of dangerous medicines. The Antiquities Act of 1906 and the expansion of national parks and monuments helped establish the precedent for future conservation activities.

378. (C) During the Roosevelt administration, Congress passed both the Elkins Act (1903) and the Hepburn Act (1906), increasing the federal government's ability to regulate the railroad industry. The Elkins Act forced railroads to notify the public if they changed their rates, and it made it illegal for railroads to offer or receive rebates. The Hepburn Act allowed the Interstate Commerce Commission (created under the Interstate Commerce Act of 1887) to set maximum rates for the railroads. It also limited the railroads' ability to give out free passes and forced them to adopt a uniform method of accounting.

379. (B) In 1908, Theodore Roosevelt handpicked William Taft to be his successor and continue his policies. One area in which Taft was successful in continuing Roosevelt's policies was in breaking up trusts. While Roosevelt distinguished good trusts from bad trusts, Taft actively went after all trusts that were in violation of the law. This created tensions when he pursued U.S. Steel, a trust allowed by Roosevelt. Overall, while Taft had many character traits that would make him ideal for his later role on the Supreme Court as a justice, he fell short of many of Roosevelt's expectations. His secretary of the interior, Richard Ballinger, sold many of the lands protected under Roosevelt's conservation program and fired Gifford Pinchot as head of the U.S. Forest Service. In foreign policy, Taft adopted what was called Dollar Diplomacy instead of Roosevelt's Big Stick Diplomacy. While Taft did not support women's suffrage, Roosevelt did not truly make it part of his platform either until he ran for president again (this time against Taft) in 1912 under his New Nationalism platform.

380. (B) The Federal Reserve was created under the 1913 Federal Reserve Act, which was passed to reorganize American banking by creating a decentralized private banking system under federal control. This new system addressed the pressing financial needs of the country at the time, which included moving credit out of eastern banking centers to make it more widely available, as well as better controlling the amount of money in circulation. Wilson did address the needs of farmers by signing the 1916 Farm Loan Act, which set up regional banks that could offer loans to farms at low interest. He also signed the Clayton Antitrust Act in 1914 to give the Federal Trade Commission (created under the Federal Trade Act) more power to enforce antitrust laws. The 1913 Underwood Tariff was significant because it marked the first substantial lowering of U.S. tariffs since the Civil War. From this point, the U.S. government's main source of revenue shifted from tariffs to money received through the federal income tax. The income tax had just been established as legal under the Sixteenth Amendment.

381. (C) While Roosevelt's platform of New Nationalism shared many similar ideas with Wilson's New Freedom, the two platforms differed in their views of how trusts should be dealt with. Wilson did not believe that trusts should be regulated; instead, they should be broken up. He argued that businesses should be made smaller, but government should not be made bigger in the process. However, both Roosevelt and Wilson believed in the importance of a strong president, as illustrated by the progressive reforms instituted by both Roosevelt and Wilson domestically, as well as their actions in foreign policy. Also, both Roosevelt and Wilson believed in lowering the tariffs, especially after Taft's poor dealing with the Payne-Aldrich Tariff of 1909, which further increased tariffs, hurting western farmers. Wilson's 1913 Underwood Tariff was the greatest lowering of federal tariffs since the Civil War.

382. (A) Jane Addams's Hull House was a settlement house founded in 1889. Located in a poor immigrant neighborhood in Chicago, it provided services and classes to the community to help immigrants succeed. Some of the services offered were English language courses, assistance to widows, and basic health services. While the house began as a limited operation, it expanded over time to occupy numerous buildings and increased its services to offer college extension courses, summer programs for children, and lectures on current issues.

383. (C) The 1911 fire at the Triangle Shirtwaist factory was one of the largest industrial disasters in New York City history. Nearly 150 men and women died in the fire. This high number was due to the common practice of locking factory workers inside the building during the workday to avoid theft and unnecessary breaks. In response to the fire, progressive reformers such as Frances Perkins pushed for increased workplace safety laws as well as the passage of workers' compensation laws. The fire also caused the International Ladies' Garment Workers' Union to increase in size and prominence as the union joined the fight for reform. Political machine bosses such as Al Smith, who was the Democratic presidential candidate in 1928, also joined the call to reform labor conditions in New York City factories.

384. (D) Susan B. Anthony was a prominent leader in social reforms during the 19th and early 20th centuries. She fought for women's suffrage and was arrested during the 1872 presidential election after she was caught illegally voting, even after she promised the arresting officer that she had voted for the Republican candidate. Earlier, she had worked with Elizabeth Cady Stanton in the temperance movement as well as for women's rights. She also worked with William Lloyd Garrison's American Anti-Slavery Society and alongside Frederick Douglass in his push for black suffrage. Margret Sanger, another advocate for women's rights, was arrested in 1916 for attempting to distribute birth control and other forms of contraception to women. Mother Jones, a prominent mining town mother, gained national prominence for organizing strikes for mining and railroad workers' unions in the 19th and early 20th centuries.

385. (B) While Taft was handpicked by Theodore Roosevelt to continue his progressive policies, Taft found himself unable to retain the support of progressive Republicans. This was illustrated by his support of the Payne-Aldrich Tariff of 1909. Originally, the bill was supposed to lower tariffs on certain goods coming into the country, but the bill was altered by Senator Nelson Aldrich, who removed many of the provisions reducing tariffs, and instead of lowering the nation's overall tariffs, it increased them. This went directly against Roosevelt's initial request. Taft's failure of leadership alienated many of the former supporters of Roosevelt and helped convince Roosevelt to run as a third-party candidate for president in 1912 as a member of the Bull-Moose or Progressive Party. The McKinley tariff, which hurt western farmers, along with the 1902 coal strike settled by Roosevelt, occurred prior to Taft's administration.

386. (C) Although George Washington Carver served as one of the Tuskegee Institute's best-known and most influential instructors, the school was founded by Booker T. Washington in 1881 to provide vocational training for African-Americans. Carver was an accomplished scientist, botanist, educator, and inventor who helped poor southern farmers grow cash crops that could yield a profit but also provide nourishment to the planters. This led him to successfully experiment and discover multiple industrial uses for the peanut, sweet potato, cashew, and numerous other crops. While these plants could be used as cash crops, they also provided an inexpensive high-protein diet for the poor farmers who could not afford a regular diet of meat. He also developed an improved method of crop rotation that would allow southern farmers to grow certain traditional crops without exhausting the soil as quickly, as well as a method of creating synthetic dyes from plants such as soybeans and peanuts, which allowed the United States to end its reliance on European-manufactured dyes. Early on, much of his work was not acknowledged, but by the 20th century, he had become a prominent leader within the international scientific community, becoming a member of the Royal Society of Arts in 1916.

Chapter 14

387. (D) Fascism is a political ideology that places the nation and its often autocratic leader above the individual citizen. It is often accompanied by fanatic nationalism and rejection of the socialist political ideology. In the wake of World War I, numerous European states began to adopt fascist regimes. After Italy received what it believed was an unfair deal with the Treaty of Versailles, Benito Mussolini rose to power and installed a fascist regime. It forcefully destroyed the socialist party and created a single-party authoritarian state. Hitler's rise to power through his Nazi Party in Germany also illustrates the creation of the fascist state in the years following the First World War. While the assassination of the Archduke Franz Ferdinand by Serbian nationalists in 1914 ultimately led to the first shots of the First World War, numerous underpinnings served as the "long fuse" that created the environment for the largest military conflict in history to that point. The rise of imperialism during the 19th century, as illustrated by the race to Africa and the partitioning of Asian markets, created tensions among European nations. One expression of these tensions was the First and Second Moroccan Crisis, in which Germany attempted to intervene in French-held Morocco. To better control and protect their empires, nations created large armies and navies. These large militaries were made possible by an increase in populations as well as by factories, which made mass production possible. Furthermore, nations began to create interconnected secret alliances for military protection, as well as to isolate rival powers. After the assassination of the Austrian archduke, other nations were brought into a conflict that did not directly concern them. Finally, jingoism, or extreme nationalism, created immense patriotism that fueled popular support for wars.

388. (B) Interwoven treaties brought the major nations of Europe into the First World War, while the United States' policy in the early 20th century still in many ways followed George Washington's call to avoid creation of intertwining treaties. Wilson was elected in 1916 in part because of the notion that he had kept the nation out of war. In doing so, he hoped he could lead the peace following the conflict. This is illustrated through Wilson's Fourteen Points, which laid out his plans for maintaining international peace. Neutrality was also initially important because the U.S. population consisted of people from all nations. Ethnic Germans and Irish supported the Central Powers (Germany, Austria, and the Ottoman Empire), while Slavic peoples supported the Allies (Great Britain, Russia, and France). Furthermore, the connection of a common language caused others to support Britain and its allies. Businesses also found it profitable to maintain neutrality because it allowed them to openly trade with both sides of the conflict.

389. (B) In 1915, the passenger ship *Lusitania* was sunk by German submarines, killing 128 Americans. Wilson called the action an act of barbarism but continued his push to keep the United States out of war. He demanded the end to the unrestricted use of submarine warfare. Eventually, in March 1916, after the sinking of the passenger ship *Sussex*, Germany issued the Sussex Pledge, stating three important promises: (1) German submarines would no longer target passenger ships; (2) merchant ships would not be attacked unless they were known to be carrying weapons; and (3) provisions would be made for personnel and passengers of merchant ships to get off the ship safely prior to its destruction. Germany's resumption of unrestricted submarine warfare in January 1917 and interception of the Zimmerman Telegram, which outlined an attempted alliance with Mexico against the United States, eventually led the Americans to enter the war against Germany on April 6, 1917. Wilson issued his Fourteen Points on January 8, 1918, after the United States had entered the war, to assure the American people that the United States had entered the conflict for moral reasons and to guide the world to postwar peace.

390. (B) On January 22, 1917, President Wilson made one last attempt to call for the end of the First World War with a "peace without victory." Germany had recently begun to make considerable gains in the fighting in Europe, and on January 31, 1917, Germany announced it would resume unrestricted submarine warfare. The announcement led Italy to join the Allied forces, because it was worried that it would lose access to the Adriatic Sea. This use of unrestricted submarine warfare would also challenge the naval blockade Britain had had in place since 1915. For the United States, the use of unrestricted submarine warfare gave the nation little choice but to go to war, but Wilson waited for an "actual overt act" to take place. This act occurred when German submarines sunk seven unarmed American merchant ships and British intelligence agents intercepted the Zimmerman Telegram, which called for Mexico to ally with Germany against the United States (see answer to question 389).

391. (C) John J. Pershing was appointed commander in chief of the American Expeditionary Force in 1917 and led the American troops during the First World War. During that time, he obtained the rank of General of the Armies, the highest rank to be awarded to a member of the U.S. Army. Nicknamed "Black Jack," he earned a strong reputation as a leader, and his actions guided many generals during the Second World War, including Eisenhower, who led the invasion of Normandy and served as the Supreme Allied Commander. Before leading the American Expeditionary Force, Pershing served in the Spanish-American War and the Philippine-American War, and he led the ill-fated expedition into Mexico to capture Pancho Villa during the Mexican Revolution. Ferdinand Foch, a French marshal, served as the commander of all Allied troops during World War I, but Pershing convinced Foch to have the American troops fight as a separate army and not be put under the command of a foreign government. Field Marshal Douglas Haig led the British Expeditionary Force throughout World War I. Smedley Butler was a U.S. Marine during the First World War, though while stationed in Europe, he was not directly involved in the fighting. After the war, he advocated for the Bonus Army at the start of the Great Depression.

392. (C) The Great Migration during the First World War refers to the mass migration of African-Americans from the South to cities in the North and Midwest. Between 1910 and 1920, nearly 1.75 million individuals relocated. The reason for this migration was the increased demand for factory workers, especially in war industries. An example of new access to industrial jobs was Ford's opening of his factories to African-American employees in 1914. Furthermore, the southern agricultural economy was experiencing an extended period of agricultural decline. Matters were made worse by the boll weevil, an insect that decimated southern crops. Finally, many African-Americans had become fed up with the continued discrimination and segregation that had become institutionalized in the southern states. However, these new immigrants in the North were often faced with extreme prejudice in their new homes as well. The competition with white workers for jobs created tensions that often erupted into violence, as illustrated by the 1919 Chicago race riot, in which 38 people were killed and 520 injured. This migration did help the formulation of cultural movements such as the Harlem Renaissance and allowed the early civil rights movement to expand.

393. (C) On November 11, 1918, the fighting in World War I officially ceased. Yet the challenges created by the conflict were by no means over. By 1919, nearly 4,000 American servicemen were returning home per day, yet the government had made no plans to help them merge back into society. With wartime production slowing, government regulation of industries ending, and the job positions filled during the war, the nation faced massive job shortages. Women, who had played a major role in the war industries during the conflict, were pressured to resign or were fired to free up positions for returning men. Returning white soldiers found they had been replaced in their civilian jobs by African-Americans. The resulting economic recession marred the first part of the 1920s and further fueled racial tensions within the United States.

394. (D) In May 1917, the U.S. government passed the Selective Service Act, authorizing a draft of young men to fill the shortage of soldiers needed for military service. After the United States initially declared war on Germany, the U.S. military was still relatively small, and only roughly 32,000 new soldiers had enlisted. When General Pershing arrived in Europe with America's initial force, he quickly realized that many more soldiers would be required. The Selective Service Act required that all men ages 21 to 30 register for military service, and the following year, the requirement was extended to include all men 18 to 45. In a departure from earlier uses of the draft, such as during the Civil War, the men called to service could not hire a substitute. Furthermore, while the Civil War draft led to massive riots, the World War I draft met with relatively little resistance; it generally had great support.

395. (B) As part of Wilson's Fourteen Points for creating peace after World War I, he called for the creation of the League of Nations. The league was to be an organization that would represent the countries of the world and help ensure security and peace among its member states. Many in the United States rejected the idea of the league, feeling it would interfere with the independence of America's foreign policy. Article X in particular became a sticking point, especially for many Republican senators. The article stated that an attack on one member state would be considered an attack on all other members. The senators felt that this type of agreement could potentially drag the nation into another world war. Ultimately, the United States rejected membership in the League of Nations. Without the United States, and given Russia's rejection of membership, the league's success was greatly limited. Most notably, it was unable to prevent the Second World War. It did, however, serve as a working model for the later creation of the United Nations following World War II.

396. (A) The Battle of Château-Thierry took place on July 18, 1918, and was one of the earliest military actions of the American Expeditionary Force (AEF) under General John "Black Jack" Pershing. Prior to the battle, the German army had advanced its position to only 50 miles outside Paris. Russia's departure from the war following the Bolshevik Revolution freed up German soldiers who had previously been fighting on the eastern front, allowing them to increase their assault in the west. The arrival of fresh American troops, however, allowed the Allies to bolster their position and launch a massive counteroffensive as part of the second Marne Campaign. The combined forces of the Americans and French were able to break through the German line, eventually causing the German military to pull back, and Paris was saved from German occupation. While Château-Thierry is often called a turning point in the war, heavy fighting would continue until November of that year, and Americans would suffer over 250,000 casualties by the time an armistice was signed.

397. (E) The War Industry Board was created on July 28, 1917, after the United States had declared war on Germany and its allies. In January 1918, it was reorganized under the direction of Bernard M. Baruch. The major focus of the board was to coordinate the purchase of war supplies, set price controls at wholesale levels, and mediate between labor and business to avoid strikes. Another agency set up during the war was the Food Administration, which was created under the Lever Food and Control Act and led by Herbert Hoover. His task was to ensure the production of food. He fixed the price of American grains, which greatly bolstered the income of American farmers. His work in this agency gained him national prominence as a great pragmatist, which eventually won him the presidency. The Lever Food and Control Act also created the Fuel Administration, which instituted daylight savings time to reduce the use of lamp oil during the summer months. The government also created the Committee of Public Information (CPI), which was headed by the journalist George Creel. The CPI had the job of ensuring public support for the war through films, speeches, radios, and other uses of media. The CPI also held massive rallies to promote the sale of war bonds, which helped finance the war. In 1917 and 1918, the government also passed the Espionage and Sedition Acts, which were designed to quell vocal opposition to the war.

398. (B) The Espionage Act, passed in 1917, made it a crime to interfere with military operations and recruitment. It also outlawed acts that promoted insubordination within the military or any other action that might support America's enemies during the war. In 1918, this law was amended to include the Sedition Act, which prohibited many forms of speech that were considered derogatory toward the government or the military. Eugene V. Debs, a labor organizer and perennial socialist presidential candidate, was arrested for violating this act in 1918 for giving a fiery speech against the draft. He was sentenced to 10 years in prison but was pardoned after 3 years by President Harding.

399. (D) On January 8, 1918, Woodrow Wilson issued his Fourteen Points, which illustrated the president's vision for sustained peace following the First World War. The Fourteen Points addressed what Wilson believed to be the causes of the war, promoted self-determination among nations, and created the League of Nations to help maintain peace and security in the postwar world. The league would prevent future conflicts through disarmament agreements, peacefully resolving disputes between members and working for the common defense of member states. The league was ultimately rejected by the United States over concerns that it would interfere with American independence in its foreign policy and possibly drag the nation unwillingly into future European conflicts. While the league ultimately failed, it served as a prototype for the future United Nations.

400. (B) During the 1920 presidential election, the Republicans had an excellent chance of victory. The Wilson administration was blamed for problems left from the First World War, which included abuses of civil liberties under the Espionage and Sedition Acts, the League of Nations controversy, and the strikes and inflation that followed the war. Warren G. Harding was nominated as the Republican candidate for president, and Governor Calvin Coolidge of Massachusetts was the vice presidential nominee. Their platform opposed the League of Nations and promised low taxes and high protective tariffs. They also called for restrictions on immigration to achieve what Harding called a return to normalcy. The actions illustrated the move toward isolationism and the pro-business environment that would define the three Republican administrations of the 1920s.

401. (C) From November 1919 through January 1920, the U.S. Department of Justice attempted to capture and deport what they saw as leftist radicals and anarchists. These raids, led by Attorney General Mitchell Palmer, were in the context of the greater Red Scare (fear of communist and socialist subversion) taking place within the nation. This Red Scare was triggered in part by the Russian Revolution of 1917, as well as by tensions with organized labor following the First World War, as illustrated by the strike and bombing plots in Seattle during 1919. Palmer set up a special force to monitor and arrest those suspected of being against the U.S. government, especially those accused of being communists, socialists, or anarchists. On January 2, 1920, federal agents stationed in more than 33 cities arrested several thousand people suspected of having radical or leftist beliefs. The Red Scare and the Palmer Raids began to lose momentum by May 1920, and many of those arrested were ordered to be released.

402. (D) The United States faced a severe recession from mid-1920 until 1921. However, the economy improved rapidly in 1922 and remained strong until 1929. Unlike earlier boom periods, which had involved large expenditures for capital investments such as railroads, the prosperity of the 1920s depended on the sale of consumer goods. Purchases of costly items such as cars, refrigerators, and a myriad of electric gadgets were made possible by credit allowing installment or time payment. The idea of credit or the installment plan was not new, but the availability of credit was greatly expanded during the 1920s. Other trends contributing to the high consumer sales that helped fuel the economic prosperity of the 1920s were improved wages, heavy advertising, and an increased market of newer products at lower costs.

403. (B) The Supreme Court's *Schenck v. United States* decision of 1919 upheld the constitutionality of the 1917 Espionage Act, stating in an opinion written by Oliver Wendell Holmes Jr. that speech presenting a "clear and present danger" is not protected under the First Amendment. The case was in response to the arrest of Charles Schenck, who violated the Espionage Act by mailing leaflets to people in an attempt to interfere with the government's efforts under the Selective Service Act. Holmes argued that Congress has a right to protect society from words that could cause needless endangerment of the greater population, such as falsely shouting "Fire!" in a crowded theater. The *Schenck* decision was modified by the 1969 *Brandenburg v. Ohio* decision, which stated that the government cannot punish subversive speech unless it directly incites a lawless act or crime. The *Brandenburg* decision also states that First Amendment rights also protect the rights of subversive groups such as the Ku Klux Klan. "Separate but equal" was constitutional in the *Plessy v. Ferguson* decision in 1896, but that decision was repudiated by the 1954 decision in *Brown v. Board of Education*.

404. (B) The 1920s were a period where the ideas of isolationism and nativism became once again prominent. Though the Ku Klux Klan had been mostly wiped out during Reconstruction, it began to reemerge starting in 1915. Yet unlike the organization of the late 19th century, the new Klan used modern recruitment and funding techniques and expanded greatly in size. Also, it was no longer isolated to the South but dominated politics in northern states such as Indiana. Furthermore, the targets of this hate group were no longer just African-Americans. The group also began terrorizing Catholic and Jewish communities, along with immigrant populations. The activities of the Klan began to decline after the leader of the Indiana Klan was found guilty of raping a minor in 1925. The National Origins Act further illustrated nativist feelings during the 1920s. The law, passed in 1924, established the first permanent limitation on immigration into the United States and established the first quota system based on national origin. While many of the American policies during the 1920s illustrated isolationism and nativism, other actions, such as the Washington Naval Conference and the Kellogg-Briand Pact, were attempts to maintain peace through international agreements. The Volstead Act of 1918 and the Eighteenth Amendment, ratified in 1919, illustrated the final success of the temperance movement to outlaw the general consumption of alcohol.

405. **(E)** During the 1920s, Harlem became the epicenter for an artistic and literary awakening among the African-American population that has become known as the Harlem Renaissance. In the decades from 1914 to 1929, the population of African-Americans living in the Harlem area of New York City grew to nearly 200,000. Jazz musicians such as Duke Ellington and Louis Armstrong, poets such as Langston Hughes, and writers such as Alain Locke created works that celebrated the African-American culture and greatly influenced American society as a whole.

406. **(D)** Sacco and Vanzetti were immigrants from Italy who were also believed to be anarchists. In 1920, they were convicted of killing two men during an armed robbery in Massachusetts. In 1927, they were executed for the crime. Many critics at the time believed that the authorities and the decisions in the trial were strongly influenced by prejudice against immigrants and fears of subversives brought about by the Red Scare. The execution of the two men was protested internationally as well as within the United States.

407. **(B)** In 1924, Congress passed the Fordney-McCumber Tariff, which raised America's protective tariffs on imports from other nations to historically high levels. The Hawley-Smoot Tariff (1930) increased these levels further. This hurt Europe's ability to pay off its debts, because it became nearly impossible to raise money by exporting goods to the United States. Furthermore, many European nations responded by passing retaliatory tariffs that made it difficult to sell American goods abroad. As a result, international trade declined drastically, leading to the economic instability that resulted in the prolonged global depression of the 1930s. The tariffs further hurt farmers because prices of manufactured goods increased at the same time it became harder for them to sell agricultural products to foreign markets. Consequently, much of the financial prosperity of the 1920s would never be realized by midwestern farmers.

408. **(A)** The Kellogg-Briand Pact, signed in 1928, prohibited the use of war except in matters of self-defense. The idea was originally drafted by Secretary of State Frank B. Kellogg and French foreign minister Aristide Briand. Fifteen nations initially signed the pact, and later they were joined by 60 additional countries. The pact's assertion of outlawing war was idealistic, and it eventually proved ineffective as the underpinnings to the Second World War emerged in the late 1930s. The 1921 Washington Conference resulted in three disarmament treaties (the Four-Power Treaty, the Five-Power Treaty or Washington Naval Treaty, and the Nine-Power Treaty), which limited the size of the world's largest navies. Starting with Herbert Hoover, but most notably championed by Franklin Roosevelt, America adopted the Good Neighbor Policy toward Latin America. Under the Good Neighbor Policy, the United States would promote security and peace within the Western Hemisphere through nonmilitary means. See answer to question 410 for background about the Nineteenth Amendment.

409. (C) Horizontal integration is a business strategy in which one company takes over other businesses within the same industry. Henry Ford used this strategy to dominate the industry during the 1920s. General Motors and Chrysler also practiced this model, creating the big three automotive companies during the 1920s. By 1929, the three companies produced 83 percent of all American vehicles. Ford also helped his company expand rapidly during the 1920s by greatly improving the automated assembly line. Though he strongly resisted unions in his factories, he did open the doors to African-American workers in 1914.

410. (D) The Nineteenth Amendment, ratified on August 18, 1920, prohibited the federal or state government from denying a citizen's right to vote based on gender. The ratification of this amendment marked the final success for many of the suffrage movements that had worked for the right to vote since the early 19th century. The Eighteenth Amendment, ratified on January 16, 1919, along with the Early Volstead Act, fulfilled the goals of the temperance movement by outlawing the general sale and consumption of alcohol. This amendment was repealed with the ratification of the Twenty-First Amendment on December 5, 1933. The Sixteenth Amendment, ratified on February 3, 1913, allowed for the creation of a federal income tax, and the Seventeenth Amendment, adopted on April 8, 1913, stipulated that all states would choose senators through direct elections.

411. (A) The 1925 Scopes Trial illustrated the debate over conservative and fundamentalist religious beliefs verses modern scientific notions of human evolution and natural selection. The trial occurred after a teacher named John Scopes challenged a Tennessee law that banned the teaching of evolution in public schools. The nationally acclaimed lawyer Clarence Darrow defended Scopes against the state's representation by the famous politician William Jennings Bryan. Though Scopes lost the case, the media circus surrounding it brought the struggle between traditional values and modern beliefs to the national level.

412. (D) The Teapot Dome Scandal involved President Harding's secretary of the interior, Albert Fall, who was accused of illegally leasing an American petroleum reserve to a private company. This was seen as one of the nation's largest scandals prior to the Watergate Scandal, during the Nixon administration, and it was one of many that tarnished Harding's administration. Some also believe that the strain of these scandals may have contributed to the heart problems that led to Harding's early death in 1923. The execution of Sacco and Vanzetti in 1927 did create a national controversy, but it occurred after Harding's death. See the answer to question 306 for information on the Crédit Mobilier Scandal, Whiskey Ring Scandal, and Star Route Scandal.

413. (C) The notion of the Lost Generation was first coined by author and poet Gertrude Stein and was later popularized by Ernest Hemingway in his novel *The Sun Also Rises*. This group of authors had become disillusioned by the First World War and its aftermath, rejecting many aspects of American culture. Many authors in this movement went so far as to live as expatriates in Europe, most notably Paris. Authors in this movement included Ernest Hemingway, F. Scott Fitzgerald, and John Steinbeck. The Harlem Renaissance was an artistic, literary, and social emergence of African-American culture during the 1920s that was focused in Harlem, New York. The Beat Generation refers to American authors who emerged after the Second World War and were prominent during the 1950s. Central elements of their work include a rejection of materialism, drug experimentation, and sexuality. Romanticism and transcendentalism were movements of the 19th century.

414. (C) In 1928, the Republican candidate, Herbert Hoover, easily won the election against the Democratic candidate, Al Smith. Many Americans were suspicious of Smith, the former governor of New York, because he was Catholic and spoke with a distinct New York accent. Many feared that because Smith was Catholic, he would take orders from the pope, which would hurt American sovereignty. Smith also called for the repeal of Prohibition, a view that was unpopular to many conservatives. Hoover, in contrast, was extremely popular and nationally known as a great pragmatist for his role in providing aid to Europe following the First World War. Hoover campaigned on the notion of continued prosperity based on the Republican platforms that defined the decade.

Chapter 15

415. (D) October 29, 1929, has become known as Black Tuesday because nearly 16.5 million shares of stock investments were hurriedly sold, causing the market to plummet. Prior to that day, bankers attempted to pool their money to buy enough stock to stabilize the increasingly volatile markets. Despite their efforts, the market continued to crash. Numerous factors are blamed for the crash. Some economists see high tariffs of the 1920s and failed policies of the Federal Reserve as major catalysts of the crash. Others blame the practice of buying on margin (buying stocks with loaned money) as a major cause because it artificially inflated stock prices. Still others blame irresponsible banking practices mixed with a decline in consumer spending.

416. (C) The Dust Bowl occurred in the Midwest from 1931 to 1940. It resulted from intensive farming practices that stripped the ground of the prairie grasses. When a massive drought hit and crops failed to grow, high winds sweeping over the plains carried off much of the remaining soil into massive dust clouds. These storms became known as "black blizzards" that reached as far as the East Coast. Nearly 60 percent of midwestern farmers lost their farms during this period, many migrating to California to find work as agricultural laborers. John Steinbeck captured the plight of these displaced farm families in his celebrated novel *The Grapes of Wrath*.

417. (B) Many of the federal relief programs developed during the Depression furthered racial segregation in the country. African-Americans often found themselves barred from professional and skilled-labor job opportunities. The Social Security Act, passed in 1935, excluded farmers and domestic workers, an area of employment that contained a majority of African-American workers. Furthermore, policies during the Depression did little to address discrimination in private businesses. White businesses would often fire minority workers to open job opportunities for whites. Roosevelt, who appointed numerous African-Americans to midlevel government posts and created an unofficial "Black Cabinet," rejected anti-lynching laws and the banning of poll taxes. A. Philip Randolph, an influential civil rights leader, did convince Roosevelt to create the Fair Employment Practices Committee, which enforced a ban on discriminatory hiring in the federal government and in corporations that received federal contracts.

418. (D) When the market crashed in 1929, Hoover believed the key to recovery was a renewal of confidence in the economy. He felt the best way to address the economic conditions was through the voluntary controls put into place by private businesses. He organized a meeting of the nation's economic leaders at which they promised to maintain wages and employment. However, as the economy worsened, this plan failed. Hoover also attempted to protect American businesses by signing the Hawley-Smoot Tariff into law in 1930. This protective tariff, the highest in the nation's history, ended up further stifling international trade, which worsened the Depression. He also established the Reconstruction Finance Corporation in 1932 to prop up large corporations and banks. Despite these efforts, banks continued to fail, and unemployment rose.

419. (A) During the summer of 1932, nearly 20,000 veterans of the First World War and their families gathered in Washington, D.C., to ask for the immediate payment of a pension bonus they had been promised. The pension was not to become available until 1945, but the marchers found themselves unemployed and penniless following the stock market crash and ongoing Depression. The House of Representatives agreed to their request, but the Senate firmly stood against it. While some of the marchers left, many stayed and established "Hoovervilles," shacks constructed of cardboard and scrap metal. General Douglas MacArthur was ordered by Hoover to remove the Bonus Army. MacArthur used force to do so, and many of the veterans were injured. This image of excessive force being used against downtrodden veterans of the U.S. military contributed to Franklin Roosevelt's landslide election in 1932.

420. (B) The Reconstruction Finance Corporation (RFC) was established by Herbert Hoover in 1932 to provide credit to banks, railroads, farm mortgage associations, and other businesses to prevent further failures and collapse in these areas of the economy. The other goals refer to programs that were part of Franklin Roosevelt's First and Second New Deal. The program that provided relief to homeowners facing foreclosure was the 1933 Home Owners' Loan Corporation (HOLC), which offered low-cost mortgage refinancing. The program that attempted to increase the prices of agricultural goods by paying farmers to produce less was the Agricultural Adjustment Administration, also created in 1933. Several programs provided work relief for the unemployed by hiring them to complete public works projects such as roads and buildings and by funding arts programs; these programs included the Civilian Works Administration, Public Works Administration, and Works Progress Administration. To provide old-age pensions, disability payments, and unemployment benefits, the government established the Social Security Administration in 1935.

421. (B) The election of 1932 marked a significant change in the way Americans viewed the role of government and the individual citizen. Hoover himself stated in 1932 that the election would be a "contest between two philosophies in government": Hoover's belief that the federal government could not and should not try to fix the average citizen's problems, versus Roosevelt's view that the Great Depression could be solved only through direct government action in the form of far-reaching programs and direct relief. Hoover's attempt to address the Depression through limited assistance and voluntary self-regulation of business seemed to fail, so Roosevelt was elected in a landslide, promising the nation a New Deal. The New Deal consisted of a wide range of government relief programs, new regulations, and recovery acts that affected all aspects of American business and society.

422. (B) The practice of buying on margin was a system where investors could purchase a stock at a fraction of its actual price and borrow money to cover the rest of the stock's cost. Brokers could charge high rates of interest and at any time could demand full payment for the remainder of the money owed. If the stock price rose, the investor could sell the stock, repay the money, and still make a profit. If the stock price declined, however, investors were still responsible to repay the broker.

423. (C) The National Recovery Administration (NRA) was established in June 1933 as part of the National Industrial Recovery Act (NIRA). The purpose of this New Deal agency was to respond to the decline of industrial prices, the failure of many businesses, and the corresponding unemployment. The agency established industry codes to ensure fair business practices and regulated wages, working conditions, and working hours. The agency's symbol was the Blue Eagle, and businesses that participated with the NRA placed Blue Eagle posters in their storefronts. However, the Supreme Court's 1935 decision in *Schechter v. United States* declared the program unconstitutional, and NIRA was replaced by the National Labor Relations Act, which shifted government support to unions. The Civilian Conservation Corps and the Works Progress Administration provided direct relief to America's unemployed by offering government jobs in federal works projects. The Home Owners' Loan Corporation offered relief to homeowners by allowing them to refinance their mortgages at a lower cost to avoid foreclosure. The Tennessee Valley Authority developed the Tennessee Valley and brought electricity into the region.

424. (B) The "Brain Trust" was the nickname given to President Roosevelt's unofficial advisers, whom he assembled during his campaign. They included prominent academics and leaders of business such as economist Rexford Tugwell and political scientist Raymond Moley.

425. (A) In 1935, President Franklin Roosevelt launched what has become known as his Second New Deal, or Second Hundred Days in part to respond to his critics who stated he had not done enough for the average citizen's welfare. This was clearly illustrated through the 1935 Social Security Act, which established the Social Security system. Under this system, the government would provide support to those unable to support themselves. It included old-age pensions, unemployment insurance, and aid for the disabled. Furthermore, programs under the Second New Deal imposed tighter controls on business and gave more support to unions, as illustrated by the 1835 Wagner Act. This legislation protected union practices such as collective bargaining while outlawing spying on union activity and blacklisting union members. The Second New Deal also offered further job relief for the poor, such as the Works Progress Administration, which provided government jobs to nearly eight million adults, and the National Youth Administration, which offered education, recreation, employment, and counseling for young adults (ages 16 to 25). The Second New Deal, like the first, had many critics. The Revenue Act of 1935 was also called the Wealth Tax because it created a series of higher taxes on the rich. Other acts, such as the Tennessee Valley Project, were seen as socialist. A large number of critics saw both New Deals as an overexpansion of government. Meanwhile, other critics said the two New Deals did not go far enough in improving the lives of the poor, women, and minorities.

426. (E) Upton Sinclair, the muckraking author of *The Jungle*, and Huey "Kingfish" Long, a senator from Louisiana, initially supported Roosevelt's rise to the presidency. Yet they soon began to rally against the president because they felt he did too little to address the needs of the poor or address the imbalance of wealth in the nation. Sinclair, in his bid for the governorship of California, called for higher inheritance and income taxes as well as pensions for the elderly. Huey Long called for a minimum income for all families of $5,000, paid for by dividing up the wealth of millionaires. Long was considered a possible challenger for the presidency in 1936 but was shot and killed at the Louisiana statehouse in 1935. Another notable critic of Roosevelt's New Deal was Father Charles Coughlin, a radio evangelist, who used his weekly broadcasts to openly criticize the president's policies. He held a strong stance against international banking and called for nationalizing banks, utilities, and natural resources. Not all critics supported nationalization and redistribution of wealth. William Randolph Hearst, a onetime supporter of the Democratic Party, criticized Roosevelt's heavy taxes on the wealthy and the inheritance tax. Other politicians, including Robert Taft, the Republican senator from Ohio, saw the New Deal as creeping socialism. The American Liberty League, which emerged in 1934, spearheaded much of the New Deal opposition. The league was headed by Alfred Smith, the former Democratic challenger to Herbert Hoover. It included numerous heads of business and politicians, who argued that the New Deal violated the Constitution and was leading the nation to Bolshevism.

427. (A) During the 1920s and 1930s, the famous British economist John Maynard Keynes argued that the government could best address economic crises such as the Depression through spending. He felt that if the government gave money to consumers, either with direct government payments or indirectly through government jobs, people would purchase more consumer goods, and the economy would begin to grow. This idea is the basis for what is called Keynesian economics and also has been referred to as pump priming. Later, during Ronald Reagan's presidency, this theory was rejected, and the idea of supply-side economics was adopted. Under this theory, also known as trickle-down economics, the government should cut taxes to businesses and investors, allowing the businesses to expand and hire more workers, thereby allowing the economy to grow.

428. (A) While the New Deal programs were often racially discriminatory, Roosevelt often sought the advice of African-American public-policy advisers, often called the "Black Cabinet" or the Federal Council of Negro Affairs. The cabinet focused on civil rights and racial inequality. However, Roosevelt, not wanting to alienate southern Democrats, declined to support anti-lynching legislation or bans of the poll tax in the South. Members of the Black Cabinet included Dr. Robert Weaver, a Harvard economist who advised on race relations. In 1966, Weaver became the first black cabinet member, serving under Lyndon Johnson as secretary of housing and urban development.

429. (D) In 1933, Frances Perkins was appointed secretary of labor, making her the first American female to hold a position in the presidential cabinet. Perkins had gained notoriety earlier as a leader of the New York Consumers League, where in response to the Triangle Shirtwaist factory fire in 1910, she fought for improved conditions and working hours. Fiercely loyal to Roosevelt, she and Interior Secretary Harold Ickes were the only cabinet members of the Roosevelt administration who served for his entire presidency. The photographer famous for capturing images of families displaced by the Depression was Dorothea Lange, who became one of America's most highly regarded photographers. The first African-American to hold a cabinet position was Dr. Robert Weaver, who was appointed secretary of housing and urban development in 1966 under Lyndon B. Johnson. Eleanor Roosevelt, the wife of President Franklin Roosevelt, arranged to have the great concert singer Marian Anderson perform in front of the Lincoln Memorial after the Daughters of the American Revolution refused to let her sing in Constitution Hall, located in Washington D.C., because she was black.

430. (C) The Lend-Lease Program began in March 1941 with the passage of the Lend-Lease Act. Its intent was to allow the U.S. government to lend, lease, or sell military supplies and defense aids to any nation that the United States deemed vital for the defense of America. Roosevelt compared the policy to lending a hose to a neighbor if one saw that the neighbor's house was on fire. During the war, nearly $50 billion in goods were appropriated to this program. Aid was initially offered to Britain and France. Later, the Soviet Union was also permitted to take part in the program after it entered the war following Hitler's June 22, 1941, invasion of nearly three million men crossing the German-Soviet border. While economic recovery was not initially the program's intent, the increased wartime production that was in part due to the Lend-Lease Program helped to pull the United States out of the Great Depression. In September 1939, prior to the start of the Second World War, the United States was already providing aid to protect democratic governments on the European continent. During the Spanish Civil War, the United States provided non-weapon goods to the republican government's Loyalists against Franco's fascist uprising on what was called a *cash and carry* basis. This was done with the passage of the Third Neutrality Act in May of 1937.

431. (B) The Atlantic Charter was an agreement signed by President Franklin Roosevelt and the British prime minister on August 14, 1941, off the coast of Newfoundland on a battleship. The document was drafted secretly and contained several main principles that outlined the two nations' war aims. They included that neither nation would pursue territorial expansion during the conflict, no territorial changes would be made without the agreement of the region's inhabitants, and both nations would promote self-determination for all people, free trade, promotion of better future cooperation between nations to avoid aggression, and the disarmament of the aggressor nations. Within 15 months after the Atlantic Charter's release, 15 other nations endorsed the document. This is similar in many ways to the principles of the Fourteen Points issued by Woodrow Wilson as the United States entered the First World War. Furthermore, the Atlantic Charter later served as the basis for the formation of the United Nations after the Second World War.

432. (E) In response to the 1931 Japanese invasion of the iron- and coal-rich Chinese province of Manchuria, the United States issued the Stimson Doctrine. The doctrine stated that the United States would not recognize any territorial gains taken by force. The doctrine had little effect on Japanese policy. The Japanese proceeded to set up a puppet government in Manchuria. When the League of Nations protested, Japan withdrew from the organization. Japan then violated the 1922 Five Powers Treaty and began to enlarge its navy. After Japan forced the Vichy government (the puppet government established in France by Germany) to allow it to construct military bases in southern Indochina (modern-day Vietnam) in 1941, Roosevelt froze all Japanese assets within the United States. Japan responded by doing the same to U.S. assets in Japan. This brought trade between the two nations to a halt. The United States ultimately declared war on the Japanese on December 7, 1941, after its planes bombed the U.S. naval base at Pearl Harbor. This action brought the United States into the Second World War. The Good Neighbor Policy refers to a program started by Coolidge and Hoover but most notably continued by Roosevelt. The Good Neighbor Policy, as announced at the conference of Latin American nations in 1933, aimed to end

American armed intervention in the region. The United States instituted this policy in 1934 by ending the Platt Amendment and withdrawing U.S. forces from Haiti. The first Neutrality Act, passed in 1935, was one of three neutrality acts passed before the United States' entrance into the Second World War. The act was written in response to the Italian invasion of Ethiopia. The first Neutrality Act stated that the United States would not sell or ship arms to nations involved in a conflict and warned U.S. citizens traveling to such regions that they did so at their own risk. The 1936 second Neutrality Act expanded the first to include prohibitions on loaning money or credit to warring nations. The third Neutrality Act, passed in 1937, gave the government more flexibility by allowing the president to permit the sale of non-war-related materials on a cash-and-carry basis. This was in response to the civil war in Spain, where fascist forces under General Francisco Franco overthrew the republican government in the summer of 1936.

433. (A) After Japan's successful attack on Pearl Harbor on December 7, 1941, the Japanese military began to absorb the islands of Guam, British-held Hong Kong, and Singapore. In the spring of 1942, the Japanese military defeated a combined force of American and Filipino troops. General Douglas MacArthur was forced to retreat from the island on March 10, 1942. At that point, he delivered his immortal promise, "I shall return," and escaped with his troops to Australia. MacArthur was true to his promise and launched his Philippines campaign in October 1944, securing the island nation with the conclusion of the war.

434. (B) Founded in 1940, the America First Committee (AFC) was one of the largest antiwar movements in American history. The committee used its massive membership to create a petition to force President Roosevelt to maintain neutrality. The group staunchly fought against the Lend-Lease Program and rejected the Atlantic Charter. Other goals of the organization further illustrate its isolationist ideals: the AFC supported heavily fortifying the United States by pursuing an impregnable system of defense, as well as ending all aid to warring nations. The AFC contained many notable members, including future president Gerald Ford, but the organization fell apart after the Japanese surprise attack at Pearl Harbor.

435. (C) The Nazi Party, which took control of Germany in 1933 under the leadership of Adolf Hitler, illustrates an extreme form of fascism. Though the party's full name was the National Socialist Workers' Party, it rejected the ideologies of socialism and communism. During the practice of genocide known as the Holocaust, the Nazi Party targeted known communists and socialists along with Jewish people and other groups Hitler deemed to be impure. Fascism is a political ideology characterized by the belief that the state is more important than the individual, and fascists usually support a strong, centralized government run by a dictator with absolute power. Benito Mussolini of Italy and Francisco Franco are other examples of fascist leaders during this period.

436. (B) The Office of War Mobilization was established to oversee and coordinate the nation's industrial production of war goods. This agency, headed by former Supreme Court justice James Byrnes, oversaw other government agencies such as the War Production Board, which decided what raw materials would be received by what industries. It limited the amount of gasoline and rubber that could be used, and it organized nationwide drives to collect scrap metals and even fats, which were used to make soap and lubricants. The government also established the Office of Price Administration (OPA) to prevent inflation. The OPA rationed consumer goods such as meats, shoes, butter, and coffee. The Selective

Training and Service Act was passed in 1940 to recruit men into the military. This action was taken more than a year prior to Pearl Harbor in response to the expansion of the global war. This made it the United States' first peacetime draft.

437. (A) Roosevelt's Executive Order 9066, dated February 19, 1942, gave the military the authority to relocate citizens of German and Italian descent to internment camps established within the United States. Japanese-Americans received the harshest treatment under this order; nearly 120,000 Japanese citizens and many Nisei (second-generation American-born U.S. citizens of Japanese descent) were taken from their homes and put into camps that lacked adequate resources and sanitation. The prohibition of wartime strikes was a result of Congress passing the Smith Connelly Act over Roosevelt's veto in 1943. The act stated that unions had to give 30 days' notice before striking and made it a federal crime to strike in an industry being run by the government. A. Philip Randolph convinced President Roosevelt to create the Fair Employment Practices Committee (FEPC), which banned discriminatory hiring in the federal government and in corporations that received federal contracts.

438. (D) The Battle of Midway, which took place between June 4 and 7, 1942, is considered to be one of the most important battles in the Pacific Theater and a turning point in the campaign. The U.S. Navy inflicted massive damage on the Japanese navy, decisively defeating them. During the battle, the Japanese lost four aircraft carriers, over 250 fighter planes, and a battleship that they were unable to replace during the duration of the war.

439. (A) Early in the war, the Allies decided that their forces would primarily focus on defeating Hitler in Europe and after that would use their combined military strength to crush the Japanese in the Pacific. The reason for this decision was concerns that Germany might be able to defeat the Soviet Union while simultaneously isolating Britain from the United States. After Germany was defeated, the Allied forces would use their combined strength to fight the Japanese to an unconditional surrender. The 1943 Tehran Conference held between the Big Three (Roosevelt, Stalin, and Churchill) formalized this agreement. During the conference, Stalin, the premier of the Soviet Union, agreed to formally declare war on Japan and coordinate the Soviet offensive alongside the British and American invasion of France.

440. (C) Following a coordinated Soviet offensive into Eastern Europe, the Allied forces on June 6, 1944, launched the largest amphibious assault in history, code-named Operation Overlord, on the beaches of Normandy, France. The planning for the assault began with the meeting of Roosevelt, Churchill, and Stalin during the 1943 Tehran Conference, and it was commanded by the supreme allied commander, Dwight Eisenhower. The beaches were stormed by 176,000 troops with the support of 4,000 landing craft, 600 warships, and nearly 11,000 planes. By July 4, nearly four million men had landed on the beachhead. To avoid German detection, the Allies set up a decoy invasion under the code name Operation Quicksilver, which was an attempt to trick the Germans into thinking the invasion would take place farther north in the French region of Pas-de-Calais. Operation Barbarossa was the code name for Germany's invasion of the Soviet Union in 1941. Over 4.5 million Axis troops stormed the Soviet border, making it the largest military operation in military history in both number of troops and total casualties. Over 1.5 million men died in the campaign. Operation Torch was the code name for the Allied invasion of North Africa that began on

November 8, 1942. Operation Cartwheel was the military strategy developed by General Douglas MacArthur in the Pacific Theater during the Second World War.

441. (C) The Manhattan Project was the code name given to the United States' development of an atomic bomb, which took three years and relied on the work of over 120,000 people, making it one of the largest government-funded research projects of all time. The idea was first set into motion in 1939, when physicist Albert Einstein wrote a letter describing the possibility of a new type of weapon that could be created by splitting uranium atoms. The first atomic bomb was tested on July 16, 1945, near Alamogordo, New Mexico, ushering in the Atomic Age. Later, two atomic bombs were used against Japan, one in Hiroshima (August 6, 1945) and the other in Nagasaki three days later. The bombs were used to force Japan into an unconditional surrender without an American-led invasion of the island nation. This marks the only time nuclear weapons have been used in direct warfare, and many people still debate the morality of the attack. Over 110,000 people were killed in the initial attack, and countless other survivors suffered from radiation poisoning.

442. (B) The Fair Employment Practices Committee (FEPC) was created by Franklin Roosevelt when he signed Executive Order 8802, which opened jobs and job training in defense plants to all Americans regardless of race. Under this order, the FEPC was also created to investigate complaints concerning discriminatory hiring in the federal government and in corporations that received federal contracts. The FEPC had only limited success because it lacked enforcement power, but it did bring the issue of combating discrimination to the highest national level. The executive order and the creation of the FEPC are credited to the civil rights leader A. Philip Randolph. He pressured the president into issuing the order to avoid a massive civil rights march on the nation's capital in 1941. The Congress of Racial Equality began in Chicago in 1942. It was an organization committed to promoting racial equality through nonviolent means. It would later pave the way for the postwar civil rights movement. The Women's Army Corps, which was started in 1941, marked the first time in American history that women could volunteer for the armed services, and over 200,000 women volunteered.

443. (D) Tehran, Yalta, and Potsdam were the sites of conferences where the Big Three—Roosevelt of the United States, Churchill of Britain, and Stalin of the Soviet Union—met to discuss the Allied strategy in World War II. Tehran, the earliest meeting of the three leaders, began in November 1943. At this conference, it was decided that the Allies would work together to defeat Hitler in Europe first and then concentrate on Japan. After this conference, the Soviet Union agreed to officially declare war on Japan, which it did on August 8, 1945. The Yalta Conference took place in February 1945. At Yalta, the Big Three laid out plans for postwar Europe, which included free general elections and the creation of the United Nations, where the United States, France, the Soviet Union, and China would be given permanent seats on the Security Council. The Soviet Union also furthered its pledge to support the Allies against Japan after Germany was defeated. The Allies also made plans to divide Germany into occupied zones. The Potsdam Conference began in July 1945. Stalin was the only member of the original Big Three to attend. Roosevelt had died of a stroke earlier, and Harry Truman succeeded him. Churchill was replaced by Clement Atlee as prime minister of Britain. During this conference, Truman ordered the use of the atomic bomb on Hiroshima and Nagasaki in Japan. This conference was fraught with disagreement. Stalin stated that he would not support free elections in Eastern Europe, and Poland's boundaries remained disputed. In many ways, this conference hinted at the tensions that would define the Cold War.

444. (A) On August 14, 1945, Emperor Hirohito contradicted key Japanese military leaders and agreed to an unconditional surrender. The formal surrender was signed on September 2, 1945, on the U.S. battleship *Missouri*. Japan at this time had experienced two devastating attacks on Hiroshima and Nagasaki, the deployment by the United States of the first and only atomic weapons ever used directly in combat. The terms of the surrender included the total disarmament of Japan, limitation of Japan's size to four main islands, and the occupation of the island nation until Japan proved it had fully adhered to the terms of the treaty.

Chapter 16

445. (D) In 1946, former British prime minister Winston Churchill gave a speech in Fulton, Missouri. He announced that an "iron curtain" had been spread across Europe, dividing the continent between free democratic nations and countries forced under authoritarian rule. This notion of a divided Europe was furthered in April 1949 with the creation of the North Atlantic Treaty Organization (NATO) by the democratic nations, and in 1955 with the formation of the Warsaw Pact by the Soviet Union and its satellite states. Presidents Truman and Eisenhower both instituted policies to address the threat of authoritarian states on the other side of the iron curtain through their administrations. The Truman Doctrine was created in 1947 to contain the spread of communism into Greece and Turkey. This policy was continued to protect other nations throughout the Cold War. Truman's secretary of state, George Marshall, unveiled his reconstruction plan for Europe (called the Marshall Plan) in part to strengthen European democracies in order to protect them from Soviet influence. Eisenhower's presidency also took on the fight against the spread of communism, adopting a policy of massive retaliation and the Eisenhower Doctrine, which attempted to keep Soviet influence out of the Middle East.

446. (A) George F. Kennan was a diplomat, stationed in Moscow, who wrote what has become known as the Long Telegram in 1946. In this telegram and a later essay entitled "The Sources of Soviet Conduct" (1947), he argued that the Soviet Union was expansionist and its influence needed to be contained. He especially stressed the containment of Soviet influence in areas that were of strategic importance to the United States. Kennan's idea of containment became the basis for the Truman Doctrine, issued in February 1947, and the Marshall Plan, announced in June of the same year. His notion of containment also influenced the formation of NATO in 1949, American military activities during the Korean and Vietnam Wars, U.S. policy toward Cuba after the rise of Castro, and other defining aspects of U.S. diplomacy throughout the Cold War.

447. (B) Following the Second World War, the United States adopted policies that were intended to help rebuild war-torn Europe, promote self-determination, and contain the spread of Soviet influence. After Great Britain announced in 1947 that it could no longer afford to aid the Greek government's fight against the communist insurgents, President Truman asked Congress for nearly $400 million in military and economic aid for Greece and Turkey. Truman stated that it was the duty of the United States to support free nations that were fighting to resist communist domination. The Marshall Plan, also known as the European Recovery Program, was instituted in 1947 in response to fears that communist organizations were gaining strength in democratic nations across Europe. The Marshall Plan illustrated the United States' belief that American aid in reconstruction would allow for economic recovery and create strong democracies. The Soviet Union openly rejected the Marshall Plan and pressured its satellite nations to not participate in the program.

448. (C) The Berlin Airlift describes the delivery of nearly 13,000 tons of supply aid by British and American aircraft following a Soviet blockade of the portions of Berlin controlled by the western allies. Following the end of the Second World War, Germany was divided into four occupied zones. The three western zones were controlled by the United States, Britain, and France, while the eastern zone was occupied by the Soviet Union. In 1948, the western allies agreed to merge their occupied territories into one democratic German state called the Federal Republic of Germany (West Germany). The Soviet Union responded in 1949 by creating a communist state called the Democratic Republic of Germany (East Germany). A problem arose, however, because the western allies also had claim to the western part of the German capital of Berlin. After East Germany was created as a communist state, many East Germans fled the nation by traveling to western Berlin and flying to a free state such as the United States or Canada. Stalin responded by creating a blockade around the city to stop the western allies' access to the capital. The people of West Berlin would quickly run out of food and other necessities without western support, but Truman decided to avoid war by forgoing the use of military force. Instead, the United States and Britain began an airlift of these supplies. It lasted until 1949, when the Soviet Union agreed to end its blockade.

449. (B) NATO was created in April 1949, and the Warsaw Pact was established in 1955. Both held a policy of mutual military assistance and collective security against an attack made by a nation outside of the treaty organization. Though the United Nations was created to promote peace in the postwar world, the Soviet Union's position as a member of the Security Council allowed it to veto many of the organization's intended actions. Western nations began to feel that another institution was needed to protect them from potential Soviet aggression. In 1949, the United States, Canada, France, Great Britain, and eight other nations formed the North Atlantic Treaty Organization to protect the West from possible Soviet-led communist aggression. This marked a significant shift in American foreign policy, which since the Monroe Doctrine had avoided permanent military alliances with European powers. In 1955, the Soviet Union retaliated by issuing the Warsaw Pact with its satellite states in Eastern Europe, which also held a policy of mutual assistance, thus furthering the notion of Churchill's "iron curtain."

450. (E) In 1949, the popular communist armies under the leadership of Mao Zedong captured the Chinese capital of Peking (Beijing), defeating the Nationalist leader Jiang Jieshi. Jiang Jieshi and his followers set up a provisional government in exile on the island of Taiwan. The United States was shocked by the fall of China to communism, and this furthered the government's resolve to prevent the further spread of communism in Asia. This resolve was illustrated by the efforts to defeat the communist leader Ho Chi Minh in Vietnam. Beginning in 1954, the United States began providing assistance to the anticommunist government in Vietnam, and after the Gulf of Tonkin incident in 1963, the United States began the long-term military escalation that became the Vietnam War. Deng Xiaoping came into power in China in 1981. He adopted some progressive reforms for China, highlighted by the Four Modernizations, which focused on agriculture, industry, science, and defense, and allowed for limited ownership of private property and some free market policies. Kim Il Sung was the leader of North Korea through much of the Cold War. He forged alliances with both the Soviet Union and the People's Republic of China. In the 1950s, his military invaded the democratic South Korea, sparking the Korean War.

451. (B) The House Un-American Activities Committee (HUAC) was originally established in 1938 to investigate German-American involvement with the Ku Klux Klan and the Nazi Party, but it is better remembered for its postwar activities in trying to probe for communist infiltration of the government and Hollywood. This was illustrated in 1947 when leading writers, directors, and actors were called before a House committee meeting to address the perceived communist infiltration into the film industry. A group of ten participants, who later became known as the Hollywood Ten, refused to participate and were held in contempt by the committee, jailed, and later blacklisted within the film industry. The actions of HUAC are often confused with the actions taken by Senator Joseph McCarthy. While both HUAC and McCarthy's committee sought to root out communist infiltration, HUAC was run by the House of Representatives, and McCarthy operated exclusively through his Senate committee. The funding provided to returning veterans so they could pursue college or vocational training after leaving the military was a provision of the Montgomery G.I. Bill, which Congress passed in 1944.

452. (C) The American author and playwright wrote *The Crucible* in early 1950s in response to the actions taken by a Senate investigative committee led by Joseph McCarthy. Miller compared the witch hunts of Salem, Massachusetts, during the colonial period with McCarthy's actions toward American citizens during the nation's second Red Scare. Like Arthur Miller's victims of the Salem witch hunt, the victims of McCarthyism were forcefully submitted to interrogation where they had little option but to confess, regardless of their guilt, and release the names of coconspirators. McCarthyism quickly declined in 1954 after Senator McCarthy attempted to investigate the U.S. Army for communist infiltration. This alienated even his staunchest supporters, and in December 1954, the Senate censured McCarthy for the remainder of his term.

453. (B) In 1953, Julius and Ethel Rosenberg were executed for passing information about atomic weapons to the Soviet Union during the Second World War. This was the second of two spy cases that defined the era. The first began in 1948, when Alger Hiss, a State Department official, was investigated and found guilty of being a former member of the Communist Party and a spy. In 1950, he was found guilty and imprisoned for four years. Julius and Ethel Rosenberg were known members of the Communist Party and found guilty on charges of wartime espionage. Many critics questioned whether the trials of Hiss and the Rosenbergs were fair or merely the product of Red Scare hysteria. Records made available after the Cold War, however, seem to confirm the guilt of Hiss and Julius Rosenberg; Ethel Rosenberg's involvement remains unclear.

454. (A) From 1945 to 1960, the American gross national product increased from around $212 billion to over $500 billion. This economic prosperity was also reflected in the homes of Americans, as the per capita income of the American family rapidly increased. Corporate expansion was also consistently growing during this time period. Combined, these types of growth contributed to a strong consumer economy. To avoid the risky investment practices that had led to the Depression, companies began to form conglomerates—corporations that owned diversified businesses. Franchises, or businesses contracted from a larger company, also began to emerge. Together, they helped fuel the consumer economy that defined the postwar years in the United States.

455. (D) The Montgomery G.I. Bill preceded the Korean War. It was signeed into law in 1944 to provide funds for soldiers returning from the Second World War so they could pursue an education after they finished their service. The Korean War began in June 1950 with the invasion of the communist North Korean army into the democratic nation of South Korea. The Korean peninsula had been divided at the 38th Parallel following the conclusion of the Second World War. Though President Truman had desegregated the military in 1948, this war marked the first time that African-American and white soldiers fought side by side in combat. The war was fought until 1953, when an armistice was signed, and the peninsula remained divided at the 38th Parallel. Because of the conflict, the United States adopted a policy of permanent mobilization, which led to the creation of a military-industrial complex. This was a powerful partnership between the military, the scientific community, and private industry. Furthermore, the Korean War directly affected the United States' relationship with Japan. The once bitter enemy of the United States during the Second World War officially became its partner against the spread of communism with the signing of a formal treaty in 1951.

456. (E) Issued in 1957, the Eisenhower Doctrine was a response to fears that the Suez Canal could fall under Soviet control with the absence of a British or French presence in the region. This threat was intensified by the U.S. economy's growing dependence on petroleum, which made the Middle East more vital in the nation's foreign policy and economy. This policy continued the ideas of the Truman Doctrine and Marshall Plan in that it promised military and economic support to countries that might become targets of communist states. Eisenhower's fears of the spread of communism in Asia were illustrated by his domino theory, first described in a speech delivered in 1954. He stated that if one nation in the region fell to communism, that event could spark a chain reaction. This theory helped to fuel the United States' involvement in Vietnam.

457. (B) President John F. Kennedy introduced his "flexible response" doctrine in 1961 as a skeptical response to Eisenhower's New Look Policy, because the introduction of inter-continental ballistic missiles (ICBMs) made Eisenhower's policy obsolete. Eisenhower's approach was limited to a policy of deterrence, stockpiling a large quantity of nuclear weapons that could be deployed through conventional means. Flexible response was created to address what Kennedy saw as a "missile gap" created by Eisenhower's strategy and opted for a more diverse and flexible approach to a Soviet threat that extended beyond just deterrence. The policy was created to introduce variable options other than the threat of nuclear weapons to respond to enemy aggression. The three main stages provided for in this policy included the use of direct defense of a Soviet attack using conventional military force, deliberate escalation in cases where a Soviet attack might possess an advantage in a strike against a NATO nation, and a general nuclear response, which reflected the policy of mutually assured destruction.

458. **(A)** In 1945, President Truman outlined a 21-point plan for domestic policy that, by 1948, developed into what Truman called his Fair Deal. It continued, strengthened, and expanded many of the programs that defined Franklin Roosevelt's New Deal, which had defined presidential public policy during the Great Depression. Initially, Truman's Fair Deal continued to push for progressive policies such as universal health care coverage and government-provided incomes for working farmers. Both of these measures were defeated by members of both parties in Congress. Truman did achieve some notable goals under the Fair Deal. He increased the national minimum wage, expanded social security coverage to more Americans, increased government works projects involving flood control and irrigation, and provided financial support to poor urban communities. The Square Deal was the domestic policy of Theodore Roosevelt, which included better regulation of business and the dismantling of trusts, greater consumer protection, and conservation of the nation's natural resources. The New Frontier was the name of the program announced by President Kennedy upon winning the presidential election in 1960. Like Truman's Fair Deal, it called for far-reaching progressive reforms. These reforms included greater federal aid to education and urban renewal, health care for the elderly, and the creation of a Department of Urban Affairs. As with Truman's plan, these far-reaching reforms were rejected by Congress. Kennedy did manage to increase the minimum wage and provided some increased support through the Area Redevelopment Act and the Housing Act, both signed in 1961 and providing funds to depressed urban areas. The Great Society was introduced by Lyndon B. Johnson in 1964. In many ways, the Great Society included and expanded upon ideas of the Fair Deal and New Frontier, but unlike the two earlier presidents, Johnson experienced much greater success in turning his planned policy into law. The Great Society included the 1965 Medicare Act, which provided health care for the elderly through the Medicare program and care for the impoverished through Medicaid, a policy that it shared with the goals of the New Frontier. Johnson also created the Department of Housing and Urban Affairs, which also had been a proposed part of the New Frontier.

459. **(C)** In 1956, President Eisenhower signed the Federal-Aid Highway Act, creating the U.S. interstate highway system. With over 41,000 miles of roads, this project was the largest public works program in American history. Ninety percent of the funds for the project were provided by the federal government, with the remaining 10 percent coming from state governments. Eisenhower was inspired to construct the system after seeing the German highway system during the Second World War. The completion of the interstate highway system further fueled suburban sprawl and marked the decline of the nation's railroad system. Eisenhower, like the earlier Republican administrations of Harding, Coolidge, and Hoover, supported the deregulation of business and smaller government and opposed the expansion of the Tennessee Valley Authority, created as part of the New Deal. Medicare (health care insurance for the elderly) and the Department of Housing and Urban Development, while first introduced as part of the New Frontier under Kennedy, were passed into law under Johnson as part of his Great Society.

460. **(A)** Beginning in Long Island in 1947, William J. Levitt introduced the first mass-produced housing development, which became known as Levittown. His system of constructing homes was in some ways similar to the method Henry Ford used to produce cars, focusing on standardization. Levitt's first Long Island development consisted of nearly 11,000 standardized, prefabricated homes, and his model was copied widely throughout the nation, helping to fuel the growth of suburban America. Further promoting suburban sprawl was the Federal Housing Administration, established during the New Deal. It provided government-insured loans to homebuyers and was used by numerous Americans in the postwar era. The interstate highway system introduced under the Eisenhower administration, as well as the increased number of automobiles in the United States, also allowed for the expansion of suburbs by providing efficient means for people to commute to their jobs from greater distances.

461. **(C)** Both Friedan and Spock had a massive impact on postwar American society. In 1946, Spock released his popular book, *The Common Sense Book of Baby and Child Care*. The book inspired many women to settle into a domestic role and focus on raising their children. In many ways, this reintroduced the Cult of Domesticity, which had been prominent during the 19th century. This defined a woman's role as being a homemaker and taking care of children. In 1963, Betty Friedan shattered this view with the release of *The Feminine Mystique*. She directly challenged the idea of a women's innate passive and subservient nature and encouraged women to pursue their goals outside of the home. In many ways, she was a leader in sparking the women's right movements of the later 20th century that included the work of organizations such as the National Organization for Women (NOW). NOW, whose founders included Friedan, pushed for an Equal Rights Amendment that would end discriminatory practices faced by American women.

462. **(B)** While the 1950s are often thought of as times of social conformity, groups such as the beatniks emerged. The Beat Generation was defined by authors such as Allen Ginsberg, who introduced poems such as *Howl*, and Jack Kerouac, who authored *On the Road*. In their works, as well as in their lifestyles, they rejected social conformity and consumerism in favor of spontaneity, drugs, sexual freedom, and often spirituality through Eastern religion. The 1960s also saw the emergence of a counterculture, which became known as the hippies. Like the beatniks of the 1950s, hippies rejected social conformity and often were part of the drug culture of the time. Some also adopted policies of social dissonance, rejecting the Vietnam War. An offshoot of the 1960s counterculture was the Youth International Party (Yippies), founded by Abbie Hoffman in 1968. This group challenged social conformity and politics through large-scale theatrical public events that mocked the Establishment. The term *yuppie* emerged in the 1980s and referred to young urban professionals.

463. **(A)** While the 1950s are often described as a time of cultural and social conformity, it was in fact a period of cultural divergence. Many people experienced a religious reawakening, as illustrated by the rise and popularity of televangelists such as Oral Roberts and increased overall church attendance. At the same time, the decade witnessed the emergence of a new youth culture that popularized the rock-and-roll music of performers including Elvis Presley, Chuck Berry, and Buddy Holly.

464. **(D)** In April 1961, the U.S. government, led by President John F. Kennedy, attempted to overthrow Cuba's communist government of Fidel Castro by launching the failed Bay of Pigs invasion. In response, beginning in 1962, Castro agreed to allow the Soviet Union to construct missile bases on the island nation in order to ensure trade with the Soviet Union and create a deterrent for possible future U.S. attacks. This led to military escalation between the United States and the Soviet Union that became known as the Cuban Missile Crisis. For 14 days, the world waited as it seemed that nuclear war had become a real possibility as the two superpowers faced off against each other. Finally, on

October 28, 1962, the world breathed a sigh of relief when the United States and the Soviet Union created an agreement to resolve the confrontation peacefully. Kennedy agreed to the removal of strategic nuclear missiles from Turkey, and Nikita Khrushchev withdrew the Soviet missiles from Cuba. The two nations also established a Moscow-Washington hot line, also known as the "red phones," to provide direct communications between the two nation's leaders.

Chapter 17

465. (A) In 1954 the U.S. Supreme Court issued its decision in *Brown v. Board of Education*, effectively overturning the constitutionality of "separate but equal" established in the 1896 *Plessy v. Ferguson* decision. The NAACP lawyer Thurgood Marshall successfully proved that segregated educational institutions were inherently unequal, and the Supreme Court ordered school districts to integrate their schools with all "deliberate speed." The 1964 Civil Rights Act further ended discrimination in the United States by outlawing racial discrimination by employers as well as unions. In 1952 the Supreme Court's *Youngstown* decision limited the power of the president to seize private property. The case was based on an attempt made by the president to seize a steel production facility that was threatening to strike during the Korean War. The *Dred Scott* decision of 1857 ruled that Congress could not outlaw or limit the expansion of slavery into states and territories and that slaves were not citizens and were not protected under the Constitution. This decision was nullified by ratification of the Fourteenth Amendment in 1868. The 1947 Taft-Hartley Act limited the power of unions by outlawing closed shops and required anti-communist oaths to be taken by union officials.

466. (C) The Congress of Racial Equality (CORE), founded in 1942, and the Southern Christian Leadership Conference (SCLC), founded by Dr. Martin Luther King Jr. and others in 1957, both advocated challenging discrimination within the United States through nonviolent means. The founders of CORE and the SCLC were inspired by the nonviolent or passive resistance adopted by Mohandas Gandhi in India. CORE established Freedom Rides, in which African-American and white volunteers traveled through the South, challenging Jim Crow laws. The SCLC's first major action was the Montgomery bus boycott in 1957. Both movements worked together through the 1950s and 1960s to fight against segregation and for racial equality. In 1963 the two groups organized the March on Washington, where King delivered his now immortal "I Have a Dream" speech. The massive march eventually led to the passage of the 1964 Civil Rights Act and the 1965 National Voting Rights Act.

467. (C) In many ways, Martin Luther King Jr. and Malcolm X illustrated a split within the African-American population during the 1960s. While King fought for desegregation and racial equality, Malcolm X advocated black nationalism, which called for a separate identity and racial unity within African-American communities. This reflected the ideals expressed by Marcus Garvey, a major influence on Malcolm X, during the 1920s. Later, Malcolm X's calls for black nationalism would be adopted by Stokely Carmichael, a leader of the Student Nonviolent Coordinating Committee who modified these views into a movement that became known as black power, which also called for establishing a sense of pride and independence within African-American communities.

468. (C) During the summer of 1964 and in March 1965, civil rights organizations launched movements to bring attention to the lack of voting rights in African-American communities in the South. The 1964 event known as Freedom Summer saw more than 3,000 African-American and white volunteers register voters in Mississippi. In 1965, Martin Luther King Jr., recognizing that many black residents of Alabama were still being denied the right to vote, organized a march to raise awareness. Alabama law enforcement officials, however, used violent means to break up the march. News agencies captured images of the brutal tactics being employed against the peaceful protestors, raising sympathies among many northern whites. These two events helped push the passage of the 1965 Voting Rights Act, which eliminated barriers to voting such as literacy tests and allowed federal officials to register voters if the local government refused. The 1964 Civil Rights Act, which banned discriminatory practices in employment, education, and public accommodations, was passed partly in response to the 1963 March on Washington. The black-power movement and the Black Panthers illustrated the formation of a more militant arm of the civil rights movement that emerged after 1966. Stokely Carmichael popularized the notion of black power through his organization, the Student Nonviolent Coordinating Committee. The Black Panthers were founded by Bobby Seale and Huey Newton. Both organizations reflected Malcolm X's call for black pride within independent black communities. The Southern Manifesto was issued in 1956 by white southern leaders, pledging to fight desegregation in the wake of the *Brown v. Board of Education* decision.

469. (E) The ratification of the Twenty-Fourth Amendment in 1964 officially made poll taxes unconstitutional. Poll taxes had been used by several southern states to keep poor African-Americans from voting. This constitutional amendment, along with the 1965 Voting Rights Act, politically empowered many African-Americans, creating a new voting population in the South. The Civil Rights Act of 1964 outlawed discrimination in jobs, education, and public accommodations, and it supported early attempts to help African-Americans register to vote.

470. (B) Even though President Johnson believed the United States could simultaneously fight in the Vietnam War and continue his ambitious Great Society domestic policy, the heavy costs of Vietnam drained money from Johnson's domestic programs and undermined the Great Society. The Great Society did have a wide-reaching impact, which included Medicare programs, the Elementary and Secondary Education Act, the creation of the Department of Housing and Urban Development, and clean-air and clean-water regulations, while at the same time cutting taxes. After Martin Luther King Jr. was killed in 1968, race riots broke out in numerous American cities. Johnson created the National Advisory Commission on Civil Disorders, also known as the Kerner Commission, to investigate the causes. The commission found that the nation was deeply divided along racial lines. Johnson responded by pushing for the passage of the 1968 Civil Rights Act, which barred discrimination in the sale or rental of housing. In a program started by Kennedy, Johnson's administration successfully completed a manned lunar shuttle landing on July 20, 1969, through the Apollo program.

471. (D) The 1960s were a time of political activism in many areas of American life. One example was the publication of *Silent Spring* by Rachel Carson, a leader in the environmental movement. Carson's book helped bring about the banning of the pesticide DDT, which had a deep and deadly impact on the environment by contaminating water supplies and killing off or endangering many species of fish and birds, including the bald eagle, which almost became extinct. Her book also prompted President Johnson to include environmental reforms in his Great Society program. Carson was not, however, involved in the efforts of Japanese-American citizens who had been forced into internment camps and later fought to be compensated for losses they had suffered. The Japanese American Citizens League began to push for legislation for monetary compensation for losses during the Second World War, which they finally settled in 1965. Author Betty Friedan reawakened the women's rights movement with the publication of her book *Feminine Mystique* in 1963. In 1966 Friedan went on to help form the National Organization for Women (NOW), which campaigned for equal rights for women. César Chávez created the United Farm Workers (UFW) during the 1960s to improve the labor conditions and treatment of migrant workers. Dennis Banks, along with George Mitchell, established the American Indian Movement (AIM) in 1968 to fight for treaty rights as well as better conditions and opportunities for the Native American people. Ralph Nader emerged during the 1960s as a leader in consumer rights. His 1965 work *Unsafe at Any Speed* helped bring about new automobile safety standards. Nader also led movements to address environmental concerns, practices of the meatpacking industry, and other areas of public concern.

472. (C) When President Kennedy took office, he attempted to keep communism from spreading into southern Vietnam. He did this by sending several thousand military advisers and other military assistance to prop up the government led by Ngo Dinh Diem against the communist northern Viet Cong, led by Ho Chi Minh. After the 1964 Second Gulf of Tonkin incident, in which the American destroyer *Maddox* was allegedly attacked by Viet Cong torpedo boats, Congress gave President Johnson the authority to send more troops into the region, officially starting the Vietnam War. In 1970, President Nixon began a bombing campaign in Cambodia, a neighboring country to Vietnam, to disrupt Viet Cong supply routes known as the Ho Chi Minh Trail.

473. (B) The major escalation of American troops in Vietnam began after an American destroyer, the *Maddox*, was allegedly attacked 30 miles south of Vietnam in the Gulf of Tonkin. Congress responded in 1964 by passing the Gulf of Tonkin Resolution, which gave the president nearly complete control of American military actions in Vietnam without officially declaring war. While the Vietnam conflict officially began for the United States with the 1964 Gulf of Tonkin Resolution, American involvement had begun much earlier when the French withdrew from the region in 1954 and the United States became involved to keep the Viet Cong from leading a communist revolution in southern Vietnam. The My Lai Massacre refers to a mass killing of unarmed citizens in South Vietnam by the U.S. Army including a soldier named William Calley, who was later sentenced to three years in prison. The Pentagon Papers, a military report on American military actions in Vietnam, were leaked to American newspapers in 1971. They exposed that the military had expanded the war by bombing the neighboring countries of Cambodia and Laos and by launching coastal raids on North Vietnam. This caused a further decline in support for the war and hurt the Nixon administration.

474. (C) Many historians consider the Vietnam War to have been the first truly televised war. As violence escalated in the conflict, the brutality of the fighting became a major focus of the evening news, bringing the events into the living rooms of American households.

In 1965, one network showed a story of American soldiers setting fire to the thatched roofs of a Vietnamese village with lighters and mistreating the residents, creating a massive public outcry. In 1968, during the Tet Offensive, broadcasts were aired showing a South Vietnamese colonel executing a prisoner on the streets of Saigon. Furthermore, in 1972, American television audiences were able to witness firsthand the effects of an accidental napalm bombing of Vietnamese refugees fleeing a village. These images, along with the cost of the war both fiscally and in human lives, began to greatly turn American public opinion against the war and fueled an antiwar movement in the nation.

475. (D) Even though American troops withdrew from Vietnam by the end of March 1973, the fighting between North and South Vietnam continued until April 1975, when the Viet Cong, the army of North Vietnam, captured Saigon, the capital of South Vietnam. At this time, they were able to take control of the entire southern nation. President Nixon did perform heavy bombing of Cambodia, hoping to disrupt the Ho Chi Minh Trail in 1970, but Congress ended this operation by June 1970. In 1954, a conference held in Geneva divided Vietnam at the 17th Parallel, creating the state of North Vietnam, led by Ho Chi Minh, and the southern state of South Vietnam, initially led by Bao Dai. Dai was quickly overthrown by the fiercely anti-communist Ngo Dinh Diem.

476. (B) In 1970, millions of American college students protested President Nixon's ordering of American troops into Cambodia. One such protest took place on May 4 at Kent State University in Ohio. After several protestors began throwing rocks at National Guardsmen stationed at the campus, the guardsmen fired into the crowd, killing four students and injuring nine others. This tragedy triggered even more protests, including a gathering of nearly 100,000 students on the White House lawn less than a week later. The event at Kent State also inspired the song "Ohio" by Neil Young, an example of the use of popular music by the antiwar movement.

477. (C) In 1968, during the Vietnamese New Year celebration, North Vietnam and Viet Cong forces launched a massive offensive attack known as the Tet Offensive. It included numerous surprise attacks on South Vietnamese cities and American bases, including the capital city of Saigon. The My Lai Massacre was the brutal killing of several hundred Vietnamese citizens by American soldiers. Operation Rolling Thunder refers to an aerial bombing campaign of North Vietnam introduced by the Johnson administration. The operation continued from 1965 to 1968. The Ho Chi Minh Trail was the supply route of the Viet Cong that stretched through Cambodia. To disrupt this supply route, Nixon ordered the carpet bombing of the region and a short-lived invasion of the region by American troops. Domestically, these actions increased antiwar sentiments within the United States. In Cambodia, the instability caused by Nixon's actions, as well as the war in general, allowed for the emergence of the Khmer Rouge, led by Pol Pot, which maintained control of the country from 1975 to 1979 by use of extreme force and genocide.

478. (D) William Calley was the lieutenant in charge of a group of soldiers who on March 16, 1968, brutally attacked and killed more than 300 Vietnamese villagers in what became known as the My Lai Massacre. News of the event led to a massive international public outcry. While 26 of the soldiers involved in the event were charged with criminal acts during the event, only Calley was found guilty, and he served three years for his actions. The event further strengthened the antiwar movement in the United States and internationally.

Robert McNamara served as secretary of defense under Presidents John F. Kennedy and Lyndon B. Johnson. He helped coordinate America's military escalation in Vietnam, first through the use of military advisers under Kennedy and then with conventional forces after the Gulf of Tonkin Resolution. However, as the war progressed, he developed mixed feelings about continuing to build troop levels and eventually resigned in 1968. At that point, he was replaced by Clark Clifford, who also became doubtful about the conflict. In 1968, Eugene McCarthy and Robert Kennedy (John Kennedy's brother as well as his attorney general) both challenged President Johnson in the Democratic primaries for the presidential election. Robert Kennedy's popular run was cut short, however, when he was assassinated in June 1968. McCarthy was unable to secure his party's nomination, and Johnson's vice president, Hubert Humphrey, became the Democratic candidate. However, in the end, the Republican candidate, Richard Nixon, narrowly won the election under the slogan of "peace with honor."

479. (E) In January 1973, the United States, North Vietnam, and the Viet Cong met in Paris and negotiated a peace settlement. The United States agreed to remove its military force from the region, and all parties agreed to stop military action in Cambodia and Laos, release all prisoners of war, and recognize the 17th Parallel as the border between North and South Vietnam. No agreements were made on the holding of free elections, and North Vietnam eventually defeated South Vietnam.

480. (B) Article I of the U.S. Constitution states that only Congress has the power to declare war, yet the president is the commander in chief of the nation's military forces. In response to the nation's disillusionment with the conduct of the Vietnam War, Congress passed the 1973 War Powers Act over the veto of President Nixon. The act limited the president's use of the nation's armed forces by requiring the president to notify Congress of any overseas troop deployment and to provide justification for the action. It also stated that troops could not be deployed for more than 60 days without congressional approval, and it allowed Congress to force the president to recall troops if the legislators felt it was necessary. The War Powers Act was first used when President Ford attempted to supply military aid to South Vietnam in 1975. The nation as a whole, like Congress, did not want to become militarily involved in the region again, so Congress used the War Powers Act to deny the president's request. As a result, South Vietnam fell to the North Vietnamese in April 1975.

Chapter 18

481. (B) After receiving less than 12 percent of the African-American vote in 1968, Nixon felt he had little to gain by advancing civil rights, so he began to relax desegregation laws. Instead, he focused on gaining the support of the former southern Democrats who felt alienated by the Great Society and civil rights programs of the Johnson administration. John Mitchell, Nixon's attorney general, attempted to prevent the extension of provisions found in the 1965 Voting Rights Act. Nixon also allowed the restoration of funding to school districts that were still segregated. Furthermore, he tried to interfere with the *Swann v. Charlotte-Mecklenburg* Supreme Court decision, which called for the use of busing to help end school segregation. He also loosened restrictions in earlier fair-housing laws.

482. (A) President Nixon with his secretary of state, Henry Kissinger, adopted a policy of détente, or the relaxing of tensions with the nation's two biggest rivals, China and the

Soviet Union. Under détente, he and Kissinger (one of his most trusted advisers) bypassed Congress and pursued often-secret dialogue with the two nations, changing the direction of American postwar policies. Détente was in many ways an extension of Kissinger's realpolitik, or practical politics. This new approach to foreign affairs allowed for the first presidential visit to the People's Republic of China and the ending of the embargo with that nation and the lifting of travel restrictions. It also allowed for Nixon to travel to the Soviet Union in 1972. At this meeting, Nixon and Premier Leonid Brezhnev worked together and finally agreed to sign the Strategic Arms Limitation Treaty (SALT I). This agreement froze the number of intercontinental ballistic missiles and restricted the development of antiballistic missile defense systems.

483. (C) SALT stands for Strategic Arms Limitation Treaty, and the two agreements served to slow the arms race between the United States and the Soviet Union, the world's two superpowers. SALT I was signed by President Nixon and Soviet Premier Brezhnev in 1972, freezing the number of intercontinental ballistic missiles at the 1972 levels, limiting the number of atomic weapons that could be launched from submarines, and limiting the development of antiballistic missile defense systems. SALT II was signed by President Carter and Premier Brezhnev. This agreement set a limit on the number of nuclear devices that either nation could possess. The agreement was never ratified by Congress and deteriorated after the Soviet invasion of Afghanistan in 1979.

484. (B) In June 1972, four members of the Committee to Re-Elect the President (CREEP), led by James McCord, broke into the Democratic Party headquarters located in the Watergate Hotel in Washington, D.C. Their mission was to steal Democratic election files and install wiretapping devices to better monitor the Democratic Party's actions during the 1972 election campaign. The men were discovered, and President Nixon denied involvement; but as investigations continued, Nixon's involvement became more apparent. Eventually, when it was discovered that Nixon had used the CIA to block an FBI investigation of the case, Nixon was forced to resign, which he did on August 8, 1974.

485. (B) To restore lands they had lost to Israel during the Six Days War, Middle Eastern states created an oil embargo to pressure Western nations that supported Israel in 1973. Henry Kissinger managed to negotiate an end of the embargo, but the Organization of Petroleum Exporting Counties (OPEC)—which included Venezuela, Saudi Arabia, Kuwait, Iraq, and Iran—drastically increased the price of oil. This caused the cost of gasoline to double and pushed inflation above 10 percent in the United States. The incident became a dark mark on Nixon's foreign-policy record, unlike the opening of talks with China and the Soviet Union through détente, as well as the signing of SALT I with Russia in 1972. The Camp David Accords were a foreign-policy success of the Carter administration: negotiation of a peace deal ending the war between Egypt and Israel.

486. (B) Shortly after taking office in 1974, President Ford issued a presidential pardon to Richard Nixon, ending all investigations into the Watergate Scandal. While this action marred the rest of Ford's term, he felt it was necessary for allowing the nation's healing process to begin. The presidential pardon was only the first challenge Ford faced as president. When he assumed office, the nation faced increasing unemployment and inflation, a combination that was termed "stagflation." Ford called for voluntary restraints and asked supporters to wear buttons that said WIN, which stood for Whip Inflation Now. This did little to help the problem, as unemployment increased along with the federal deficit. Ford had mixed success with his foreign policy. When he asked Congress to supply military aid to South Vietnam, legislators used the 1973 War Powers Act to deny his request. However, he did sign the Helsinki Accords, in which the United States, the Soviet Union, Canada, and roughly 30 other nations agreed to economic cooperation, respect for territorial boundaries, and promotion of human rights. He also continued SALT negotiations with the Soviet Union.

487. (C) In the wake of government distrust following the Watergate Scandal, Jimmy Carter was able to win the 1976 presidential race by presenting himself as a political outsider. Carter had graduated from the U.S. Naval Academy and served as an engineering officer, and he later went on to serve as the governor of Georgia. He became known for rejecting many of the formal and ceremonial practices of the presidential office. This, however, generated criticism from those who thought he was downplaying the dignity of his office. After his election, however, he found that being a political outsider had its disadvantages. He and his inexperienced advisers had difficulty promoting his agenda. He did find some success in deregulating certain parts of American industry such as the railroads and lifting price controls on oil and natural gas. This further alienated him from fellow members of the Democratic Party who supported these regulations. His attempt to raise taxes on gasoline sales further hurt his popular support. He felt that convincing people to use less energy and drive less would make the nation less vulnerable to OPEC's price increases, which had plagued the nation since 1973. Despite opposition, he did manage to pass the 1978 Energy Act, which imposed higher taxes on cars that inefficiently used gas, called for alternative energy sources, deregulated prices on domestic oil and natural gas, and offered tax incentives for homeowners who pursued energy efficiency in their homes. The Moral Majority, a conservative Christian political organization, played a major role in the 1980 election, helping to elect Carter's Republican challenger, Ronald Reagan.

488. (D) One successful action of the Carter administration was ending the war between Egypt and Israel with the signing of the Camp David Accords in 1978. The Middle East had become unstable as the Arab nations and Israel had engaged in several conflicts between 1967 and 1973. In 1978, Carter was able to get the Egyptian leader, Anwar el-Sadat, and the Israeli leader, Menachem Begin, to sign the Camp David Accords, a treaty that would lay the groundwork for peace. Under the treaty, Israel agreed to withdraw from the Sinai Peninsula, and in return, Egypt formally recognized Israel as a sovereign nation. The Helsinki Accords were signed by Ford in 1975. The agreement between nations called for economic cooperation, protection of human rights, and respect for territorial boundaries. The Geneva Accords were created in 1967 as an attempt to solve the Israeli-Palestinian conflict. The SALT I and II agreements were created first by Nixon (SALT I) and then by Carter (SALT II) with the Soviet Union's Brezhnev to slow the nuclear arms race between the two superpowers.

489. (C) Jimmy Carter's inability to solve the Iran hostage crisis in 1980 helped the Republican presidential challenger win the election in 1980. For decades prior to the incident, the United States had backed the shah of Iran, Mohammed Reza Shah Pahlavi. However, in 1979, a fundamentalist Islamic revolution erupted in the nation. The shah fled the nation and was replaced by the religious leader Ayatollah Khomeini, who was strongly anti-Western and planned to make Iran into a conservative state. Carter allowed the deposed shah to seek refuge in the United States. This caused Iranian revolutionaries to seize the American embassy in Iran and take 52 Americans hostage. Carter took several steps to free the hostages, including freezing Iranian assets in the United States and launching a failed military rescue mission. Unlike the Iran hostage crisis, the Camp David Accords illustrated a success for Carter: negotiation of a peace deal between Israel and Egypt. SALT I was signed by President Nixon with the Soviet leader Brezhnev to limit the production of nuclear weapons. The Iran-Contra Affair was a scandal during the Reagan administration. The president's office was caught in 1986 selling arms to Iran despite an embargo on weapons sales to that nation. The First Persian Gulf War took place in 1991 during the administration of President George H. W. Bush in response to Iraq's invasion of Kuwait.

490. (D) Ronald Reagan's election in 1980 marked a resurgence of the conservative movement that wanted to lower taxes and reduce the size of the federal government. Reagan and fellow conservatives were critical of the New Deal and Great Society programs, believing they led to an overexpansion of the federal government and increased the tax burden. In doing so, Reagan began to cut funding to many government programs such as urban development and the federal assistance programs for the poor through the 1981 Budget Reconciliation Act. This act cut funding to education, welfare, and other social assistance programs. Reagan did, however, increase the size of the military budget by nearly $12 billion. Conservatives such as Reagan rejected Keynesian economics, which believed economic growth resulted from the government providing jobs and financial assistance to workers, and adopted an economic theory known as supply-side economics. According to supply-side economics, also known as trickle-down economics, economic growth is best achieved by deregulation and government tax cuts to business and investment. This would allow companies to expand, increase production, and then hire more workers. While the nation did make some economic gains under the Reagan administration, the gap between the rich and poor greatly increased, the conditions of America's urban centers drastically declined, and the national deficit soared, reaching over $3 trillion in 1990.

491. (B) In 1981, Ronald Reagan appointed Sandra Day O'Connor to the Supreme Court, making her the first woman to serve in the nation's highest court. Reagan also appointed the conservative Antonin Scalia to the Supreme Court in 1986, as well as Anthony Kennedy in 1988. In 1986, Reagan appointed Justice William Rehnquist to be Chief Justice. These appointments helped establish a strongly conservative court that in many ways mirrored Reagan's political beliefs and catered to his political support in the conservative movement as well as in the religiously conservative Moral Majority. Ruth Joan Bader Ginsburg was the second female appointed to the Supreme Court. She was appointed by President Clinton in 1993. Sonia Sotomayor was selected for the Supreme Court by President Barack Obama in 2009, making her the third woman to serve. And in 2010, Obama selected Elena Kagan to be the fourth female Supreme Court justice. Frances Perkins was the first female to serve in the president's cabinet. She served as secretary of labor under Franklin Roosevelt. Margaret Thatcher was the first female prime minister of Britain, serving from 1979 to 1990.

492. (C) Perestroika and glasnost were the basis of the policy initiated by Soviet Premier Mikhail Gorbachev during his tenure from 1985 to 1991. Perestroika refers to restructuring, and glasnost refers to openness. This policy illustrated Gorbachev's push to reform the Soviet's government practices and provide greater transparency. The result, however, was that the communist nations, which for years had run single-party police states, lost their grip, and the Eastern European regimes began to collapse, marking the end of the Cold

War. In 1989, Poland held its first free elections; during the same year, the Berlin Wall fell, and Germany reunited. Ultimately, the Soviet Union also collapsed after a failed coup in 1991.

493. (D) After Iraq invaded the independent nation of Kuwait in 1990, the United States and its allies attacked Iraq to liberate the tiny, oil-rich state. President Bush hoped that the liberation of Kuwait and the defeat of the Iraqi-led invasion would lead to a revolution within Iraq that would result in the overthrow of Saddam Hussein. Yet Bush did not support supplying Iraqi rebels with military aid, and the later uprisings were quickly crushed by Saddam's forces. Saddam Hussein remained in power until he was overthrown by the United States during the Second Gulf War, led by Bush's son, President George W. Bush, in 2003.

494. (A) In 1992, Bill Clinton won the presidency in a three-way race against the incumbent president George H. W. Bush and independent candidate Ross Perot. As he began his term in 1993, he focused his domestic program on reforming the nation's health care system by providing over 37 million uninsured Americans with health care coverage. He called for the creation of a government-supervised health care system, which would provide affordable coverage to all Americans. Insurance companies and medical companies lobbied heavily against the measure, and after nearly a year of debate, the plan ultimately failed.

495. (C) During the midterm elections in 1994, House Republicans under the leadership of Speaker of the House Newt Gingrich launched what they called the "Contract with America." In the contract, the Republican candidates promised a balanced budget within seven years by drastically cutting public services. Most of their plans failed, as their intended cuts were rejected by both parties in the Senate, as well as rejected by Clinton through vetoes. Ultimately, the battle between House Republicans and the president led to a brief shutdown of government in 1995. The Republicans' attacks on public services and social spending measures raised Clinton's popularity in the polls while causing their own to decline. The Star Wars program, a nickname for the Strategic Defense Initiative, was a costly nuclear defense developed by the Reagan administration, which added to further increases in military spending during his two terms.

496. (C) In both the 1824 election and the election of 2000, the candidate who received the largest percentage of the popular vote lost the overall presidential election. During the 1824 election, the House of Representatives decided the election in favor of John Quincy Adams over Andrew Jackson. In the 2000 elections, the final decision fell into the hands of the Supreme Court. On the election night of 2000, the race became too close to call, and neither candidate received enough electoral votes to win the presidency, though Democratic candidate and former vice president Al Gore won in the popular vote over the Republican candidate, George W. Bush. Eventually, Florida emerged as a battleground. After the two candidates waged legal battles for nearly a month, the Supreme Court decided the election with its decision in the *Bush v. Gore* case, which ended the vote recounts in Florida, awarding the presidency to Bush.

497. (A) In November 1986, it was discovered that senior officials in President Reagan's administration were secretly selling weapons to Iran despite a congressional embargo. The officials hoped the arms sales would aid in the release of hostages and provide funds to aid rebels in Nicaragua against the Sandinista government. The savings and loan (S&L) crisis involved the failure of more than 700 financial institutions in part caused by the climate created by the deregulation policies approved by the Reagan administration. Nearly $160 billion in federal funds were used to avoid collapses in the financial sector, leading to a large increase in the national deficit. In the HUD scandal, members of the Department of Housing and Urban Development gave large contracts to political supporters of the Reagan administration. In the Inslaw Affair, officials in the Department of Justice under Reagan were accused of committing software piracy and deliberately driving the Inslaw information technology company into bankruptcy. The Whitewater Scandal plagued the Clinton administration. Clinton was accused of unethical investment practices in a failed real estate investment venture.

498. (E) President Bill Clinton was the second president in U.S. history to be impeached. The first was Andrew Johnson, in February 1868. The Radical Republicans in the House of Representatives charged Johnson with violating the Tenure of Office Act of 1867. Clinton was charged with perjury and obstruction of justice in an investigation concerning allegations of sexual harassment in a suit brought by Paula Jones, a former Arkansas state worker. While Johnson avoided removal by a single vote, 55 senators voted against Clinton's removal.

499. (D) The Oklahoma City Federal Building bombing took place on April 19, 1995, and was carried out by Timothy McVeigh, who was a sympathizer of the American militia movement. The bombing of the Alfred P. Murrah Federal Building in Oklahoma City killed 168 people and injured nearly 700 others. It was considered the largest terrorist attack on American soil until the Al Qaeda attacks of September 11, 2001.

500. (A) The USA PATRIOT Act, or Uniting and Strengthening America by Providing Appropriate Tools Required to Intercept and Obstruct Terrorism Act of 2001, was signed into law by President George W. Bush on October 26, 2001. The law was created in direct response to the Al Qaeda terrorist attacks on the World Trade Center and the Pentagon on September 11, 2001. The law was designed to reduce restrictions on law enforcement and intelligence agencies' ability to gather intelligence concerning future terrorist threats. The law was deemed controversial because it contradicted earlier legislation such as FISA, the Foreign Intelligence Surveillance Act of 1978, which was signed into law by President Carter. FISA was created specifically to limit intelligence agencies' ability to use surveillance on American citizens in the wake of the Watergate Scandal under President Nixon. The McCain-Feingold Act, or Bipartisan Campaign Reform Act of 2002, was a bipartisan attempt to regulate the financing of political campaigns. Portions of the law were struck down as unconstitutional in 2010 with the Supreme Court decision in the case *Citizens United v. Federal Election Commission*. The Brady Bill, or the Brady Handgun Violence Prevention Act, was signed into law by President Bill Clinton in 1994. The law required federal background checks on people wishing to purchase a firearm.

BIBLIOGRAPHY

Alderman, Ellen, and Caroline Kennedy. *In Our Defense: The Bill of Rights in Action*. New York: Avon, 1991.

Ayers, Edward L. *American Passages: A History of the United States*. Vol. 1. Fort Worth: Harcourt College, 2000.

Cayton, Andrew R. L. *America: Pathways to the Present*. Boston: Pearson/Prentice Hall, 2007.

Cayton, Andrew R. L., Elisabeth Israels Perry, and Allan M. Winkler. *America: Pathways to the Present*. Needham, Mass.: Prentice Hall, 1998.

College Board. "AP: Subjects—U.S. History." *College Board Tests*. 13 June 2010 (http://www.collegeboard.com/student/testing/ap/sub_ushist.html).

Davidson, James West. *Nation of Nations: A Concise Narrative of the American Republic*. New York: McGraw-Hill, 1996.

Ellis, Elisabeth Gaynor, and Anthony Esler. *World History: Connections to Today*. Upper Saddle River, N.J.: Prentice Hall, 1997.

Hall, Kermit, David Scott Clark, James W. Ely, Joel B. Grossman, and N. Hull. *The Oxford Guide to American Law*. Oxford: Oxford University Press, 2002.

Jordan, Winthrop D., Miriam Greenblatt, and John S. Bowes. *The Americans: A History*. Evanston, Ill.: McDougal Littell/Houghton Mifflin, 1996.

Kennedy, David M., Lizabeth Cohen, and Thomas Andrew Bailey. *The American Pageant: A History of the Republic*. Boston: Houghton Mifflin, 2006.

LaFeber, Walter. *America, Russia, and the Cold War, 1945–1996*. New York: McGraw-Hill, 1997.

O'Neill, William L. *A Democracy at War: America's Fight at Home and Abroad in World War II*. Cambridge, Mass.: Harvard University Press, 1995.

Stokesbury, James L. *A Short History of World War I*. New York: Morrow, 1981.

Tindall, George B. *America*. Vol. 2. New York: Norton, 1993.

Tindall, George Brown, and David E. Shi. *America: A Narrative History*. New York: W. W. Norton, 1993.

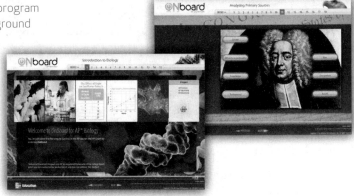

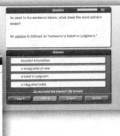